Economics of African Agriculture

Economics of African Agriculture

**John Levi and
Michael Havinden**

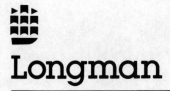

Longman

Longman Group Limited,
Longman House, Burnt Mill,
Harlow, Essex, UK.

© Longman Group Ltd 1982

First Published 1982

British Library Cataloguing in Publication Data

Levi, John
    Economics of African agriculture.
    1. Agriculture – Economic aspects – Africa,
    Sub-Saharan
    I. Title   II. Havinden, Michael Ashley
    338.1'0967   HD2117

    ISBN 0-582-64147-0
    ISBN 0-582-64148-9 Pbk

Printed in Great Britain by Butler & Tanner Ltd,
Frome and London

Contents

List of tables

List of figures

1 Introduction

The ultimate concern of this book is with economic development. Needless to say, that term can have different meanings. Here we take it as a long-term improvement in the standard of living, as felt and judged to be so by most of the people in a country. Differences in views as to what development means can produce conflict between the actions of development agencies and the desires of the people themselves. For example, a newly introduced technology may result in greater agricultural output and cash income. This may be considered an improvement in living standards by the introducers but the technology might involve harder work on the part of those adopting it, and perhaps undesired changes in the traditional way of life. Thus, the people who actually receive the new technology might consider it a mixed blessing and not at all an unambiguous 'development' or improvement.

Our definition or criterion of economic development is in that spirit and implies our value judgements as to what kinds of changes are good, bad, indifferent or unclear as to their effects. Many readers will agree with our values; some will not. But it is necessary to state what they are at the outset so that, at least, readers will understand our analyses and conclusions even if they do not agree with them.

Economic development is as urgent and elusive as ever. This is in spite of the fact that there has been, during the last 15 years or so, and quite rightly, an increase in the degree of attention paid to agricultural development, as a prerequisite both for more general economic development and for providing at least some 'basic needs' (a term which has become something of a slogan). In particular, agricultural development is necessary to provide a minimum reasonable level of food consumption. Food is of course the most basic need of all.

Unfortunately, despite this greater attention towards agriculture, especially in the form of more external aid and an internal financing of more and more development projects and programmes, significant widespread improvement in rural living standards by no means has been the result. Indeed evidence in the last section of the next chapter suggests the reverse: a widespread deterioration. What are we to make of this, and what to do? There are no easy answers, of course, but the main objective of the following pages is to provide at least some basis from which it might be possible to begin formulating answers.

Although the last two chapters are concerned with 'development' as such, or rather with 'attempts to develop', the essence of our approach is to look at the positive economics of agriculture rather than the normative. In other words, we are mainly concerned with the economic workings of agriculture as it is and has been, not with what it ought to be. This is not to say there is no assessment of policy – far from it, for even if we are looking mainly at positive economics, government policy and the policies of other outside agencies have had a major influence on the behaviour of the agricultural economy, for good or ill. Also, a central theme of the book is that of the nature, supply of, and changes in, resources; for development must surely come, in some way, through reorganising resources, changing resources or introducing new ones, while it seems self-evident that if development means change, then one should understand what it is one is trying to change. To give a simple, and in practice all too common, example, an innovation such as a new cash crop may require the application of labour just at a time when labour is most needed for food production. Such innovations have, needless to say, failed to make much of an impact – because of a failure to understand the nature of, and constraints on, the existing resources. Another example, which illustrates the kind of approach that is needed, was seen on British television a few years ago. A social anthropologist tried to persuade some Dogon villagers in Mali to accept a new type of water tank that would save a large amount of time spent by women in head-loading water from distant sources. The design of the tank had to be such as to blend with the characteristic Dogon architecture. Furthermore an 'oracle', involving the scattering of bones and examination of the pattern they made, had to be consulted. It was found that a fox had walked across the oracle patch during the night, which event was considered a good omen; so the tank was deemed acceptable. A final touch was a wooden door on the top of the tank, carved with a picture of the fox and other elements of the story. This was true development, according to our criteria. (Notice that there was actually no direct increase in output, although the time saved could be used to produce more.)

In summary, then, the book is an attempt to shed light on the problem of achieving economic development in agriculture. We try to do this by analysing the economic behaviour of farm families and their response to the major forces that impinge on them, such as government policy, development strategies, population growth, etc.

Chapter 2 largely is intended for those who have little or no knowledge of the technical aspects of African agriculture or of the major environmental conditions bearing on it. Readers who have such knowledge may, therefore, prefer to skip or skim through the chapter, at least as far as the last section. There is no intention to be in any way authoritative, but the attempt is made to give a general picture of the diversity of African agriculture and, by describing in greater detail a few case studies, to impart the 'flavour' of agricultural systems mainly, but not only, for the benefit of non-African readers. The chapter was included also for the sake of completeness. After all, climatic and other ecological factors do have a major influence on the African rural economy, and to ignore them simply because they are non-economic would give a misleading impression.

To a greater or lesser extent the state of agriculture now can be explained by what has happened in the past, and Chapter 3 gives some indication of how crucial this can be. Chapter 5, too, in its discussion

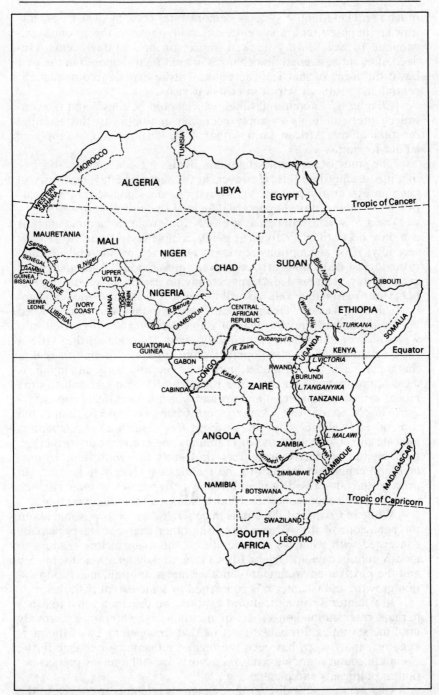

Fig. 1.1 The countries of Africa

of land and land tenure systems demonstrates how, in some cases, historically imposed tenure systems, especially those of the colonial era, continue to have a very marked impact on present-day events. (Indeed, it could be argued that changes in land rights imposed in the past lay at the heart of much of the political strife experienced in eastern, central and southern Africa in post-war years.)

Chapter 4, 'Labour and time', which could be considered the central chapter, attempts to apply economic reasoning to the essential function of the African farm – that of producing food by applying labour to land.

The study of economics simplifies, by using models and we believe that it is useful to do this. However, at the same time it is necessary to keep an eye on the real world, so that one does not become too carried away by the appealing internal logic of theoretical abstractions – a weakness to which economists are only too prone. Economic analysis can only be justified firstly, if it is not completely *contrary* to reality; secondly, if its assumptions represent reality reasonably well; thirdly, if the logical deductions arrived at were not obvious in the first place; and fourthly, if these deductions actually do explain or predict human behaviour reasonably well. As will be seen, too, it is not enough simply to apply 'Western' economic analysis, for this has been devised mainly to explain the workings of economies that are organised in a way which on the whole is totally different from that of the African rural economy. Many development economists are coming to realise that a particular type of model, until quite recently fairly unfamiliar, is most appropriate to much of the rural Third World,[1] and this is the model we use in Chapter 4 and around which a good deal centres.

Closely linked with Chapter 4 are Chapters 5 and 6, 'Land' and 'Capital and change'. The titles chosen for these three core chapters indicate our intended theme of examining the economically orthodox, fundamental productive resources or factors of production, labour, land and capital, in relation to the realities of African agriculture. In practice they do provide a useful framework on which to build, though some may find their conceptual shortcomings a little disconcerting.

While in Chapter 4 the aim is to generalise as far as possible about the behaviour of the African farm, the other chapters are principally concerned with what we consider to be the main factors tending to modify that behaviour. Apart from those already mentioned – history and the physical environment – another important influence is population growth, and Chapter 6 is concerned to some extent with this.

In Chapter 7, on agricultural exports, we discuss a topic that has perhaps received the lion's share of attention in the literature, certainly until the seventies. Probably it is true that the opening up of the markets for export crops has been the biggest influence for change in the twentieth century, and agricultural exports are still a major preoccupation of politicians and planners.

Chapters 8 and 9 discuss the numerous attempts to 'develop' the agricultural sector. We try to extract the essentials from these experiences, as represented by a few major case studies and tentatively suggest some directions in which policy might move, as well as those to avoid.

As for geographical coverage, the boundaries are not precise. We use the terms 'sub-Saharan' and 'black' Africa loosely, even though the former might strictly exclude much of, say, Niger to which there are references, while the latter might exclude South Africa and the northern parts of Sudan, both of which are referred to in the text. 'Tropical' Africa might have been a compromise, but again this would exclude, for example, Botswana and the Transkei; or perhaps 'sub-Cancer Africa' might be the best single label. In any case, boundaries do not matter too much in the extraction of general principles; indeed much of our analysis should be applicable, *mutatis mutandis*, to parts of the world other than Africa. Countries excluded from our purview are the North African fringe: Western Sahara, Morocco, Tunisia, Algeria, Libya and Egypt. Also we refer only to the mainland and not to Madagascar or the smaller islands.

References

1 See, for instance, in a recent textbook, D. Colman and F. Nixson, *Economics of Change in Less Developed Countries*, Philip Allan, London, 1978, pp. 138–143 and E.K. Fisk, 'The response of non-monetary production units to contact with the exchange economy', in L.G. Reynolds, ed., *Agriculture in Development Theory*, Yale University Press, New Haven, 1975, p. 28.

2   Descriptive background

The task of generalising about the systems of agricultural production in this vast continent is a daunting one, but generalise we must if we are to get anywhere in economics. On the other hand, the detailed deviations from the generality must always be borne in mind.

We can conceive of two sides to an agricultural system from the viewpoint of economics: the 'output side' and the 'input side'. The output side of a system involves the commodities produced and their relative quantities and values – what we call the 'product mix' – while the input side refers to the use of the factors of production, mainly land and labour. The major factors affecting these two aspects of a system are four: climate, and in particular, rainfall; the quality of the land and environment; population density; and the degree to which agriculture is commercial. These four attributes of an agricultural system may be interrelated – the quality of the land and the environment determines the density of population to some extent; climatic factors determine which, if any, commercial crops can be grown, and so on. There are other attributes that we might include such as the degree of geographical isolation, but our intention here is merely to provide a simple framework which we can use to classify agricultural systems.

The influence of rainfall, the major element in the climatic attribute, on agriculture is all-pervasive. Roughly speaking, there is a middle belt of high and seasonally prolonged rainfall centred on the equator (modified in the east of the continent), which gradually peters out the further south or north we go. A further pattern is imposed on this basic one in that the wet season not only becomes shorter and less intense, but tends to split into two with a short dry season in between, the further north or south we move from the equatorial band. Also the wet season is concentrated on the middle months of the calendar year north of the equator, and in the late and early months, south of the equator. Very broadly, the effect of this is to concentrate root crops such as yams, sweet potatoes and cassava, together with bananas and plantains, near the middle, while there is a very wide area of grain crops, especially sorghum and millet in the drier zones. Also cattle appear to a greater extent in the drier parts. This over-simplified scheme is modified in various ways; for example, on the eastern side, the cattle belt spreads downwards into the Lake Victoria region, the middle wet belt being interrupted in an easterly direction by the Ruwenzori mountains and the Rift valley; in the far Western region there is an area of very heavy rainfall that is capable of supporting rice. There are many other important details but these are best dealt with in a geography book rather than a book on economics.

The other major effect of rainfall, in particular, its seasonal distribution, is on labour use; in fact the labour applied in most African agricultural systems depends crucially on this. Usually, planting is carried out as soon as the first rains start to fall and this operation has in most cases to be done very quickly because timing in relation to the commencement of rainfall affects the productivity of labour very significantly. This is for two main reasons. The first is that the moistness of the ground affects the ease with which it can be worked; the dry season can make the earth hard. The second is that a small amount of rain generally provides the optimum conditions for seed germination; also it is important for plants to get a quick start in developing leaves so that they can make the maximum use of sunlight and, therefore, can compete more effectively with weeds. Where productivity is sensitive to the rain in this way, the whole seasonal pattern of labour input is dictated by the timing of the initial rains, for the weeding, pest control, harvesting and processing all follow on from this and are entirely determined by how and when nature is affecting crop and weed growth during the growing season. We shall have more to say about this in Chapter 4.

The variability in the amount of rainfall from year to year, and in its timing, is sometimes of great importance. This is because a high degree of variation creates uncertainty for farmers as to the decisions they make regarding the crops they should grow, the particular operations they should undertake and the timing of those operations. Under such circumstances there is a strong tendency for farmers to 'play safe' – to plant crops that are less susceptible to variations in the weather, for example, and can be depended on to yield enough food to keep going in the event of drought or flood, rather than devote too much effort to crops that are more desirable but less dependable.

The second and third attributes, quality of land and environment, and population density, can be taken together, for, as has been suggested, the one may influence the other.[1] Numerous things influence the first of these attributes, for example, soil fertility, the desirability of the climate from the point of view of human comfort, the presence or absence of tsetse flies or mosquitoes, proximity to markets for produce (including ports, for produce that is sold on world markets), and so on. To a large extent, population has been drawn, over the years, to the most desirable regions, and variation in the density of population simply reflects this fact. On the other hand, movements of population have often been constrained: in modern times, by political boundaries, and in the past, by wars, tribal boundaries and so on. Therefore in some regions the density of population is not a reflection of the economic and physical advantages of those regions, but of extraneous forces, that have caused people to congregate in greater numbers than if they had chosen freely. Furthermore, the physical characteristics of a region may change adversely, owing to, for example, changes in weather conditions (e.g. the Sahel drought of recent years – see below), or to the effect of the natural growth in population in bringing about soil erosion due to over-farming or over-grazing. The population of such regions may then become trapped to some degree, depending on other social and political forces that prevent them from moving out. Under those circumstances, it would seem reasonable to say that 'high' population densities reflected the pressure of population on resources – but only under those circumstances. Clearly, to look upon all high population-density areas as high population-pressure areas and low density areas as low pressure areas is very much mistaken. A density of two persons per square kilometre in Mauritania may well represent a high degree of pressure on the land resources of Mauritania, while a density of 100 in Rwanda may be well within the capacity of the land there and give people a fair standard of living on all counts.

In viewing agricultural systems on the basis of these two features, then, we need really to look at the one, population density, in relation to the other, the productivity of the land and the potential of the environment; and the second is certainly not easy to assess except in a very broad way. We can perhaps compare densities as between regions that are physically similar, and expect to find differences in agricultural systems, as indeed appears to be the case, but if we are comparing physically different regions, it may be more sensible to look upon differences in density as mainly reflecting differences in the endowments of good environment and productive land – unless it is known that population movement is, or has been, constrained in some way. More will be said about population density and pressure in Chapter 6.

The fourth major factor affecting agricultural systems is the existence of external markets for products and the degree of response to them. In most cases the market is international – for commodities such as cocoa, coffee, cotton, groundnuts, tea and oil palm products – while internal markets, especially for food are perhaps a weaker influence, but not to be neglected. Yet another relatively less significant influence is the market for labour. In some parts this is of great importance, as in Malawi where large numbers of rural people move out seasonally to work in South Africa and Zimbabwe; another is Upper Volta, whence many people migrate southwards especially to work on coffee farms in the Ivory Coast.

We shall deal with these forces in greater detail in following chapters. For the moment, we are simply looking at them as the major attributes with which we can establish a broad framework for classifying African agricultural systems, and we concentrate on the four dominant features, rainfall, population, natural resources and market orientation, while bearing in mind other things that may be in evidence in any particular environment.

The general nature of land and labour use

Before going into greater detail, it is perhaps worth saying something in very general terms about African agricultural systems, and especially with regard to the nature of *resource use*, i.e. the 'input side'. For the outstanding economic feature of African rural economies is that they are *land-intensive*; i.e. the area of cultivable land relative to labour input is high, as compared with most Asian countries in particular. This is nearly the same thing as saying that population densities are relatively low, except that the labour input referred to is not merely the number of workers, but the amount of effort that those workers tend to apply, which is also low as compared with the general tendency in other countries. Of course, in a situation where land is in abundance relative to labour it is economically rational to use plenty of land relative to labour, contrary to the view that often used to be held by Western and colonialist observers of African agriculture, who were overly influenced by their own labour- and capital-intensive systems. Of course, in the extreme case of very abundant land, the optimum system of food production is based on hunting, fishing and gathering of wild produce, which is still the major system for some African people, such as the pygmies of the Zaire basin, and is a supplementary (and often enjoyable) system for many more. But far and away the dominant systems of land-intensive production are based on the burning of natural vegetation before cultivating, which is followed by natural fallows of at least two years duration (and usually much longer).

A note about terminology

The terms applied to these fire and fallow types of agricultural system tend to be rather confusing to the uninitiated, and moreover, there does not seem to be complete agreement as regards terminology. In particular, some writers distinguish between what they call 'rotational bush-fallow' systems and 'shifting cultivation' systems, while others would not make such a distinction and simply use 'shifting cultivation' as a general term. For instance W.B. Morgan[2] characterises shifting cultivation by short periods of cultivation and long periods of fallow, with field boundaries marked only during the cultivation periods; thus, when a new field is being cleared, its boundaries will not generally be the same as the old boundaries marked before the land was left fallow.[3] (This is partly because the natural growth of vegetation during the fallow period obliterates any signs of the old boundaries.) On the other hand under rotational bush-fallow, rights to a particular field area are maintained throughout the fallow period, so that old fields are returned to after fallowing and recultivated. In some farming systems, the settlement site itself may be moved from time to time, and some authors restrict the term shifting cultivation to that type of system (although Morgan does not). Clearly these characteristics, singled out as the basis for terminology, are important economically, but other features are just as important (e.g. the length of the fallow period and the length of the cultivation period);[4] so we shall adopt what appears to be the most common practice and refer to all systems using fire clearance and 'long' natural fallow periods as shifting cultivation, while not using it as a very precise term.

There may also be some confusion about the use of the term 'intensity' of cultivation. Generally, this is used to indicate the intensity of land use. Thus 'intensive cultivation' is taken to refer to a system of farming in which most of the (cultivatable) land is used for growing crops in any year and, conversely, not much of it is idle or fallow. This also implies that the amount of labour applied per unit of land area is relatively high; and it may thus also be called a 'labour-intensive' system. At the other end of the spectrum we have 'extensive' systems, such as shifting cultivation or transhumant pastoralism, where the ratio of land to labour is relatively high. Alternatively these may be called 'land-intensive' – the area of land combined with a unit of labour being relatively high.

Using shifting cultivation in a loose sense, then, we can say that it accounts for most of the land use in tropical Africa, although the precise form it takes varies greatly, and indeed it is often combined with various kinds of permanent cultivation. It should be remembered, however, that although shifting systems account for the great proportion of land *area* (very roughly, about two-thirds to three-quarters of the area of Africa between the tropic lines), the proportion of *production* it accounts for and the proportion of the rural population dependent on it must be lower – because more intensive systems are in regions of high population density, so that their populations and yields are high even though land areas are small.[5] (We are here excluding pastoral systems which are even more land-using – or, perhaps, space-using – than shifting agriculture.)

A further important qualification needs to be made to these simple generalisations about African farming systems, however, and that is that shifting cultivation may often not make up an entire system, but rather be part of one. A common form of farming in Africa – and indeed throughout the world, at the present time and historically – is what has been called 'concentric-ring' farming. Under such a system, the intensity of agricultural production is relatively high near to the village or dwelling and decreases with distance from the village. For example, land may be permanently cultivated, with manuring and composting, in the immediate vicinity of the houses, while land further away has shifting cultivation; or in more densely populated areas, the more distant land may be used for grazing cattle, while the 'in-fields' are ploughed and permanently cultivated, with manure and compost (e.g. in parts of Uganda and Ethiopia). It is probable that some form of concentric-ring farming system supports more rural Africans than any other system, although the most common way in which the 'outer-rings' are farmed is by shifting cultivation. Perhaps it is more reasonable to call shifting cultivation a method or technique rather than a system, although of course it may be a system if it is the sole technique used.

An agricultural round trip

Figure 2.1 shows the distribution of the main types of natural vegetation – a simple indicator of general ecological conditions. Starting in the north-west corner in Mauritania and northern Senegal, and moving eastwards, we have a dry belt of land, going through the two countries mentioned, plus Mali, Niger, Chad and Sudan. The vegetation is mostly dry savannah in the south merging into thornbush steppe and then desert in the north. The economy is based on pastoralism and the population is very sparse. In the northern, desert parts nomadism predominates while transhumance is the rule further south. Under nomadic conditions, stockmen lead their herds, which are mostly camels, sheep and goats, to areas of patchy vegetation, where the amount of forage depends on irregularly distributed rainfall. There is thus no reg-

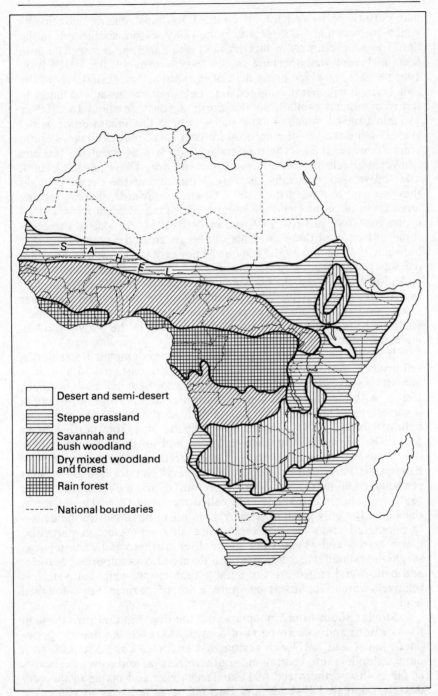

Desert and semi-desert

Steppe grassland

Savannah and
bush woodland

Dry mixed woodland
and forest

Rain forest

----- National boundaries

Fig. 2.1 Zones of major natural vegetation

ular pattern of movement, in contrast to transhumance movements which are seasonal – northwards in the rainy season, southwards in the dry. The southern part of this dry land, the Sahel, has achieved a grim fame in recent years because of the terrible drought that lasted from 1965 to 1973, in which many died of starvation. The boundaries of the Sahel are not generally agreed on, but they are usually defined in terms of annual rainfall. In the north it starts at about the 100 or 150 mm isohyet, which is more or less where the Sahara ends; its beginning is marked by the appearance of a small plant known as cram-cram. Towards the southern boundary, which is at about the 600 mm isohyet, agriculture becomes more in evidence. These rainfall boundaries move geographically, however, and during the recent drought they are said to have drifted 100–150 km southwards, thereby turning large areas of pastureland into desert. This kind of event has occurred in the past, too, in 1910–1916 and in 1940–1944. An idea of the geographical impact of these droughts can be got from the observation that between 1941/42 and 1951/52 about 30 per cent of the area of Mauritania was turned from pasture into desert.[6] There is little in the way of agriculture in the region, but some staple crops, mainly sorghum and millets, are grown. Irrigated rice is important on the Senegal and Niger rivers, and the irrigated Gezira between the Blue and White Niles, south of Khartoum, is the major cash-crop area in the Sudan, producing chiefly cotton.

It would be neat and convenient for the geographer if the northern dry belt extended simply from west coast to east coast, but it does not. It bends sharply south-eastwards into Somalia and northern Kenya, with the Ethiopian highlands forming an interruption. Ethiopia is something of an island; it is separated from the mainland – the moist bulk of tropical Africa – by the dry strip running from north-west to south-east, through south-eastern Sudan and northern Kenya (where there is even some desert, east of Lake Turkana).[7] The western half of Ethiopia is fairly densely populated (generally more than 20 persons per square kilometre), with fairly high rainfall and high altitude. In the south-western parts a staple crop called the ensat or ensete is grown, this being the only place in Africa where it can be found. In the densely populated areas, several cereals are also important, in particular maize, barley and wheat, while in the drier northern and eastern parts, sorghum and millet are dominant. Cattle are also an important feature, and cotton and coffee are the notable cash crops, while cultivation is relatively intensive, involving quite a lot of permanently ploughed land.

Moving south from Ethiopia across the dry strip that runs through the northern and eastern parts of Kenya, we reach the densely populated, moist and fairly rich region that encircles Lake Victoria, with limbs extending into central and southern Kenya, and south-westwards as far as the northern end of Lake Tanganyika and taking in the very densely populated Rwanda and Burundi. It is not easy to generalise regarding the staple foods in this region, but roughly speaking, bananas and plantains predominate on the north-western shores of Victoria (Uganda), cassava (manioc) in Rwanda and Burundi, sorghum and millet in the north-western corners of Tanzania and in eastern Uganda and maize in the remainder of the region, i.e. the eastern and southern sides of the Lake. Cotton and coffee are major cash crops, and maize is also important on the north-east of the Lake (Kenya). Cattle are much in evidence throughout this region and one often finds them used for ploughing. Shifting cultivation is the exception. To the east of the Lake Victoria region, the pastoralism of the dry north-eastern region, which is in effect a kind of extension of the Sahelian and Saharan zones, merges into the agriculture of the eastern and central plateau, which extends right across from Angola to Mozambique and southern Tanzania. Pastoralism is still important in eastern Kenya and north-eastern Tanzania, and it is exemplified by the famous Maasai (or Masai) people, whose way of life is coming into conflict with the harsh realities of population growth and the incursions of agriculture.

The eastern and central plateau includes southern Tanzania, Mozambique, Malawi, Zimbabwe, Zambia and Angola, and is rather variable agriculturally, not least because of political circumstances in the past, especially in Zimbabwe and Angola, but also because of differences in altitude and rainfall. It is perhaps best to look at each country in turn, rather than try to generalise for the whole region.

In southern Tanzania and Mozambique there is mostly shifting cultivation with woodland fallow. Maize is important in Tanzania, in the area of Mozambique on either side of Malawi and in the southern third of Mozambique. Millet and sorghum predominate down the central band of Mozambique but, towards the coast, cassava takes over in an area straddling the border with Tanzania. At the northern end of Lake Malawi there is an area of fairly intensive cultivation, including a banana and plantain area and an area where agriculture and livestock-rearing are both of importance. Malawi is relatively densely populated and intensively cultivated, especially in the south and along the shores of Lake Malawi; it is also very diverse agriculturally as a result of the mountainous terrain. The chief agricultural feature of Zimbabwe has been the division into white and black (tribal) land. The former, whose area is out of proportion to the number of European farmers, follows the central uplands with their more desirable climate, which run diagonally across the centre of the country from south-west to north-east. In Zambia, cassava (manioc) is dominant in the north-western areas of both of that country's two 'bulges'; but this phases into millets and sorghums; maize is important as both staple and cash crop along the line of the railway that serves the copper belt, and on the eastern borders. Cattle are also more in evidence in the maize areas, which tend to be more developed and commercialised, and where agriculture is more intensive than in the more sparsely populated bulk of the land where shifting cultivation is the rule. Angola has mainly savannah woodland, merging into grass and scrub, and then desert in the south and east (there is a very thin strip of desert along the coastal plain). Roots, especially cassava, are the major staples in the north, phasing into maize and then millets and sorghum, moving southward.

Moving northwards into the huge basin drained by the Zaire (Congo) and its tributaries, we find an environment that contrasts very sharply with the regions we have previously covered. Population is sparse, rainfall is high, much of the land is forested, cattle are rare[8] and long-fallow shifting cultivation is nearly universal. In the southern half of the basin, and in the west, cassava is the dominant crop, and this is so down as far as the middle of Angola. A large tract of land in the north-east of the Zaire basin, roughly following the northward and north-westward curve of the river Zaire is notable for having rice as a staple crop. North of that, maize takes over and then cassava in the Central African Republic. Bananas and plantains are major staples in the far west, especially in Gabon and Congo and in the east and north towards the Ruwenzori mountains and the Rift Valley. The foregoing gives only a very simplified and broad picture of the dominant crops grown in this large and important region, and there is considerable variation in detail. There is, too, much variation in the detail of the farming systems, crudely labelled shifting cultivation; this is brought out in Miracle's excellent book.[9] He distinguishes 12 separate sub-types of the classic tropical long-fallow system, as well as ash-fertiliser-dependent long-fallow systems (mainly northern Zambia), compost-dependent long-fallow systems (only in savannah areas) and short-fallow systems with irrigation and manuring (mainly Rwanda and Burundi). The sub-types of the classic long-fallow depend on the combination and sequence of the operations of cutting, burning, hoeing and planting; but the most common is 'cut, burn, plant' found throughout the forest zone. This consists of cutting down the forest in the patch to be cultivated, during the dry season, followed by burning after the wood has been left to dry for a few days. Seeds are then planted directly into the ash in holes made by sticks. Weeding proceeds during the growing season and birds and other pests are kept from the ripening crops by children until harvest.

Travelling westwards, we arrive in the more densely populated coastal states of West Africa, from Cameroun and Nigeria to Sierra Leone, Guinea, Guinea-Bissau, The Gambia and Senegal. This is perhaps the most complex of our regions, agriculturally, as there is great variation in the predominant staples, population densities and cultivation practices and in the degree of commercialisation. The northern parts of these countries (the 'Sudanic' zone) merge into the Sahelian zone, and sorghum and millet along with pastoralism are major features, although the latter is not generally nomadic and is not as important as it is to the north and north-east. Shifting cultivation with grass fallow is the general rule, but fallow periods are short in some areas of high population density, and both permanent cultivation and some ploughing are in evidence; this is particularly so in the north and north-west of Nigeria, especially in the country surrounding the city of Kano, and in northern Cameroun. Most of this dry belt is relatively uncommercialised, but groundnuts are the major cash crop and earn fairly high amounts per head of population in northern Nigeria. Senegal and The Gambia. Cotton is also important, mainly in northern Cameroun.

The southern, or coastal halves of these West African countries contain the most densely populated and highly commercialised agricultural areas in tropical Africa. Population is especially dense in southern Nigeria and along the coasts of Togo, Benin (formerly Dahomey) and Ghana. Dominant cash crops are oil palm in south-eastern Nigeria and Benin, cocoa in south-western Nigeria, Ghana and Ivory Coast, and coffee in Ivory Coast. In addition a trade in food crops has developed, produced in the middle belt of the countries from Ivory Coast eastwards to Nigeria, and supplying the export crop areas and towns to the south. Shifting cultivation (or rotational bush fallow) is still the most important agricultural technique, despite the high population densities, although, of course, fallow periods tend to be short and concentric-ring farming is taking over, with more and more permanently cultivated lands. Staple crops are varied, but broadly, the region can be divided into four: the western quarter from The Gambia and southern Senegal to the western half of Ivory coast, where rice predominates; the middle-western quarter, from eastern Ivory Coast to Benin, where dominant staples are in great variety, including yams, cassava, bananas and plantains, sweet potatoes and maize; the middle-eastern quarter, which is the southern half of Nigeria, where yams are especially important. Southern and western Cameroun, making up the eastern quarter, also have a varied collection of predominant staples.

Having thus covered very broadly the salient agricultural features, we now proceed to look at a few concrete examples of farming practice. The choice of examples and the amount of space devoted to each one, is constrained more by what is available in the literature than by their relevance or economic importance. This rather unsatisfactory approach is enforced by the very mixed nature of the available material; little of it was written with economics primarily in view and few of the studies are as detailed as we would like. There is, therefore, some danger of being misled into believing that one agricultural system is more complex than another, when in fact it is simply that the evidence is more detailed for the one than for the other. Also, of course, the systems described are based on studies in the past, so current conditions may be quite different. We have tried to keep a reasonable geographical coverage, with examples from the main types of agricultural region.

A few stops

1 A good description of the economy of a village situated in Mali, on the banks of the Niger, is given by W.I. Jones,[10] and it is worth summarising here (although justice cannot be done in the space available). The basis of the farming system is a kind of shifting cultivation of sorghum, although fields have quite long periods of cultivation and are only left fallow – again for long periods – when they are quite exhausted. These upland fields (*foroba*) are not scarce and rights to use are maintained as long as they are cultivated. The operational unit in *foroba* cultivation is an extended family (*lu*), with the male elders taking the decisions, and although there are small, individually controlled plots called *dyomforo* for growing sauce ingredients and men's cash crops like tomatoes and groundnuts, priority is given to the staple, sorghum, on the *foroba* land. In addition some rice is grown close to the river where the land is seasonally flooded, but the yields are extremely variable because of variation in the flooding behaviour of the river, so that rice cannot be depended on for food supply. Also a rice

irrigation project was set up with outside help, but it was not particularly successful for various reasons.

Rainfall averages about 1 000 mm but, as is so often the case in Africa, is very variable, especially as regards the timing and amount of the crucial first showers of the rainy season (May to October). Before the rains start the fields are cleared – by burning, if cultivation is following the period of fallow. When the first rain arrives it becomes possible to work the moistened soil, which is heaped into mounds. Formerly this was always done with hand hoes, but nowadays ploughs are increasingly being used and they allow the operation to be performed much more quickly. However, an interesting observation of Jones's is that although the farmers by using ploughs are enabled to plant a bigger area, they cannot always fully weed it, whereas under the old manual system, weeding labour was not a constraint because the area was smaller. Sowing is done by making holes in the earth mounds to take the seeds, and the timing of this task in relation to rainfall is of great importance as the seed will not germinate if the rain fails to continue. Weeding follows in the rainy season, two or three times, and the harvest is in October and November when the weather becomes drier. Harvest work is communal and accompanied by drumming, to make it more enjoyable. Other crops are interplanted with sorghum, and less fertility-demanding crops follow the sorghum-dominated mixtures in the later years of cropping – for example, millet, fonio and sometimes cassava. The precise mixtures grown and their succession depend on various micro-agricultural factors, such as location, slope, etc., and the degree of soil exhaustion, as indicated by the type of wild vegetation that appears.

2 In the southern Ethiopian highlands are areas of high population density and intensive agriculture in medium rainfall conditions. The agrarian economy is exemplified by the community of Chento, the subject of a study in 1968,[11] which consists of 137 dwellings and occupies 2.59 km^2 (one square mile). Apparently 400–500 people are supported by this land (150–200 persons per km^2). We have here the method based on grazing of cattle on common grasslands and using the manure they produce in night-stalls for permanent cultivation of in-fields.

The staple food is the root of the ensete, a banana-like plant (the fruit is not eaten) which is also used for clothing and furnishings; barley, wheat and pulses are also important, these being grown in fairly flexible rotations. None of the land is unused; 30 per cent of it is grazing land.

A great deal of labour is involved in carrying manure from the stalls to the fields (the task of the women) and in taking fodder from meadowland, and in the form of weeds from the barley fields, to the cattle. Terraces and lateral drainage ditches for preventing erosion on the fairly steep slopes are in evidence and there is some irrigation by stream diversion. Ploughs are relatively unimportant here (although there are more of them in nearby Holo), cultivation being by hand hoe. There is rather little in the way of marketed production.

3 Masii location in Machakos District, Kenya,[12] has a high population density (over 116 per km^2) and fairly low and very variable rainfall (averaging about 635 mm per year). Agriculture is intensive, with indi-

vidual ownership of both arable and grazing land. Ox-drawn ploughs are used for nearly all cultivation, though weeding is by hand, and quite a lot of effort is devoted to terracing and fencing of land. Much of the land is of very poor quality or even unusable so that the average holding size of about 4 hectares does not represent an abundance, the greater part being used as grazing land. Maize is a preferred crop but, because it is sensitive to the variations in rainfall, the more drought-resistant millet, sorghum and *wimbi* are also grown. Little milk is obtained from the cattle which are used mainly for ploughing and as a store of wealth, though some sheep and goats are also kept.

4 The part of Africa around Lake Victoria is a region of relatively high population density, matched only in this respect for such a large area by parts of Nigeria with its neighbouring coastland, and Ethiopia. An example of the kinds of farming practised there is found in the Bukoba district of north-west Tanzania, on the western shores of Lake Victoria.[13]

Rainfall is plentiful and reliable and land is used fairly intensively, individual rights to land being strong. The essence of the farming system is in the division of land into grassland of low fertility, grazed by cattle, on the one hand, and on the other, plots cultivated intensively using the hand hoe, and containing combinations of bananas, the predominant staple crop, coffee and other food crops. On average, the cropped plot is about 0·8 hectares and the grassland about 0·6. The cattle are stabled at night and their manure is applied to the cultivated land, thereby effectively bringing fertility from the grassland pasture and concentrating it in a smaller area around the dwelling. (Only a minority of farmers (37 per cent) actually own the cattle, but the animals are hired out to those who do not own, for the purpose of obtaining manure.) The average number of cattle per farm is 1 to 2, including non-owning farms (4 per owning farm). Two other features of the system are interesting. One is the fact that the fertility of the banana land is gradually built up over a period of years, by the continuous addition of manure and by the practice of mulching (i.e. covering the soil with grass and leaves to reduce evaporation). The other is the greater intensity of cultivation nearer to the homestead – a rough pattern of concentric rings prevails with declining intensity of cultivation moving away from the hut; bananas receive most attention in the inner rings and coffee and secondary food crops are phased in further away. (A small area of food crops is also grown by shifting cultivation on the grassland.) The coffee is, of course, all sold, and it accounts for most of the cash income, which was estimated at about 40 per cent of total income – quite a high degree of commercial production for Africa.

5 The Ndendeuli of Southern Tanzania[14] are shifting cultivators and populate the land at a low density (about 2 per km^2). Rainfall is moderate at about 1 000 mm, falling for the most part between mid-December and April, and the major crop is maize.

Because they live in fairly tight communities of 30 to 50 households, the cultivation of the land is more intensive and soil-exhausting than it would be if the people were more scattered. This means that not only is the bush-fallow technique practised on the land surrounding the community, but that households have to move to more fertile areas every now and then when the local land becomes over-cultivated. A household may shift to the outskirts of its community, join another community or start a new one. Gulliver estimates that it takes about 15 years until community land becomes exhausted, when the shifting of households becomes necessary.

There is very little in the way of livestock, because of tsetse fly, nor is there much hunting or any fishing. Gathering of wild fruits and vegetables is not much in evidence either. There is a small amount of tobacco grown for cash.

The method of production follows the standard shifting cultivation pattern. Wood is cut on new fields in the dry season from June to September, followed by the burning of piled wood and vegetation and the scattering of ashes. The ground is hoed and cleared when it becomes soft with the onset of rain in December and the planting is done. The wet season from January to May is spent weeding and thinning, with more and more time devoted to pest-scaring as the grain ripens. Harvesting and storage by the women is done in May/June.

6 An interesting variant of shifting cultivation is the *citemene* system found in Zambia and described at length by Allan.[15] Population densities are generally less than 4 per km^2 and rainfall is fairly low. Here, woodland from a wider area than is to be planted is cut and carefully stacked on the cultivation site during the dry season. There are different kinds of wood stack appropriate to different situations and they require some skill in construction. The farmers are also expert meteorologists in that they have to forecast the onset of irregularly timed rains accurately, so that the burning of the wood is under really dry conditions while not being too long before the rain. If it is too long the fertilising ash formed from the burn tends to be blown away before planting can be carried out, and if rain falls on the stacked wood, of course, it does not burn properly. Their skill is such that the crops rarely fail. There is a number of variants of the technique.

Allan has an interesting discussion of the scientific logic of the system. It seems that nitrates (which increase fertility) in the soil form to the greatest extent when conditions change from dry to moist – the drier the soil is, the greater the quantity of nitrate formed. Thus the burning of the wood not only provides ash fertiliser, but also increases the dryness of the soil and the subsequent formation of nitrates. Experiments showed that either a burn alone or ash alone resulted in much lower yields than is the case with ash and burn.

7 One of Miracle's many useful descriptions of agricultural systems in Zaïre[9] concerns a village of the Sakata tribe located in the forest zone. The burning of forest in the area to be cultivated is carried out in the dry season, from July to September, with undergrowth cut first, followed by the felling of trees except those that are too hard, big or valuable. After leaving the wood to dry for about two weeks, the burn may be done in one of two ways depending on the main crop to be planted; for bananas and plantains, only partial burning is required and so the wood is lit on the windward side to stimulate a rapid spread of fire; for cassava the reverse process is better, ensuring a complete conflagration. After the first rain has fallen, in the case of cassava, mounds of earth are raked up, about one metre across and half a

metre high, and cassava cuttings are stuck into them (about three per mound). Other crops – bananas, plantains, maize and tobacco, principally – are planted between the mounds, at different times. Cassava has the advantage that it can be left growing in the ground for a long time without harm, so that harvesting lasts from about one year until about two years after planting. Weeds are removed when they start to grow large, by hoeing between the mounds and pulling from the mounds.

Yams are an important supplementary crop and are grown in separate fields mainly as pure stands and without mounds, as are sugar cane and rain-fed rice. Gardens containing vegetables, maize, tobacco, bananas and plantains, and sweet potatoes are situated around the houses, and are fertilised with ash from burnt refuse and with compost; they may also be fenced. Other food sources are a number of fruits, such as citrus, pineapple, avocado, mango, etc., and goats, sheep and poultry.

8 In the south-east of Nigeria lies the Uboma Local Council area containing six villages, the subject of a detailed socio-economic study carried out in the mid-sixties.[16] The whole region in which Uboma is situated is one of very high population densities – over 200 persons per km^2. Rainfall is high and there is a four-month dry season.

The rural economy is based on the root crops, cassava, yams and cocoyams as staples, with palm oil and kernels as cash earners. Cultivation is by bush-fallow, but fallow periods are of course rather short with such high population densities, for the most part being from one to three years, but increasing to seven years in more sparsely populated parts. The root crops are grown on earth mounds and are intercropped with maize, vegetables, groundnuts, etc. There is a strong element of concentric ring farming here as elsewhere. More attention is paid to crops on compound land in that they are manured and composted and planted first with yam at the beginning of the rains. Oil palms are densest near the compound, some being in special groves with about 250 to the hectare. Further away the land is much more open and the palms are dotted about at roughly 25 to the hectare.

An indication of the extent to which the practice of shifting cultivation has been eaten away by the spread of permanent cultivation is given by the average figures for a sample of 34 farmers shown in Table 2.1.

Table 2.1 Land use in Uboma, Nigeria

Land use	Hectares
Crops	1·18
Fallow: 1–3 years	1·17
3–7 years	0·42
7–15 years	0·30
Over 15 years	0·04
Total fallow	1·93
Total arable (including fallow)	3·11
Trees	0·06
Total area	3·17

9 Northern Nigeria has some very densely populated areas, where land is under continuous cultivation. In the east of Sokoto Province is one such region (60 to 300 persons per km^2) and six villages were selected for a study by Luning in the early sixties.[17] Rainfall is 635 to 1 000 mm per year. The major crops are millet and sorghum with groundnuts as an important cash crop.

Most of the land is continuously cultivated rain-fed upland, but there is also moist land known as *fadama*, in valley bottoms and depressions, which is used for highly valued, specialist crops such as sugar cane, rice and onions. There is very little fallow land but quite substantial areas are kept as grazing land (often only suitable for that purpose) and woodland used for firewood.

The use of animal manure for the maintenance of fertility is of great importance. Goats and sheep and some cattle are the major source and much time is devoted to transporting manure by donkey from the farmyard to the fields. This occurs during the growing season when the goats and sheep are tethered in the compound and fed with weeds from the fields and other gathered fodder, while the cattle are kept on grazing land. After the harvest they are allowed to graze the cropped fields. Thus the system fairly efficiently utilises nearly all the available land fertility. Inedible vegetable matter in the form of stubble and weeds is effectively converted into a store of animal protein and fertility as manure, while vegetation on the poor land is similarly converted by the grazing of cattle.

10 In south-east Ghana, shifting cultivation dominates in an environment where moderate rainfall is erratic both in amount and in timing. Maize and cassava are the major crops, supplemented in particular by groundnuts and semi-wild oil palms. There is not much commercial production. People are for the most part concentrated in villages of 200–300 heads, and land use is distinctly of the concentric-ring variety. Table 2.2 shows data taken from a study of six villages.[18]

Table 2.2 Cultivated land as a percentage of total land area

Village	Distance from centre of village (km)					
	0–0·8	0·8–1·6	1·7–2·4	2·5–3·2	3·3–4·0	4·1–4·8
Podoe	22·9	2·9	3·1	3·3	–	–
Kpomkpo	11·4	13·8	1·6	4·0	0·1	0·5
Akpokofe	45·2	2·9	2·9	1·3	–	–
Dzalele	20·1	2·7	1·3	1·8	–	–
Waya	4·4	12·2	3·8	3·4	0·3	0·4
Toda	13·7	12·1	32·1	5·7	–	1·3

There are in fact two rainfall peaks (March–June and September–December, major and minor respectively) and this together with the extreme variability of the rain makes cultivation far from simple. Thornton's concise description of the complexity is worth quoting in full:

> Cropping and yields are affected directly by a variety of factors in the short run which cause the farmer to modify his plans and which take the result largely outside his control; the shorter the growing season the more this tends to be true. These factors include labour

availability, both family and hired at crucial times, but also particularly the weather. ...

While many quick decisions may be taken in the light of changing circumstances to affect cropping in detail, a typical sequence of cropping was a six-season sequence with maize grown first after clearing, sometimes mixed with vegetables; followed by maize and/or groundnuts in the first minor season; followed by maize in the third, later interplanted with cassava which may be allowed to continue to grow through to the fifth or sixth season, being cropped little by little over as much as 18 months while regeneration of the natural vegetation is allowed to begin.

The husbandry is characterised by certain phases which may be listed as follows:

1 the *annual clearing* of 'forest' or 'savannah' (the density of vegetation depending in part on the length of the rest period and in part on local soil and soil-water characteristics); this takes place particularly during February–March and also in August–September preceding the minor season; substantial trees, ant hills and growing oil palms frequently are left;
2 the *planting* of annual crops, concentrated at the beginning of both seasons but frequently delayed in the major season either on account of weather or to gain benefits from intercropping;
3 some alternation of extractive and restorative crops, perhaps accidental rather than intentional, in soils which quickly lose soluble nutrients by quick percolation of ground-water;
4 crop care limited chiefly to *weeding*, the frequency and timing of which is conditioned by intercropping and whether crops have been planted in rows (row-planting may apply to maize and cassava but seldom to other crops);
5 harvesting spread over time in the cases of maize (a proportion of which is commonly harvested green), cassava and vegetables, but concentrated in the case of groundnuts;
6 simple *storage* of maize and groundnuts to extend the period over which home-grown food supply is available, to spread the post-harvesting tasks (especially shelling of groundnuts), and to take advantage of seasonal price variations for that portion of the crops to be sold;
7 home-scale processing for all home-grown food ...;
8 the *marketing* [of any surplus products].[19]

Agriculture in the African economy

Having attempted to get some idea of the general nature of African agriculture and looked at examples of farming methods, can we now be more quantitative and see how agriculture fits into the general economy and assess the major aggregate changes that have been taking place in recent years? In other words, what are the results, in the aggregate, of African farming systems? What do they deliver to the people of Africa? In practice, statistics that can be relied on to tell us

Table 2.3
Statistics of Population, Labour and Agricultural Production, by Country

	Population, 1978 est., million	Population density, persons per km²	Percentage of labour in agriculture 1978	Agricultural product[1] as per cent of GDP	Agricultural production per head in 1978 as per cent of 1969–71 average	Food production per head in 1978 as per cent of 1969–71 average
Angola	6·908	6	59·0		62	84
Benin	3·341	30	46·7	38 ('77)	93	94
Botswana	0·750	1	81·7	24 ('76)	114	114
Burundi	4·068	145	83·9		103	103
Cameroun	6·855	14	81·5	31 ('76)	100	103
Central African Republic	1·912	3	88·2	32 ('71)	98	103
Chad	4·157	3	85·1	41 ('75)	95	92
Congo	1·453	4	35·7		82	81
Djibouti	0·114	5	n.a.		n.a.	n.a.
Equatorial Guinea	0·332	12	75·8		n.a.	n.a.
Ethiopia	30·350	25	80·2	46 ('76)	81	81
Gabon	0·536	2	77·4	6 ('78)	94	95
The Gambia	0·541	49	78·8		73	73
Ghana	10·775	45	52·3	51 ('76)	79	79
Guinea-Bissau	0·553	15	83·2		105	105
Guinea	4·762	19	81·1		86	87
Ivory Coast	7·248	23	80·5	25 ('78)	106	116
Kenya	14·658	25	78·5	34 ('77)	98	90

Lesotho	1·226	41	85·1	37 ('74)	88	95
Liberia	1·677	15	70·9	14 ('77)	105	109
Malawi	5·297	45	84·9	49 ('73)	114	105
Mali	6·146	5	87·9		98	95
Mauritania	1·527	1	83·8	25 ('78)	78	78
Mozambique	9·955	13	66·3		75	78
Namibia	0·965	1	49·9		88	87
Niger	5·006	4	89·0	51 ('69)	85	85
Nigeria	68·724	74	55·1	26 ('75)	90	90
Rwanda	4·631	178	90·4	49 ('76)	105	103
Senegal	5·364	27	75·5	30 ('75)	110	109
Sierra Leone	2·988	42	66·4	37 ('77)	89	89
Somalia	3·446	5	81·0		87	87
South Africa	26·904	22	29·0	82[2] ('78)	101	103
Sudan	16·693	7	77·9	34 ('75)	96	108
Swaziland	0·511	30	74·5	31 ('73)	112	109
Tanzania	16·886	18	82·1	46 ('78)	89	93
Togo	2·449	44	69·0	28 ('76)	80	81
Uganda	12·436	53	82·0	73 ('76)	80	92
Upper Volta	5·986	22	82·6	41 ('74)	94	94
Zaïre	26·445	11	75·3	19 ('75)	93	94
Zambia	5·508	7	67·9	14 ('77)	100	101
Zimbabwe	6·960	18	59·7	15 ('78)	89	97
Total population	310·139 million					

Sources: UN Demographic Yearbook, UN Monthly Bulletin of Statistics, FAO Production Yearbook.

[1] Agriculture, forestry, hunting and fishing.
[2] Includes Namibia.

what is happening are not easy to come by, but it is worth looking at those that are available for the general impression they give, while taking care to treat the data with reservation.

Table 2.3 gives a collection of these data. Looking at population first, an important feature is its very unequal distribution among countries. To begin with, out of a total population of 310 million, 69 million are in Nigeria (although it should be said that Nigerian population census figures are notoriously unreliable). Nigeria and Ethiopia contain about 100 million people, and those two countries plus Zaïre, Sudan and Tanzania account for over one half of the population of sub-Saharan Africa. Out of 40 countries, 8 have populations of less than 1 million and 21 have populations of less than 5 million.

Agriculture generally contributes less than half the gross domestic product and there is considerable variation in this proportion, as can be seen from Table 2.3. Comparatively low contributions, as in Gabon, Zaire and Zambia for instance, can generally be attributed to the existence of highly-valued mineral-extracting operations. The figures can be rather misleading, however, as that type of industry may involve a high degree of foreign ownership and operation, so that the amount of their value added accruing to the *nationals* of the countries where they are situated is often considerably less than the gross value added. Thus generally, the proportion that agriculture contributes to the gross *national* product is likely to be higher than that contributed to the gross domestic product.

In any case, when we look at agriculture's contribution to employment, i.e. approximately the proportion of a country's people that is directly supported by farming and pastoralism, we get quite a different picture. Over 80 per cent of the labour forces is in agriculture in 19 of the 40 countries, and 28 of the countries had more than 70 per cent in agriculture. Thus we can assert with good reason that agriculture (and pastoralism) is the main means of support for over 200 million people.

How has agriculture been faring over the last few years? Not very well at all, if we can believe the figures. The last two columns of Table 2.3 show the position in 1978 compared with the average of 1969–71 in terms of agricultural output per head of population and food output per head. The precise values of these figures are not to be taken too seriously, but the general impression they give is probably a fair one – and that is one of stagnation or decline. Few countries (and even fewer people) have experienced an improvement. Of the big five – Nigeria, Ethiopia, Zaïre, Sudan and Tanzania–only Sudan has shown any rise in food production per head – a mere 8 per cent; and the other four show a definite decline. The population of those countries that have experienced a decline .in food production per head amounts to 222 million – 78 per cent of the population of black Africa. Moreover, it is unlikely that these worrying statistics arise merely because of inaccuracy, or because 1978 was untypically bad. Figure 2.3 shows that, for the whole of Africa (including the Northern countries), the 1978 outcome was in line with a downward trend; and figures for the fifties suggest a similar picture, as do independent estimates made by the United States Department of Agriculture.[20]

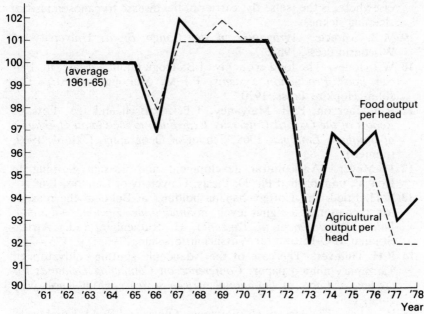

Fig. 2.2 Indices of agricultural output per head and food output per head; all Africa, 1961/1965 – 1978 (1961 – 1965 average = 100)
Source: FAO *Production Yearbook*

References

1 The rainfall regime, too, could be looked upon as one of the factors that make up the quality of the land and the environment.
2 W.B. Morgan, 'Peasant agriculture in tropical Africa,' in M.F. Thomas and G.W. Whittington (eds), *Environment and Land Use in Africa*, Methuen, London, 1969, pp. 241–272.
3 The term 'field' here denotes 'cleared and cultivated area'. Occasionally one sees the term 'farm' used in the same sense.
4 Indeed some authors distinguish 'forest-fallow', 'bush-fallow' and 'grass-fallow' as well as 'long' and 'short' cultivation periods. See E. Boserup, *The Conditions of Agricultural Growth: The Economics of Agrarian Change under Population Pressure*, George Allen and Unwin, London, 1965.
5 For instance, 'The highly populated regions of Tanganyika, with densities approximating to or exceeding 100 per square mile (39 per km²), represent perhaps 5 per cent of the territory's area and support well over a third of the population,' W. Allan, *The African Husbandman*, Oliver and Boyd, Edinburgh, 1965, p. 207.
6 E. Bernus, 'Human Geography in the Sahelian Zone', in *The Sahel: Geological Approaches to Land Use*, MAB Technical Report, UNESCO Press, 1975.
7 The word *sahel* is Arabic for seashore or edge.
8 An important factor preventing the presence of cattle, here and

elsewhere, is the tsetse fly, carrier of the disease trypanosomiasis or sleeping sickness.

9 M.P. Miracle, *Agriculture in the Congo Basin*, University of Wisconsin Press, 1967.

10 W.I. Jones, 'The food economy of Ba Dugu Djoliba, Mali', in *African Food Production Systems*, P.F.M. McLoughlin (ed.), The Johns Hopkins Press, 1970.

11 R.T. Jackson, P.M. Mulvaney, T.P.J. Russell and J.A. Forster, *Report of the Oxford University Expedition to the Gamu Highlands of Southern Ethiopia*, 1968, School of Geography, Oxford, 1969, (mimeo).

12 J. Meyer, 'Agricultural development and peasant farming in Kenya', unpublished Ph. D. thesis, University of London, 1966.

13 K.H. Friedrich, 'Coffee–banana holdings at Bukoba: the reasons for stagnation at a higher level', in *Smallholder Farming and Smallholder Development in Tanzania*, H. Ruthenberg (ed.) Africa-Studien, IFO-Institut für Wirtshchaftforschung, 1968, pp. 175 – 212.

14 P.H. Gulliver, 'The case of the Ndendeuli, shifting cultivators of Tanzania', mimeo paper, *Conference on Competing Demands for the time of Labor in Traditional African Societies*, Holly Knoll, Virginia, 1967.

15 W. Allan, *The African Husbandman*, Oliver and Boyd, Edinburgh, 1967. Allan, in fact, prefers to reserve the term shifting cultivation for those cases where the community of cultivators itself shifts, dwellings and all.

16 H.A. Oluwasanmi, I.S. Dema, *et al.*, *Uboma: a Socio-economic and Nutritional Survey of a Rural Community in Eastern Nigeria*, Occasional papers No. 6, World Land Use Survey, 1966.

17 H.A. Luning, *Economic Aspects of Low Labour-Income Farming*, Centre for Agricultural Publications and Documentation, Wageningen, Netherlands, 1967.

18 D.S. Thornton, *Agriculture in South East Ghana*, Vol. 1, Summary Report, Development Study, Department of Agricultural Economics and Farm Management, University of Reading, 1973.

19 D.S. Thornton, *op. cit.*, pp. 22–24.

20 USDA, *Indices of Agricultural Production in Africa and the Near East*, Economic Research Service, Foreign Section, various issues.

3 Historical evolution

This chapter views the evolution of African agricultural systems in the context of long-term development by concentrating on the twin themes of stability and change. Present-day systems of farming have evolved over a long period of time, which means that they are part of a stable ecological balance; but during this evolution they have been modified by recent changes, which show that they are not static and inflexible. To understand the relative importance of stability and adaptability we need to examine three major themes in the historical development of African agriculture. First, and rather briefly, its origins, to illustrate the influence of a long period of maturation on the creation of a stable ecological balance; secondly, changes in the pre-colonial period when the growth of trade with Southeast Asia, and later the Americas, brought important new crops to Africa; and finally, the important developments of the past century when the rise of export crops brought African agriculture into a prominent position within the world trading system.[1] However, before looking at these aspects in detail, a few introductory remarks on their significance will help to set them in a proper context.

Work on the origins of farming in Africa is still in its infancy and no firm conclusions can be drawn at this stage. It is important to note that the general tenor of nearly all recent research has been to push the origins farther and farther back in time and to stress the importance of indigenous discoveries and systems at the expense of the imported cultures which hitherto have received most attention. It is becoming clear that African agriculture has its own specific history and course of development, and is not merely the territorial extension of discoveries and systems worked out elsewhere. The significance of this long history and its adaptation to the various tropical ecosystems in Africa has still not been fully grasped by agricultural 'improvers' – as witnessed by the disastrous failure of some of the more grandiose schemes to introduce sudden and dramatic change. The Tanzanian groundnut fiasco of the early 1950s is merely the most notorious of many such episodes.[2]

The significance of the long period of world-wide trade in the pre-colonial era is also only just beginning to emerge. It long pre-dates African contact with Europe. Trade across the Indian ocean with the ancient civilisations of India and Indonesia has probably been going on for thousands of years. Certainly new crops and livestock were beginning to modify African farming systems from about AD 300 and possibly earlier, and the significance of the introduction of new and more productive varieties of food crops (especially bananas, plantains, Asian yams and cocoyams) may have been crucial for the later ability of African peoples to specialise in the production of crops for export. The trading connections between Africa and the Americas were also important in this respect (especially the trade between the Portuguese colonies in western Africa, from Guinea to Angola, with Brazil). Such trade was not limited to slaves, and brought some important crops to Africa from South America; most notably groundnuts, maize, cassava (manioc) cocoa and tobacco.

Finally, in the modern period it is hard to exaggerate the effects of the rise of export crops, not only on agriculture but on the entire African economy. It enabled certain countries most notably Nigeria, Ghana, Zaïre, Kenya, Uganda and Ivory Coast, to assume leading positions in world trade for some key exports, such as palm products, groundnuts, cocoa, coffee and cotton.

The rise of export crops will be examined from several points of view. It had far-reaching – but, significantly, seldom disruptive – effects on the evolution of farming systems. It also changed the economics of farming quite radically. Increasingly the emphasis on subsistence gave way to specialisation and production for the market. As this process gathered momentum it generated side effects. The cash incomes of many farmers rose, creating a rural market for products, both imported and domestically produced. Within farming both land and labour became more valuable. Where land was concerned this sometimes exerted pressure on traditional systems of tenure. For rural dwellers came the opportunity to earn wages, but this did not always arise without migration. To some extent seasonal migration increased the opportunities to raise a migrant's income without disrupting the rural economy of his home region, but in some countries, like Upper Volta, migration to cocoa-growing regions in Ghana and Ivory Coast, assumed large enough proportions to upset food production at home – so that the effects of export production were felt with differing intensity and were not always equally beneficial.[3]

The origins of agriculture in Africa

Until fairly recently it has been the accepted belief of archaeologists and historians that knowledge of crop cultivation and livestock husbandry diffused southwards into Africa from a centre of origin in Syria, Mesopotamia and Egypt about 3 500 years ago. However, recent work by David Harris and others seems to go far to confirm what some scholars (especially botanists) had long suspected – that the knowledge of crop cultivation, and probably animal domestication as well, was independently evolved in the tropics (including Africa) at a much earlier date; possibly as much as 10 000 years ago or even earlier. When it is realised that the work of Leakey in Tanzania suggests that the first men may have evolved there as much as two million years ago, an independent discovery of farming in Africa does not seem inherently improbable.[4]

Far too little archaeological work has yet been carried out in Africa to enable the evolution of farming to be understood at all clearly, but certain important crops seem to have been domesticated from wild varieties originating in Africa. Amongst these are African yams (*Dioscorea* spp.), Kaffir potatoes (*Coleus* spp.), Abyssinian bananas (*Ensete edulis*), various millets and sorghums, cowpeas (*Vigna unguiculata*) and African rice (*Oryza glaberrima*). Oil palms, sesame, pumpkins, coffee and watermelons are examples of less essential foods which also seem to have been indigenous to Africa.

It is generally thought that the domestication of animals followed the knowledge of crop cultivation (except perhaps in the case of dogs used by early hunting peoples). Few animals seem to have been first domesticated in Africa. Guinea fowls (*Numidia meleagris*) and donkeys, domesticated in Ethiopia, are amongst them.[5]

Domesticated cattle, sheep and goats are thought to have been brought into Africa from western Asia at a very early date – perhaps 7000–5000 BC and to have diffused up the Nile and around and across the Sahara. In the period 5000 to 2500 BC, the Sahara was wetter than it is now and rock carvings of cattle have been found in Wadi Zirmei in Tibesti in an area where no mammals, wild or domestic, survive today. Cattle were kept in Africa by sedentary farmers long before the nomadic dairying peoples such as the Fulani of West Africa and the Masai of East Africa entered the continent. It seems that these peoples originally stole their cattle from the settled farmers.[6] This is interesting because it is sometimes alleged that the combination of arable farming and livestock keeping (which needs to be re-established if production is to increase) would be very difficult because African farmers have never kept livestock and have no traditional skills. It is true that the skills of animal husbandry need to be learnt by many peoples who do not at present possess them; but it is apparently not true that none of the sedentary farmers have ever kept cattle in the past.

It is worth emphasising perhaps that agricultural trade has very ancient roots. Much of African agriculture is correctly described as being in a subsistence condition. This concept is useful as a broad generalisation, but it can also be a source of confusion. There probably never has been a time when farming communities were absolutely self-sufficient. Certain articles such as salt, fish, stone and iron tools, and probably condiments like kolas and peppers have been traded since agriculture began. Regional specialities have also been traded since very early times, such as the exchange of cereals and fruits for meat and dairy products, between peoples like the Hausa and Fulani in West Africa and the Kikuyu and Masai in Kenya and Tanzania; but these are no doubt merely some of the better known examples of regional trade networks which were spread widely throughout the 'subsistence' sector. Agricultural trade has increased hugely in the twentieth century, but it would be a mistake to imagine that it was a totally new innovation imposed on a previously static rural economy. A recent study of the complex nineteenth century trade patterns in the Sierra Leone/Guinea area of West Africa emphasises this point.[7]

The antiquity of African agriculture is significant in several ways. It refutes the view (still not entirely dead) that Africa has no history and has borrowed all the main features of her culture from more advanced neighbours. More importantly, it means that the basic crops have been continuously cultivated for long periods and that they have established a relationship with their environment which enables them to withstand pests and diseases (unlike the more recently introduced cocoa, for instance, which has suffered badly from swollen shoot disease). Also the basic crops can be cultivated (usually on some form of shifting system) without the dangers of declining soil fertility or erosion. This long-established ecological and genetical balance can too easily be taken for granted. Careful thought and experiment need to precede any proposals for drastic and radical changes to those traditional systems which have proved their long-term environmental viability.[8]

The development of agriculture in the pre-colonial period

The significance of this period is two-fold. First, the range of crops under cultivation was greatly extended and the capacity of farming systems to support growing populations, urban as well as rural, consequently much enlarged. Second, these developments occurred naturally and freely. They were not imposed by alien rulers (or innovators such as missionaries). They were worked out slowly over time, and new crops and cultivation systems were not incorporated until they had been thoroughly tested and acclimatised. The result is that they too were absorbed without harming the ecological balance.

The earliest crops to be introduced were those which had originally been domesticated in tropical or sub-tropical Asia. They are usually referred to as Indo-Malaysian crops, though some of them, like oranges, were Chinese. The most important food crops were probably Asian yams (*Dioscorea* spp.) cocoyams (*Colocasia* spp.) also known as taro, and bananas and plantains (*Musa* spp.). Also important in more restricted areas were Asian rice (*Oryza sativa*) which was grown in swamp areas such as the Guinea coastlands between the Gambia and Sierra Leone rivers; and breadfruits (*Artocarpus incisa*). Coconut palms (*Cocos nucifera*) and sugar cane (*Saccharum officinarum*) were also useful supplements to the diet in certain areas, though they were not extensively cultivated.[9]

These crops probably entered Africa from Madagascar (Malagasy Republic) occupied by Oceanic and Malaysian settlers at an unknown date, perhaps 2 000 years ago. We know it was before AD 400 because the Malagasy – Indonesian language contains virtually no words from Indian Sanskrit, which entered the Indonesian languages at about that time, so the migrants cannot have left Indonesia later than AD 400. Dates of around 100 BC to AD 100 have been suggested for the migration of the Indonesians across the Indian Ocean to Madagascar, but linguistic arguments based on the differentiation between modern Malagasy and modern Indo – Malayan languages, suggest that it could have been as much as a thousand years earlier. We know virtually nothing of how the Indo–Malaysian crops were diffused in Africa, but it seems the process may have been fairly rapid. They seem to have reached as far as West Africa by about AD 500. These Indo–Malaysian crops were specially significant in forest regions to which they were better adapted generally than to savannah areas. As a result the settlement of the rain forest was greatly facilitated by the introduction of these crops and the rise of some of the more famous early states such as Oyo and Benin (in Nigeria) Kongo (in Zaïre) and Monomotapa (in Mozambique) may have been made possible by the greater yields which these crops gave in comparison with their indigenous predecessors.[10]

Equally important for subsequent development was the arrival of new crops from the Americas, brought initially by the Portuguese when they began to develop trade between their African settlements (in Guinea and Angola) and their new colonies in Brazil after 1500. The arrival of these American crops was, of course, facilitated by the rapid growth of the Atlantic slave trade after 1600, but it should be remembered that the slave trade was only one of the trades between Africa and the Americas and it need not be assumed that the introduction of the American crops was dependent on the slave trade, or in any sense a 'benefit' derived from it.[11]

The American crops fell into two major groups – food crops and export crops. The food crops were initially the most important because they enabled more food to be produced for the same amount of labour on the same amount of land. They thus tended to displace existing crops and enabled production to be increased and the population to expand without using up more land. The export crops could thus be fitted into the rural economy without too much difficulty when overseas demand began to exert its influence. This was generally not till after 1900, when the most important export trades based on American introductions, such as cocoa and groundnuts, began to assume major proportions in West Africa.[12] East and Central African agricultural exports such as cotton, coffee, sisal, and sugar, in contrast, were based on crops already in cultivation. The main exception to this was Zimbabwean tobacco – an American plant.

American *food* crops, especially maize (*Zea mays*) were, however, even more important in East and Central Africa than they were in West Africa. Maize tended to displace the old cereal staples – millet and sorghum – in all parts of tropical Africa, but it assumed a special importance as a staple crop in East and Central Africa. With its relatively high yield and ease of cultivation, it increased the food supply greatly and enabled land hitherto needed for this purpose to be released for export-crop production (or it decreased the pressure to shorten the bush fallow).[13]

Other important American food crops were groundnuts (peanuts), *Arachis hypogaea* – also of course, a major export crop in countries like Nigeria, Senegal, Mali, and Niger; cassava (manioc), *Manihot utilissima*, sweet potatoes, *Ipomoea batatas*; pumpkins, *Cucurbita peop*; squashes, *Cucurbita maxima*; tomatoes, *Lycopersicum esculantum*; and papayas (pawpaws), *Carica papaya*.[14]

The major export crops were cocoa, groundnuts and tobacco. Rubber was also important in Liberia and Nigeria, while fruits like pineapples, avocados and guavas were exported in small quantities, as well as enriching the variety of local diets.[15]

It is clear that the Indo-Malaysian and American crops together played a vital role both in expanding the staple food economy of Africa and in facilitating the rise of export production. They provide an interesting long-term example of one of the most important methods of raising agricultural productivity – namely the introduction of new and higher yielding plants (or varieties) into a pre-existing cultivation system. There is still some scope for further progress along this path in present-day African agriculture, mainly by means of the introduction of improved varieties of existing species (the so-called 'green revolution'). However, the scope for such simple changes is no longer as great as it was. Increased production in future may depend on more fundamental and far-reaching changes in the agrarian structure to facilitate systems of cultivation involving fertilisers and mechanisation.

The rise of exports

From the theoretical point of view each region of the world can benefit from the exchange of those products in which it has a comparative advantage. Thus tropical Africa, which can produce certain tree or bush crops like palm fruit, cocoa, cotton, coffee, bananas and citrus, and certain field crops like groundnuts and sugar, comparatively cheaply should be able to benefit by trading these products for those of temperate regions. This would apply particularly if the exchange were for manufactured products in conditions where Africa lacked industrial capacity; and where the provision of such capacity would have been both difficult technically and very expensive. Broadly speaking such conditions existed until about 1929, when the terms of trade (the ratio between the prices of African exports and imports) were generally favourable to Africa.[16] The period between about 1900 to 1929 was the time when many African countries were able to expand their agricultural exports quite rapidly and in some cases to assume world leadership in certain crops. For instance by 1914 Ghana was already supplying nearly half the world's cocoa beans; whereas her exports in 1898 had been only a few tonnes.[17]

However, between 1930 and 1945 the terms of trade tended to move against primary producers. The considerable investments in extending both crop cultivation and means of transport during the boom period meant that the increased production of many export staples could only be sold for lower prices. For this reason African countries found themselves on a treadmill in which it was necessary to produce more and more each year in order to try to maintain their incomes. This tendency was strengthened by the growth of oligopolistic practices amongst the industries of the developed countries which enabled them to maintain the prices of their manufactured exports rather more successfully than the primary producers could do.[18]

Fortunately movements in the terms of trade are seldom in one direction indefinitely, and in the post-war reconstruction period – roughly 1945 to 1954 – they swung sharply back in favour of African agricultural exporters as can be seen from Table 3.1. Whereas the index of the quantity of agricultural exports rose from 76 to 113 between the mid-1930s and 1954 (with 1952/3 = 100), the index of their 'real value' in terms of the imports they were able to purchase rose from 45 to 122. Then the boom ended and Table 3.1 shows the 'real value'

Table 3.1
Index numbers of volume and 'real value' of agricultural exports
(1952/3 = 100)

Year	Volume	'Real value'[1]
1934–38 av.	76	45
1948–52 av.	90	89
1953	103	102
1954	113	122
1955	121	115
1956	127	112
1957	129	112
1958	130	116
1959	138	112
1960	138	106

Source: *Oxford Regional Economic Atlas of Africa*, Clarendon Press, 1965,
    p. 18
[1] Total export earnings deflated by UN index of average export unit values of manufactured goods.

gradually sagging to 106 by 1960 while the quantum of exports had risen to 138. Since then there have been further oscillations and it is clear that the fluctuating nature of the terms of trade means that African countries should not rely too heavily on agricultural exports at the expense of either domestic food production or domestic industry. Nevertheless the history of agricultural exports shows that many African countries have derived considerable benefit from them over quite long periods of time; and therefore a sensible exploitation of comparative advantage should continue to pay dividends in future, particularly if the dangerous dependence on too narrow a range of exports can be overcome.

Before considering the mechanism and dynamics of the rise in export crop production, it may be useful to start with a survey of the main developments in the process in the tropical African countries so that the discussion can be set in a proper factual perspective. First, we can look at the major African agricultural exports and their share of world trade. This information is set out in Table 3.2 which shows the share of the major exports in the 1930s, and 1950s, and 1977. It is noticeable that Africa supplied more than three-quarters of the world's palm kernels and two-thirds of its cocoa throughout the whole period. It was, and is, also a very significant supplier of groundnuts, groundnut oil and coffee, but it is noticeable that the list of African specialities is a rather limited one, and that it showed little significant change between the 1930s and the 1970s. Of course the *value* of the produce exported rose significantly, (though this was largely the result of inflation), but the market shares altered very little. The most important change was the dramatic fall in the importance of palm oil from 52·8 per cent in the 1930s to only 5·5 per cent in 1977. This was mainly caused by increased domestic consumption as the population of the palm oil-producing countries rose rapidly after 1960. Sisal also suffered an eclipse, but the falling percentage of groundnuts (from 43·2 in the 1930s to 17·9 in 1977) was more than offset by the rise of groundnut oil

Table 3.2
African share of world agricultural exports (*selected commodities*)

1934–38 av.	Percentage
Palm kernels	91·5
Cocoa beans	67·2
Palm oil	52·8
Groundnuts	43·2
Sisal	42·1
Coffee	7·9
Tobacco	6·6
Rubber, natural	0·7

1950–58	Percentage
Palm kernels	93·0
Cocoa beans	67·9
Palm oil	65·3
Sisal	59·2
Groundnuts	26·0*
Coffee	19·4
Tobacco	13·1
Rubber, natural	3·9

1977	Percentage
Palm kernels	84·0
Cocoa beans	71·9
Groundnut oil	42·3
Coffee	30·2
Groundnuts	17·9
Tobacco	10·0
Palm oil	5·5
Rubber, natural	5·3

*1958 only

Sources: M.J. Herskovits and M. Harwitz, *Economic Transition in Africa*, Routledge and Kegan Paul, 1964, p. 37 for 1930s and 1950s; and UN, FAO, *The State of Food and Agriculture, 1978*, pp. A-14, 17 and 18, for 1977 (developing African countries only).

as an export in the 1970s (from almost nothing in the 1950s to 42·3 per cent in 1977).

The significance of agricultural exports for different African countries is shown in Table 3.3, where 16 exporting countries are shown in rank order of their dependence on agricultural exports in the 1970s. If we compare the agricultural exports in Table 3.3 with the ones listed in Table 3.2, we can see that the major exports were important in many of the countries; but we can add some less important ones to the list – notably cotton, tea, gum arabic, maize, cloves, haricot beans, cashew nuts and sesame seed. Certain other products like bananas, citrus fruits, ginger, hides and peppers, are insignificant for Africa as a whole, but are included in the exports of a few countries. A striking feature of Table 3.3 is the way it reveals the dependence of most countries on two or three products, with all that this can mean when there is a sudden fall in world prices. Another interesting aspect of Table 3.3 is the variation it shows in the dependence on agricultural exports, from countries like Uganda and Sudan, with over 90 per cent dependence, to countries with important mineral and oil exports, like

Table 3.3
Percentage shares of agricultural exports in the early 1970s (in rank order of dependence)

Country	Year	Agricultural exports as per cent of total exports (by value)	Main commodities as per cent of total agriculture exports (by value)	
Uganda	1973	93	Coffee	72·7
			Cotton	17·2
			Tea	5·6
Sudan	1972	93	Cotton	63·2
			Groundnuts	7·7
			Gum Arabic	7·7
Malawi	1973	88	Tobacco	47·6
			Tea	22·2
Cameroun	1973	71	Coffee	34·1
			Cocoa	34·1
			Cocoa products	9·1
Tanzania	1973	62	Coffee	28·6
			Cotton	19·2
			Cloves	13·5
			Sisal	12·8
			Cashew	10·0
Ethiopia	1973	57	Coffee	50·7
			Haricot beans	13·4
			Sesame seed	11·5
Senegal	1972	53	Groundnut oil	69·0
			Groundnut cake	24·1
			Groundnuts	3·4
Ghana	1972	49	Cocoa	90·9
			Cocoa butter	9·1
Ivory Coast	1974	44	Coffee	52·4
			Cocoa	33·3
Kenya	1973	32	Coffee	45·4
			Tea	21·5
			Maize	7·1
Liberia	1974	24	Rubber	89·0
			Cocoa	5·5
			Coffee	5·5
Sierra Leone	1971	14	Palm kernels	46·2
			Cocoa	23·1
			Coffee	23·1
Nigeria	1973	12	Cocoa	42·3
			Groundnuts	17·0
			Groundnut oil	9·1
Zaïre	1973	12	Coffee	60·4
			Palm oil	16·7
			Rubber	12·5
Zambia	1973	1	Tobacco	64·9
			Maize	35·1
Gabon	1972	0·5	Cocoa	100·0

Source: UN, *African Statistics Yearbook*, 1974.

Nigeria, Zaïre and Zambia, for whom agricultural exports are relatively insignificant. The rise of oil in the last 20 years has, for instance, completely transformed the position in Nigeria, all of whose major exports in 1960 were agricultural.

When we look at agricultural exports on a regional basis, as in Table 3.4 and Fig. 3.1 an interesting pattern emerges. The tropical African countries have been divided into three broad regions: West Africa, Central Africa and East Africa, for purposes of comparison. Whilst it is not claimed that these particular regional groupings are the only possible ones, they have the merit of emphasising some key distinctions. The West African states have a generally admitted cultural unity. They are all linked to ports on the Atlantic and, very broadly, they are all related to the Niger river basin. The Central African states are joined again by their relationship to the Atlantic and to the Zaïre river basin, while the East African states are linked by their frontage on to the Indian Ocean and by the fact that a greater proportion of their land is in a highland zone than is the case in the other two regions. Generally the East African group do not contain any significant areas of rain forest, and they became involved in world trade at a later date than the other states – most of which had the misfortune to be involved in the Atlantic slave trade between the sixteenth and the nineteenth centuries.

The first thing to be noticed about Table 3.4 is the way in which the tropical African states have caught up with South Africa since 1907. In 1907, they had only 31·2 per cent of sub-Saharan export trade between them. By 1935 they had advanced this to 46·9 per cent, by 1958 to 66·2 per cent and by 1975 they had achieved 82·8 per cent. These figures, of course, refer only to *shares* – they tell us nothing about the growth in the total volume and value of the export trade, which, as we have seen earlier, increased very substantially in this period for all regions, including South Africa.

The second point is that the inequality of shares between the regions, which was quite noticeable in 1907, when West Africa's share was almost double that of Central Africa and substantially ahead of East Africa's, had considerably decreased by 1935, and virtually disappeared by 1958 when the difference between the three tropical regions had narrowed considerably. West and East Africa had virtually identical shares and Central Africa was not far behind. All this was completely changed between 1958 and 1975 by Nigerian oil exports. By 1975 Nigeria alone accounted for 35 per cent of all sub-Saharan exports (by value) – over twice those of South Africa. As a result West Africa had taken the dominant share in the export market (rising from 23·6 to 51·6 per cent), while Central Africa had maintained its share (16·2 to 16·8 per cent) and East Africa had fallen from 21 to 14·4 per cent.

Within the regions there was little change in the importance of individual countries between 1907 and 1958, when Nigeria, Zaïre and Zimbabwe dominated their respective regions, but since 1958 the rise of diamond exports in Angola and oil exports in Gabon has enabled them to overtake Zaïre in Central Africa; but from an agricultural point of view the most interesting country is Ivory Coast, where a considerable expansion in coffee and cocoa exports has enabled it to displace Ghana as the second-most important exporter in West Africa.

The main conclusion to be drawn from Table 3.4 is that the marked regional inequalities in the export trade, which were so notice-

Table 3.4
The shares of sub-Saharan export trade, 1907–1975, by value
(in percentages)

West Africa	1907	1935	1958	1975
Nigeria	5·4	6·3	8·1	35·0
Ivory Coast				5·2
Senegal				2·9
Guinea				1·1
Mauritania	4·8	5·3	7·5	0·8
Niger				0·4
Upper Volta				0·2
Mali				0·2
Benin				0·1
Ghana	3·8	5·2	6·4	3·2
Liberia	–	–	0·9	1·7
Togo	0·4	0·3	0·3	0·6
The Gambia	0·4	0·2	0·3	0·2
Guinea-Bissau	0·2	–	0·1	–
TOTALS	15·0	17·3	23·6	51·6

Central Africa				
Angola	1·4	1·1	2·8	5·4
Gabon				4·1
Brazzaville (Congo)				0·8
Central African Republic	1·1	1·3	2·1	0·2
Chad				0·2
Zaïre				3·8
Rwanda	3·5	5·2	8·9	0·2
Burundi				0·1
Cameroun	1·2	0·8	2·4	2·0
TOTALS	7·2	8·4	16·2	16·8

East Africa				
Zambia				3·5
Zimbabwe	3·7	7·5	8·7	2·4
Malawi				0·7
Kenya				2·0
Tanzania	2·9	6·0	7·8	1·5
Uganda				1·1
Sudan	0·7	2·6	2·9	1·9
Mozambique	1·4	1·0	1·5	0·9
Somalia	0·3*	0·1*	0·1*	0·4
TOTALS	9·0	17·2	21·0	14·4

South Africa	68·4	56·3	38·5	17·2

GRAND TOTALS	99·6	99·2	99·3	100

*Former British section only

Note: In the 1975 totals export figures were displaced by one or two years in 3
cases – Zimbabwe (1973) Angola (1974) and Guinea (1976).

Sources: Adapted from M.J. Herskovits and M. Harwitz (eds), *Economic
Transition in Africa*, 1964, pp. 29–30; UN Yearbook of *International
Trade Statistics*, Vol. I; *Trade by Country*, 1977; and *Africa South of the
Sahara, 1979–80*, Europa Publications, London, 1979.

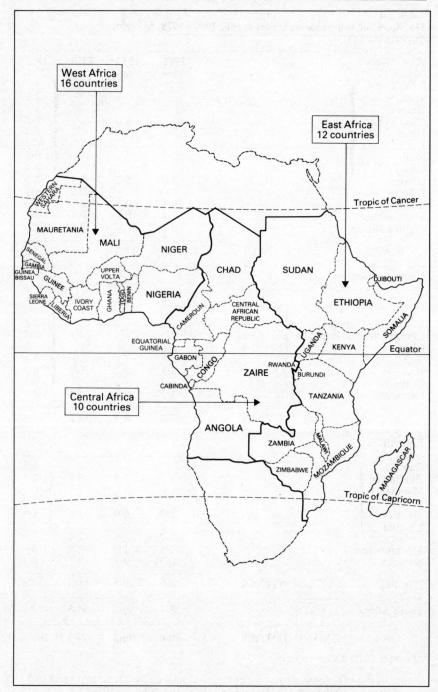

Fig. 3.1 Tropical African countries, divided by region

able in 1907, had largely disappeared by mid-century, and that even in 1975, the export of *agricultural* commodities was much more widely shared amongst the tropical African countries than it had been in 1907.

It is also clear that, speaking generally, the rise of agricultural exporting has been a considerable success story and one that has brought numerous benefits to Africa. It is necessary, therefore, to examine the conditions that made this achievement possible and especially to try to determine whether they still exist. In other words, is the expansion of the trade in agricultural exports a *process* which is still continuing, or is it one of those historical movements which were inspired and motivated by a set of circumstances which were applicable to a particular epoch, but which no longer apply? The answer to this question is of considerable importance in framing future agricultural development policies; for if there is no real scope for further expansion of the supply of agricultural exports, it is fruitless to base one's strategy on that assumption, even if the demand situation looks favourable (an assumption which does not necessarily hold). Before this question can be answered though, it is necessary to draw certain distinctions, since the causes of the growth of agricultural exports were not identical in all African countries, except at a very abstract level. They all responded to the stimulation of world demand reflected in rising prices for primary products, particularly in the periods 1900–1914, 1919–1929 and 1945–55; but their response on the supply side took different forms. Basically these can be divided into three different types – often geographically distinct, but sometimes overlapping within the same country. Probably the most important response was the one whereby it has been claimed that the indigenous rural population spontaneously began cultivating an export crop as part of, or alongside, their traditional farming system. This response has been claimed for West Africa, with products like palm oil, cocoa and groundnuts; for Uganda with cotton; for Kenya with coffee and elsewhere with various crops. This type of response is known as the vent-for-surplus theory. Until recently the theory was widely accepted but is now increasingly challenged. Since the implications of the criticisms of this theory are important, we shall return to them later after considering briefly the less important responses.

The second type of response was one whereby foreign capital and management were invested in plantations worked by indigenous labour. It was characteristic of Zaïre (Unilever's palm oil plantations), Mozambique (sugar), Kenya (sisal), Liberia (rubber), and many other examples in East and Central Africa. It was never more than a minority response in any country (except Liberia) and is one which is unlikely to have much future attraction as African countries seek to reduce direct foreign involvement in their economies. Though it can be technically efficient it has the disadvantage of tying a large capital investment to the production of a small range of crops when the world market is unstable. If the prices of those crops fall sharply, the plantations can become unprofitable and release a large quantity of wage labour on to a market where there may be no alternative demand for it. In contrast peasant producers can often diversify into new or different crops (often local foods) with much less social and economic disrup-

tion. For this reason the development of indigenously owned plantations – whether private or public – is also unlikely to commend itself
strongly. An exception, though, might be for the production of food
crops for the domestic market.

The third historical response to the demand for agricultural ex-
portation was to introduce foreign settlers to cultivate export crops.
The best known examples occurred in Kenya (mainly coffee), Zimbabwe (tobacco) and Angola (again mainly coffee). Despite technical
efficiency, the social and political disruptions caused by this process are
too well known for further comment to be necessary. Over time nearly
all these settlers have been, or will be, replaced by indigenous farmers,
so that the relevance of this phase of historical experience for the future can be assessed fairly safely as minimal.

This brings us back to the first supply response – the indigenous
adoption of export crops. This is usually considered in the light of
Adam Smith's vent-for-surplus theory of foreign trade, which was re-
fined for an African context by Hla Myint in *The Economics of
Developing Countries* (1964), but which is now increasingly attracting
criticism for being too simplistic.

The essence of the theory is that it will be possible to expand
agricultural exports rapidly and easily (once overseas demand has
made itself felt, via marketing firms linked to the agricultural area by a
simple transport system – usually railways, steamboats or tarred roads)
provided that certain predisposing conditions exist in the traditional
rural economy. These conditions are essentially two-fold. First, there
should be fertile land available which has not yet been utilised.
Second, there should be labour available to work this land – available
not because it was previously unable to find work to do, or because it
preferred leisure for traditional 'social' reasons, but because it could
produce all it needed without working full time – to have produced
more goods would have been to provide commodities for which there
was no market. If there are thus people with some spare time on their
hands and if there is land available for them to work, the theory
assumes that an expansion of agricultural exports can and will take
place without certain more fundamental changes in the economy which
might otherwise have been expected. These conditions are three-fold.
First, no expansion of the population need take place. Second, no reduction in the supply of traditional goods and services is necessary
(mainly food production) and third, no significant technical change in
farming methods is required. To these basic assumptions Myint adds
some refinements. The most important of these concern capital investment and risk-taking. He believes that because increased inputs of
land and labour are available and, because no changes in farming
technique are necessary, no great investment of capital is needed
(beyond increased labour time). In other words peasant producers
would not need to have access to previously-produced stores of capital
before they could start producing the export crops; nor would they
take any great risk by entering the export trade since it would be complementary to, and not competitive with, traditional food production.

Various writers have criticised this version of events. A.G. Hopkins in *An Economic History of West Africa* (1973) points out that the

production of export crops did not take place without an increase in the population.[19] It may be that the population of Africa did not increase very rapidly between, say, 1900 and 1950 (although the surviving demographic data for the early period is too unreliable for there to be any great certainty about this); yet it still rose from an estimated 120 million in 1900 to about 206 million in 1950.[20] This is a rise of about 86 million, or 71 per cent in 50 years. However, much more important than this overall change, was the expansion of migration, both seasonal and permanent. Already in the 1920s the harvesting of cocoa pods in Ghana was dependent on migrant labour, and the migration of labourers and farmers into Senegal and The Gambia had become an important part of the groundnut-producing economy even earlier. By the early twentieth century there were already about 100 000 migrant farmers growing groundnuts along the banks of the River Gambia.[21]

It is, therefore, not the case that cultivation for export can be expanded solely on the basis of existing under-utilised labour. Moreover, this point brings into question another assumption of the vent-for-surplus theory, namely that the production of goods and services for the domestic economy will not suffer. There is now considerable evidence that regions, like Upper Volta in the savannah region of West Africa, which have yielded migrants to exporting areas have suffered very considerable dislocation of their economies as a result. Food production has suffered, an undue burden of work has fallen on the women left behind, and, as more and more of the labour force has migrated, the whole economic climate has deteriorated with consequent depressing effects on local investment, entrepreneurship, employment opportunities and infrastructure. In a recent study of the problem, Samir Amin estimates that between 1920 and 1970 some three million people migrated permanently from the interior regions of West Africa (primarily Upper Volta, Mali, and Niger) to the groundnut-exporting regions of Senegambia and the cocoa and coffee belt of Ivory Coast and Ghana. More seriously he believes that, contrary to the views of those, like Elliott Berg, who have argued that migration is beneficial to both importing and exporting regions, it is in fact highly disadvantageous to the exporting regions. Based on a study by J. Bugnicourt, his argument is that if the value of the direct capital formation through labour inputs in agriculture which the migrants would have contributed if they had remained at home is taken into acccount, and is added to the cost of rearing and educating the migrants, their emigration represents a loss of 7 per cent of the gross national product of the interior regions per year. Even if the value of the migrants' remittances home is subtracted from this, the net loss still stands at about 5 per cent of the GNP. By contrast, the receiving regions gain about 5 per cent of their annual GNP from the migrants.[22]

Therefore, when assessing the scope for adding export-crop production to traditional farming systems, it is necessary to take a broad view. Concentration on the benefits to the immediate region concerned can obviously be misleading, if these have to be bought at the cost of increasing poverty in a wider hinterland beyond. The dynamics of export production may be much more complicated than they appear at first sight.

Nor can new crops be introduced without any innovations in farming technique. It is true that these have not been of major importance, but many of the export crops like cocoa, groundnuts and cotton, were either new to Africa or had not been grown hitherto on a large scale, so that new techniques had to be learnt and old ones adapted. For instance, in northern Nigeria minor, but significant, changes in farming techniques occurred when groundnuts were introduced after 1911. These included shorter fallow periods, increased manuring and earlier planting.[23]

More importantly, recent studies have shown that export-crop production was much more dependent on supplies of *indigenous* capital and risk-taking entrepreneurship than the vent-for-surplus theory in its simple form, would suggest. Polly Hill's study of the migrant cocoa farmers of south-eastern Ghana has shown that from about 1905 onwards they were prepared to invest quite heavily in purchases of virgin forest land for future production. Some of their farms were as large as 40 hectares and when it is realised that a cocoa tree may take seven to ten years before it yields any profit, it can be seen that this was from the outset a long-term business enterprise heavily dependent on capital investment. Where did this capital come from? The Akwapim peoples who migrated from their ridge to grow cocoa in the forests to the east of them, were no simple subsistence farmers. They had long been engaged as merchants in exporting palm oil through Accra, and it was the capital accumulated over the years in that trade which gave them their start. As palm oil exporters they had found it hard to compete with producers in the Niger Delta region: hence their shift to the new, and growing, cocoa trade.[24]

Similarly, although groundnut production in northern Nigeria appears to have arisen spontaneously when the railway from Lagos reached Kano in 1911, in reality the expansion of cultivation depended on the enterprise of Hausa merchants who were prepared to invest capital accumulated in many years of long-distance trading. They had been involved in the trans-Saharan trade and in the distribution, over a wide area of savannah country, of kola nuts from the southern forests. The role of these Hausa traders has been well summarised by A.G. Hopkins, who says they

> . . . perceived that groundnuts offered a new, and potentially lucrative, commercial opportunity. They contacted their established agents and suppliers in the villages around Kano, persuaded farmers to grow more groundnuts, or to grow them for the first time, offered financial assistance and gave guarantees regarding the purchase of the harvest. The fact that local farmers were prepared to trust the Hausa traders and to treat them as opinion leaders was vital to the success of the enterprise.[25]

We can see, therefore, that the conditions necessary for an expansion of export-crop production have not always been so elementary as the vent-for-surplus theory might suggest, and that to expect export production to increase from a *mere* extension of a modern transport network into areas where there appear still to be a relative abundance of land and under-used labour, might be to nourish an impractical hope. Historical experience suggests that a wide range of economic, social and political changes may need to occur before a successful export trade can begin. It has been suggested that the imposition of colonial rule may have been much more important in this context than has been realised previously. In Nigeria and Ghana the provision of a stable currency and banking system, and the loosening of traditional barriers to migration have been stressed. The abolition of internal slavery and the reduction of the military power of the local chiefs and emirs was also important in Nigeria.[26] The imposition of poll or hut taxes in several countries also sometimes was effective as a spur to encourage people to raise the money via export-crop production. However, there were limits to the effectiveness of colonial pressures. Around 1909 attempts were made to spread cotton production to the Langi peoples of northern Uganda, but they failed; not because the Langi declined to engage in export-crop production for sale, but because they already had a far more profitable trade exporting sesame to the Bunyoro region of southern Uganda.[27] This example also serves as a warning against the use of over-simple models of the pre-colonial rural economy, which often was far removed from the stagnant, subsistence stereotype.

So far as the contemporary encouragement of export-crop production is concerned, there is a need to make absolutely sure that domestic food production would not be affected. Senegal and The Gambia have consumed much of the foreign exchange they earned from exporting groundnuts in importing rice. If rice is cheaper than groundnuts there may well be advantages in this policy, but its implications in a world of rapidly rising population levels need careful consideration. Imported food may soon be very expensive.

Finally we may consider an important topic which has been rather neglected in the past, namely the relationship between external market prices and the provision of a transport system as causes of an increase in the production of an export crop. The authors have considered this problem in a study of the agriculture of Sierra Leone, where it was related to the rapid increase in the export of palm kernels in the period 1898–1913.[28] Our conclusion, though specific to Sierra Leone, may well be of wider interest.

During this period the annual export of palm kernels rose by 30 000 tonnes, from 20 000 tonnes in 1898 to 50 000 tonnes in 1913 – a rise of 150 per cent. Two important causes were operating simultaneously, a general increase in the prices of palm kernels and the construction of a railway into the palm belt of eastern Sierra Leone. Real prices of palm kernels (the export price deflated by an index of the prices of imported goods) rose by about 100 per cent. Meanwhile the railway was being pushed eastwards from Freetown and had penetrated 365 km by 1908, when it reached its eastern terminus of Pendembu near the Liberian border. A northern branch was then started which reached the edge of the palm belt at Makeni in 1914, adding another 134 km of rail. Rail transport was cheaper than the old

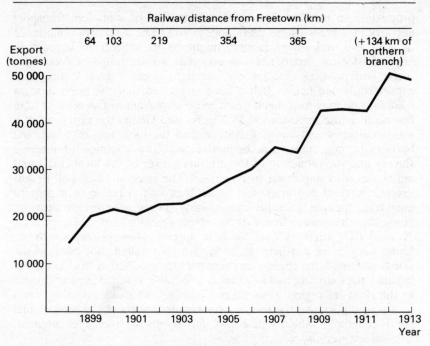

Fig. 3.2 Exports of palm kernels and railway construction in Sierra Leone

system which involved head-loading kernels to a navigable stream and sending them down river by canoe to small coastal ports where they were transhipped to Freetown for export to Europe and America. By 1913 over half the kernels were going by rail (i.e. nearly all the extra production) (Fig. 3.2).

To arrive at a precise assessment of the share of the rising prices and the improved transport in causing the increased exports would be very difficult, but it is possible to arrive at a reasonable estimate by comparing the influence of prices (price elasticity of supply) at a later period in Sierra Leone's history when improvements in transport were not occurring. This has been done for the 20 years or so following World War II, and produced an elasticity of 0·8, which means that an increase in prices of 100 per cent could be expected to produce an increase in supply of 80 per cent. If this proportion holds good for the earlier period we could say that the 100 per cent increase in real prices accounted for an 80 per cent increase in exports. This would have amounted to 16 000 tonnes (80 per cent of 20 000 tonnes exported in 1898). But exports rose by 30 000 tonnes leaving another 14 000 tonnes to be accounted for, which might be attributed to the influence of the railway. If we express these shares in percentage terms we can say that the doubling of prices caused 53·3 per cent of the increased exports and the railway caused the remaining 46·7 per cent.

Another way of expressing these calculations is to say that if the real price of palm kernels had remained constant at its 1898 level, the effect of building the railway would have been to increase exports from

20 000 tonnes in 1898 to 36 000 tonnes in 1914 (instead of the 50 000 tonnes actually achieved).

The implications behind this conclusion may not be generally applicable, of course, and would certainly need to be supplemented by similar studies of other areas; but the immediate lesson to be drawn is that one must beware of placing too much importance on the effects of *merely* linking an area where there appears to be surplus of labour and land to an international export market, regardless of price movements. For if the real price of palm kernels had been *downwards* between 1898 and 1913, it is quite possible that the railway (which, in fact, was built primarily for administrative reasons) would have had very little effect in raising palm kernel exports. Therefore the evaluation of the economic effects of extensions of transport networks needs careful consideration. The historical evidence can be misleading, if taken in the context of the vent-for-surplus theory, without an allowance being made for the influence of price changes.

In conclusion, we may return to the opening themes of stability and change. We have seen that the antiquity of African agriculture gives it a well-rounded ecological base. It has adapted to its environment over a very long period and its basic stock of crops and livestock are capable of sustained reproduction without ecological damage. On the other hand the systems are not unchanging and inflexible. They have developed, grown and adapted over time; in particular African agricultural exports have moved into a crucial position in the structure of world trade during the past century. Generally this has brought improvements in living standards, infrastructure and economic diversification, but there have also been disadvantages. Most African countries are too dependent on a narrow range of export crops. This puts them at the mercy of sudden changes in the international terms of trade and subjects them to de-stabilising shocks. Historical experience therefore suggests that in future, more attention should be given to obtaining a better balance between agricultural exports and domestic food production.

References

1 There is an immense bibliography on African agriculture. Useful studies from an historical point of view are G.P. Murdock, *Africa, its Peoples and their Culture History*, McGraw Hill, New York, 1959; William Allan, *The African Husbandman*, Oliver and Boyd, London, 1965; Daniel Biebuyk (ed.), *African Agrarian Systems*, OUP, 1963; *Oxford Regional Economic Atlas of Africa*, Clarendon Press 1965; M.J. Herskovits and M. Harwitz (eds), *Economic Transition in Africa*, RKP, London, 1964. For West Africa see also M.A. Havinden, 'The history of crop cultivation in West Africa, a bibliographical guide,' *World Agricultural Economics and Rural Sociology Abstracts,* 17 (8), August 1975.

2 A.T.P. Seabrook, 'The groundnut scheme in retrospect' *Tanganyika Notes and Records*, 47, 1957, pp. 87–91.

3 See Samir Amin, (ed.) *Modern Migrations in Western Africa*, OUP, 1974, pp. 98–124.

4 See David R. Harris, 'The origins of agriculture in the tropics', *American Scientist*, **60**, 1972, 180–93, and his chapter in P.J. Ucko and G.W. Dimbleby, *The Domestication and Exploitation of Plants and Animals*, Duckworth, London 1969. Also useful are J. Desmond Clark, *The Prehistory of Africa*, Thames and Hudson, London, 1970; J.D. Fage and R. Oliver (eds), *Papers in African Prehistory*, CUP, 1970; A.G. Hopkins, *An Economic History of West Africa*, Longman, London, 1973 and Barbara Bender, *Farming in Prehistory, from hunter-gatherer to food-producer*, Baker, London 1975.

5 Murdock, *op. cit.*

6 W.J.A. Payne, 'The origin of domestic cattle in Africa', *Empire Journal of Experimental Agriculture*, **32** 1964, 97–113.

7 Murdock, *Culture History, op. cit.*; Claude Meillassoux (ed.) *The Development of Indigenous Trade and Markets in West Africa*, OUP 1971; C.C. Wrigley, 'Speculations on the economic prehistory of Africa', *Journal of African History*, I, 1960, 189–203; and Allen M. Howard, 'The relevance of spatial analysis for African economic history: the Sierra Leone – Guinea system', *Journal of African History*, **17**, 1976, 365–88.

8 Allan, *op. cit.*

9 Murdock, *Culture History, op. cit.*

10 Havinden, *op. cit.*

11 Walter Rodney, *How Europe underdeveloped Africa*, 1972, 111–12.

12 Havinden, *op. cit.*

13 Marvin P. Miracle, *Maize in Tropical Africa*, Univ. of Wisconsin Press, Madison, Wisconsin, 1966.

14 Murdock, *op. cit.*

15 *Oxford Regional Atlas, Africa*, 1965.

16 The net barter terms of trade provide an index of the import-purchasing power of a unit of exports; while the income terms measure the import-purchasing power of total exports. See A.G. Hopkins, *op. cit.*, pp. 131–135, for a discussion of their effect in the nineteenth century.

17 Havinden, *op. cit.*; Seth La Anyane, *Ghana Agriculture, its economic development from early times to the middle of the twentieth century*, OUP, 1963; and R. Szereszewski, *Structural Changes in the Economy of Ghana, 1891–1911*, Weidenfeld and Nicholson, London, 1965.

18 E.A.G. Robinson (ed.), *Economic Development for Africa South of the Sahara*, MacMillan, London 1964; P.T. Bauer, *West African Trade*, 1954; and V. Harlow, E.M. Chilver and A. Smith, *History of East Africa*, II, Clarendon Press, Oxford, 1965.

19 A.G. Hopkins, *op. cit.*, pp. 231–2.

20 Walter Rodney, *How Europe underdeveloped Africa*, p. 106; and *Oxford Atlas, Africa*, p. 8.

21 Samir Amin, *op. cit.*, 70–78; Ken Swindell, 'SeraWoollies, Tillibunkas, and strange Farmers: the development of migrant groundnut farming along the Gambia river, 1848–1895', *Journal of African History*, **21**, 1980, 93–104.

22 *ibid.*, 98–110.

23 A.G. Hopkins, *op. cit.*, p. 220.

24 Polly Hill, *Migrant Cocoa Farmers of Southern Ghana, a study in rural capitalism*, CUP, 1963.

25 A.G. Hopkins, *op. cit.*, p. 220.

26 Barbara Ingham, 'Vent for surplus reconsidered with Ghanaian evidence', *Journal of Development Studies*, **15**, 1979, 19–37; and Sheila Smith, 'Colonialism and economic theory: the experience of Nigeria', *ibid.*, 38–59.

27 John Tosh, 'Lango agriculture during the early colonial period: land and labour in a cash crop economy,' *Journal of African History*, **19**, 1978, 415–39.

28 J.F.S. Levi, with M.A. Havinden, G. Karr and O. Johnson, *African Agriculture: Economic Action and reaction in Sierra Leone,* Commonwealth Agricultural Bureaux, Farnham Royal, 1976, 44–51.

4 Labour and time

Drawbacks of conventional micro-economic theory

It is only in recent years that economists have begun to realise that the economic behaviour of the peasant farmer requires a theory which is quite different from the micro-economic theory found in standard Western texts. And this is remarkable considering the number of people in the world whose economic environment is essentially rural. The fundamental factor that makes conventional theory unrealistic is the assumed dichotomy between firms and consumers. This may represent fairly well the realities of an industrial economy, but it is quite inappropriate to the rural economy, and in particular, the African rural economy, where there is rarely any distinction in practice between the producing firm and the consuming household. In the orthodox theory of the firm, it is assumed that the entrepreneur buys his inputs, converting them into products using the factors of production, the products being sold in some form of market. He produces and sells to the extent that his profits – sales less costs – are maximised. The consumer is assumed to decide, in the face of a given income, to purchase the combination of available commodities that maximises his utility; and the worker, for whom it is possible to work longer or shorter hours at a fixed wage rate, is assumed to choose a combination of work (thus, earnings) and leisure so as to maximise his utility. It is the assumptions underlying these theories that are incorrect when dealing with the typical, here, African, farmer. Unlike the industrial employer, he does not in general, or to any great extent, hire labour by the hour, day or week and expect a fairly homogeneous amount of work or output in exchange for a given wage; and he does not purchase much in the way of inputs of any sort. Unlike the consumer who works for a firm, or receives rent or other forms of income, he does not have a given, regular, income, expected with a high degree of certainty. Unlike the industrial worker, he is not obliged to put in a fixed amount of work (so many hours per day or week) in order to be employed at all. Rather, he makes a choice about the number of hours of work he will do in a day, about the amount of rest he will take in each hour and even about how energetic his toil will be. The choice about the amount and kind of work done is determined by how much output and income the farmer and his family want and how much time they want to devote to other occupations, such as craft work, ceremony, visiting relatives, etc. (In reality, it is not of course just 'the farmer' who conveniently takes all the decisions for the good of everyone in the farm family. For example, in some cases, women may be completely independent in taking decisions about particular crops which are by custom their domain.)[1]

So it is more reasonable to look upon the typical African farm as a sort of combination of household and firm. The consequences of doing this are significant when we try to set up a model of the economic behaviour of the farm.

Appropriate theory

An early pioneer thinker on the economics of peasant farming was the Russian economist, A.V. Chayanov, who wrote *Peasant Farm Organisation* in 1925. In it, and in his 1921 work *On the Theory of Non-Capitalist Economic Systems*, he attempted to show that, as indeed we have suggested in the last few paragraphs, the farm is in a class on its own as an economic entity, the peasant being neither true capitalist nor true proletarian. (In so doing he took issue with some of the views of Marx, but particularly with those of Lenin, who seemed to see an inevitable degeneration of the peasant economy into a capitalist one, through the evolution of classes, and who argued that the extent of 'family', or subsistence, farming in Russia was far less than the 90 per cent of farms suggested by Chayanov. He was arrested in 1930 and the team of colleagues he led, along with the research tradition he established, was broken up). The link between the paragraphs of the previous section and the theory that follows below is perhaps most easily seen by quoting from the 1966 translation:

> The greater the quantity of work carried out by a man in a definite time period, the greater and greater drudgery for the man are the last (marginal) units of labour expended.
>
> On the other hand, the subjective evaluation of the values obtained by this marginal labour will depend on the extent of its marginal utility for the farm family. But since marginal utility falls with growth of the total sum of values that become available to the subject running the farm, there comes a moment at a certain level of rising labour income when the drudgery of the marginal labour expenditure will equal the subjective evaluation of the marginal utility of the sum obtained by this labour.[2]

Mellor[3] and Nakajima[4] in the sixties, independently presented similar and original models of the peasant farm, Nakajima's being somewhat more rigorous and mathematical. These, perhaps along with that of Sen,[5] marked an important breakthrough in theory and it is on them that we base our theory herein. (With the benefit of hindsight we can see the importance of Chayanov's contribution, but few economists were aware of it in the early sixties, before the English translation became widely available.) In the text that follows we attempt to keep the theory as simple as possible. Indeed we begin with what is clearly over-simplification in order to bring out the general principles, and then gradually introduce the complexities of real life – standard practice in economics.

The first assumption is that the farm is a single decision-making unit, as if only an individual person were in complete control, deciding how much labour is to be applied and by whom, what is to be produced, and so on. The second assumption is that time is divided between only two occupations, labour and leisure, each of which is conveniently homogeneous and measured in hours or days. Labour-time is applied to farming the land in return for output. We can initially suppose that there is a single homogeneous product (food) or else that several products can be aggregated in money terms. The usual assumption of diminishing returns to labour applies, given that other productive factors, such as land and climatic conditions, and the technique of production, remain constant. The production–possibility curve, which depicts the relationship between labour and output, thus has the general form shown in Fig. 4.1.

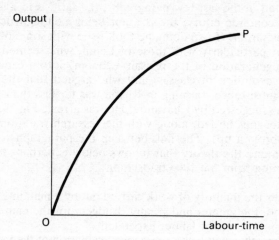

Fig. 4.1

The utility generated by any amount of output produced on the farm is offset by the loss of utility from time that could have been enjoyed in leisure activity, but which is used up in labour, and also from the fact that the labour in itself is irksome and generates disutility, or negative utility. Thus the farmer has to choose that combination of output and leisure which will give him and his family maximum utility. His choice is constrained by the production–possibility curve, i.e. the combination chosen cannot possibly lie above the curve OP.

We suppose that the farmer has a set of indifference curves with general shapes as in Fig. 4.2. The higher the indifference curve, the higher the level of utility on it.

On any given curve, utility is constant and the farmer chooses any of the combinations of output and leisure along that curve indifferently. The form of the curves is such that for each additional hour of work applied, more and more output is required to compensate, i.e. to keep utility at a constant level. Conversely, as output is progressively reduced by a constant amount, the leisure required to compensate for each reduction is increased. We have also assumed that there is a minimum, or subsistence, level of output at which no amount of leisure (or in principle an infinite amount) will compensate for a further re-

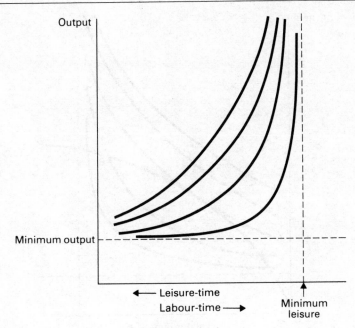

Fig. 4.2

duction. Similarly, there is a minimum amount of leisure, in the form of rest, etc.

Putting these curves – the production–possibility curve, OP, and the indifference curves (or indifference map) – on the same diagram shows how the optimum combination of leisure and output is chosen, and the diagram is useful for the logical analysis of changes in the economic circumstances of the farm (Fig. 4.3).

The highest utility level attainable within the confines of OP is that denoted by the indifference curve marked II, and the combination of leisure and output (or labour and output) chosen is at A, this being the only combination attainable on II (since any other point on II would be above the production-possibility curve OP). Or putting it another way, any other point on OP, such as B or C, would be on a lower indifference curve, as can be seen; and, of course, any point below OP would be on a lower indifference curve.

Still another way of expressing the optimum, or equilibrium, combination of output and leisure is as follows. Take a point on OP such as C. Here the indifference curve cutting OP has a smaller slope than OP. What does that mean in plain language? It means that if labour were to be increased by one hour, the amount of output required to compensate for that labour and keep utility constant is smaller than the output produced by the extra hour. This amounts to saying that the farmer finds it worthwhile putting in another hour of work. There is a net gain in utility by doing so: the extra utility from the added output is greater than the disutility of the added labour. Now this is also true of all the points on OP to the left of A, because the slope of any indifference curve cutting OP to the left of A is smaller than the slope

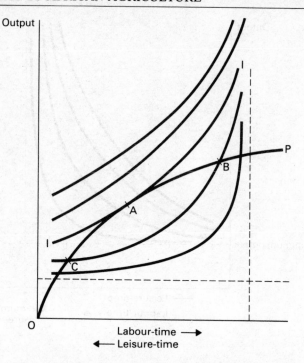

Fig. 4.3

of OP. So, to the left of A it is always worthwhile putting in more labour. The reverse is true for points on OP to the right of A, where the slope of any indifference curve cutting OP is greater than the slope of OP: the reduction in output consequent on reducing labour by one hour is not so undesirable as to offset the utility gained from diminished toil.

All of this is, of course, a gross over-simplification of reality. There are all sorts of uncomfortable qualifications that spring to mind and which together seem almost to demolish the validity or usefulness of the theory. For example, the farmer cannot know exactly how much extra output he will get from putting in an extra hour of labour, because the output from agriculture is always uncertain, dominated as it is by weather conditions. Again, the assumption that labour is homogeneous, and that another hour of labour will always affect output in the same way, no matter when or by whom it is applied or what it does, is obviously not true. But we are here only setting out the basic principles; we shall gradually deal with the complications as we proceed. Also, this approach does demonstrate clearly the difference between the economic behaviour of the peasant farmer and that of the 'firm' or 'consumer'. When the farmer has produced, or expects to produce, what he considers a reasonable income in terms of material goods, he will not bother to exert himself any further. As Galletti *et al.* put it in their study of Nigerian cocoa farmers:

> . . . palm nuts may lie uncracked because the market value of the
> kernels does not appear to a woman to be worth the labour of

preparing them for market: and palm fruits drop unharvested from the trees to rot on the ground because the family has enough oil for its present needs and the producing of more oil would add too much to the day's work.[6]

Similar observations were made with regard to cocoa, yam and cassava cultivation, in the face of income levels of around £100 per family in 1951/52, cf. the quotation from Chayanov above.

The precise location of A – the combination of leisure (or labour) and output – depends on firstly, the shape of the indifference map and secondly, on the position of the production–possibility curve. Dealing with the latter first: this will be affected by the endowments of the other productive factors that combine with labour, such as land (including its quality), tools, fertiliser and so on. It will be affected, too, by more intangible things like the techniques of production, managerial ability, health, etc. Also, if we suppose that output is expressed in value terms, rather than physical, then OP will be raised if the price of output increases (or the prices of the outputs if there is more than one product). The indifference map might be tilted, for example, so that a particular farmer had a preference for more output and less leisure than another farmer, given the same production–possibility curve. This might, for instance, be because he has more children or other dependants to feed, or simply because he is more acquisitive.

We might suppose, however, when considering broadly the labour – output combinations for whole regions, rather than individual farmers, that the position of the production – possibility curve is the dominant influence. And a superficial impression, gained from reading Chapter 2 perhaps, is that the scarcity of land (with allowance for the quality of land) and the existence and nature of markets for agricultural products might be the most important factors involved. However, the effect they have is not clear, for it depends on the shapes of the curves. Consider the two diagrams in Fig. 4.4, each of which compares a farmer possessing a small endowment of land with a farmer who has plenty.

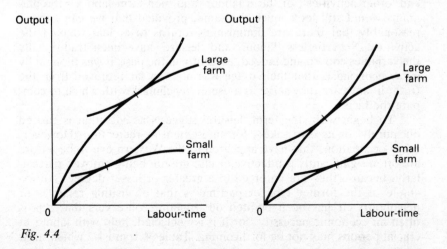

Fig. 4.4

In the first case the large farmer puts in more labour than the small farmer, but in the second case he puts in less. All depends on the shapes of the curves, i.e. on the nature of preferences and on the nature of the production relationships. The position is similar with regard to differences in the market value of farm output. A rise in the value of agricultural produce may cause farmers to put in more or less labour, depending on the nature of their preferences and on the nature of the relation between production and labour. On the other hand, it seems reasonable to suppose that for farmers or farm-families close to subsistence level (i.e. poor), they will tend to put in more effort, the lower is their land endowment, for the simple reason that they will be highly motivated by the desire to avoid hunger, malnutrition or even starvation; they thus try to keep output as much above subsistence as they can.

The realities of the use of time

The representation of the African farm by our theoretical model, with its simple division of time into labour and leisure, its decisions taken with perfect certainty and as if by a single person, is of course, artificial. Nevertheless it does serve the function of bringing out the essence of economic behaviour and enabling logical analysis, which is the function of economic theory generally. But it would be a mistake to be satisfied with theory alone even though there is a gain from abstraction, and a mistake, too, to believe that economics has little to do with describing the complexities of the real world. Although insight comes from theorising, even better insight is gained by comparing theory with actuality, which is what we now proceed to do.

First of all we have to remember that the common practice of economic theory in selecting only two variables from many, is so that the (two-dimensional) diagram can be employed. Otherwise rather more difficult mathematics are necessary. And the labelling of the two activities in the model of the farm as 'labour' and 'leisure' is not to be taken too seriously. The labels could just as well have been 'labour' and 'other activities', or 'farm labour' and 'non-farm labour': the diagrams would still look much the same, provided that we can assume reasonably that there are diminishing returns to at least one of the activities. Nevertheless 'labour' and 'leisure' have been traditionally the variables chosen and indeed, evidently in the past, it was thought by many economists that their usage was not too far removed from the truth; in any case they serve as a useful benchmark with which to compare the facts.

To begin with, the term 'leisure' suggests activity that is carried out purely for its own sake – for amusement or recreation. However, many occupations that have appeared to the Western eye to be leisure are often significantly productive or else are not being enjoyed particularly, because they are enforced to a greater or lesser degree. An example of the former type of pastime is that of visiting relatives or neighbours. It has been pointed out by some observers that this is often an economic necessity, for if it is neglected, help with labour at crucial periods may not be forthcoming. Tables 4.1 and 4.2 which show

Table 4.1
Zengoaga Village, Cameroun: Average hours per year devoted to different activities, 1962–64

	Men	Women
Sleep	3 250	3 276
Meals, hygiene	255	247
Visits, travel	1 524	1 300
Rest, chatting	1 665	1 306
Illness ·	136	153
Various unproductive	136	71

Agricultural work

	Men	Women
Plantations (cocoa and coffee)	456	19
Food	560	1 315
Various productive	61	21
Total agricultural	1 077	1 355
Hunting, fishing	187	20
Market, selling	126	172
Construction, maintenance	309	37
Housework	–	820

Source: J. Tissandier, *Zengoaga* (*Cameroun*), Atlas des Structures Agraires au Sud du Sahara, No. 3, Mouton/ORSTOM, 1970.

the aggregate use of time over the year in a Camerounian village and among a group of Ghanaian lime farmers, give some idea of the amount of time devoted to these and other occupations that might be termed leisure. These tables also demonstrate the way in which the preconceptions of the researcher may to some extent be imposed on his research, for the categories into which time is divided in the two studies are quite different; indeed there are only two or three categories that are common to both surveys: sleep, marketing and possibly housework (although the 'household activities' among the lime farmers may not be entirely the same thing as 'housework'). An example of an occupation that may be enforced is rest or 'idleness' brought on by illness; as Hammond has put it in a study of the Mossi of Upper Volta:

> Another thing the Mossi are doing when they are apparently just sitting and lying around is suffering from the painful and debilitating effects of Guinea worm, bilharzia, filaria, yaws, and a variety of other, often chronic, diseases.[7]

Some types of activity appear to be a combination of labour and leisure. Hunting, for example, is generally intended to be productive of food, but may not always be taken very seriously as such. Furthermore, there are often clear attempts to make labour less irksome by injecting an element of festivity in the form of singing, drumming, beer drinking, and so forth.

So having cast a few doubts on the notion that we know what we mean when we are talking about leisure, let us also ask the question: 'What is labour?'

Table 4.2 Lime Farmers, Southern Ghana: Average hours per year devoted to different activities, Sept. 1969–Aug. 1970

	Men	Women
Productive activities:		
Farming	992	833
Walking to place of work	373	402
Non-farming	368	232
Walking to place of work	70	22
Market	81	158
Walking to place of work	31	54
Total productive	1 915	1 701
Domestic activities:		
Sleep	3 153	3 198
Household	769	2 058
Leisure	1 238	578
Rest	711	486
Medical	72	70
Total domestic	5 945	6 390
Social obligations:		
Traditional	672	371
Non-traditional	108	177
Total social	780	548

(Figures may not add exactly, owing to rounding)

Source: H.T.M. Wagenbuur, 'Labour and development: an analysis of the time budget and of the production and productivity of lime farmers in southern Ghana', Institute of Social Studies Occasional Papers No. 23, The Hague, 1972.

In the two 'time budgets' presented above, the hours spent in what is actually classified as farm work are quite 'low' (low, that is, by the standards of typical work in a Western economy, which probably averages something around 2 000 hours per year), and Cleave[8] concludes from his study of farm surveys conducted in English-speaking Africa that the typical farm worker spends about 4 to 6 hours per day in the field over 140–160 days in the year. But should we, for example, include as labour, walking to the fields, which among the Ghanaian lime farmers takes up a considerable amount of time, as can be seen in the above table? Of course, if there were no time spent walking to the fields there would be no output. On the other hand, if more time is spent walking, we would not expect more output, unlike the case with, say, weeding, for which it is reasonable to expect a greater output – though not indefinitely greater – the more work is applied. There is no clear relationship, as in our theoretical diagrams, between walking time and output. Moreover time spent in walking to the fields is significant throughout much of Western Africa, where agriculturalists are generally settled in villages (some of which are very large, as in western Nigeria). This is in contrast to many parts of eastern Africa where settlement is in the form of scattered homesteads and walking time is negligible. Other kinds of work have the characteristic that the labour–output curve displaying diminishing marginal product cannot reasonably be applied to them. Another prime example is harvesting. Usually, the amount of harvest work put in depends entirely on the amount of the crop there is to harvest: we can almost say that labour depends on output rather than the reverse. Similar remarks can be made about processing – threshing, winnowing, drying, cooking, etc. There are instances when some of the planted crops are left unharvested, however. In Sierra Leone, for example, some intercrops are planted with the primary crop, rice, as an insurance in case the rice harvest is bad; if it is good, these crops may be ignored. This would also often apply to the harvesting of oil palm fruit, as suggested by the quotation above in regard to Nigeria.

All these activities are generally called 'work', even though, as we have suggested, they do not really comply with the notion of labour we use in the theory. Perhaps we should therefore distinguish two types of labour. The first is the type we have just discussed which we might call 'requisite' labour. Such labour is necessary in order to obtain the final product, but it is unreasonable to suppose that a functional relationship between output and requisite labour represents reality. The second type we might call 'productive' labour for which the diminishing returns curve does seem a valid abstraction. In this category are included land-clearing, hoeing, ploughing, sowing, weeding, etc.

Another point we might question regarding the validity of the theoretical model is the assumption implicit in the diagrams that labour can be both measured and aggregated, i.e. that we can both assume that time spent at some task is a consistent indicator of the labour applied and that, say, hours spent weeding can be meaningfully added to hours spent sowing seed.

Table 4.3 shows data of labour use among a sample of shifting cultivators in Sierra Leone. A large amount of time is spent by children in scaring birds and other pests away from the growing crops.

Table 4.3   Labour inputs per acre, shifting cultivation, Sierra Leone, 1970

	Workdays
Brushing	9·2
Felling	6·9
Burning and clearing	6·4
Hoeing and sowing	9·7
Weeding	19·7
Pest-scaring	20·0
Harvesting	10·0

Figures from a sample of 86 farms, with an average cultivated area of 3·9 acres and an average of 5·8 working persons per farm. Adult male and female, and child labour was aggregated by weighting. Sample size for weeding labour was 25. Pest-scaring labour is an approximate figure.

Sources: A.O. Njoku, *Labor Utilisation in Traditional Agriculture: The Case of Sierra Leone Rice Farms*, Ph.D. dissertation, University of Illinois, 1971; G.L. Karr, A.O. Njoku and M.F. Kallon, 'The Economics of the Upland and the Inland-valley swamp rice production systems in Sierra Leone', *Illinois Agricultural Economics*, **12**, 1, Jan. 1972.

Haswell, too, found that in Genieri village, The Gambia, about 10 hours per day were spent by boys in this occupation during the growing season.[9] Little is actually done during these long hours, apart from occasionally throwing stones or making a noise, but it is a vital activity, for the entire crop can disappear if it is neglected too much. Indeed, there are instances of farming systems having to be changed to a less pest-attracting mix of crops when the labour-time required for protection is no longer available owing to, for example, the advent of generally available education or non-agricultural wage employment. Yet for all that, it is obviously nonsense to aggregate pest-scaring hours with, say, planting hours. Admittedly this is perhaps the extreme example, but it does demonstrate the kind of pitfalls involved in adding together hours of labour spent on different tasks. Also, of course, hours of labour spent by different categories of worker, especially children versus adults, cannot be aggregated, although – just to complicate matters – it is possible that with some tasks, such as, indeed, pest-scaring, the efficiency of adult hours is no different from that of child hours.

We take it for granted that days of work are an unsatisfactory measure since, obviously, the number of hours of work per day can vary. However Guillard, in his comprehensive study of a Toupourri village in northern Cameroun, argues in favour of the half-day as the best compromise measure of labour.[10] This is because, he maintains, it is the concept of labour-time most meaningful to the people themselves, for they tend in fact to do tasks in half-days regardless of whether the hours needed may in fact be much less than half a day. But this approach, even if valid for the Toupourri, is not necessarily generally applicable.

Even if we are only considering one particular task performed by a single category of worker, it is still possible that hours might be an inadequate measure of the input of labour, because an hour's work can be carried out more or less energetically. Table 4.4 shows some exam-

Table 4.4
Calorie use and resting time, by different tasks, The Gambia

Task	Energy use per hour of continuous work, cal/h/kg	Per cent of time spent resting	Energy use per hour including rest* cal/h/kg
Females:			
Hoeing and broadcasting	3·2	42	2·3
Weeding rice	2·4	29	2·0
Transplanting rice	2·7	25	2·3
Pulling grass	2·7	27	2·2
Lifting rice seedlings	2·1	23	1·8
Harvesting rice	1·7	9	1·6
Males:			
Windrowing groundnuts	2·1	39	1·7
Lifting groundnuts	3·7	30	2·9
Harvesting millet	2·0	10	1·9
Stacking groundnuts	2·8	4	2·7

* Calorie use during rest is put at 1·0 cal per hour per kilo body weight.

Source: J.H. Cleave, *African Farmers*, Appendix Tables C1 and C2.

ples of rates of energy use in different tasks in The Gambia. Note that there is also a tendency for the proportion of the time spent resting to be greater, the more energetic is the work, especially for women, although this does not completely offset the rate of energy use.

Given some allowance for energy as well as time in assessing the input of effort, there are still some residual factors that need to be taken into consideration which we can lump together under the generic term: 'quality' of labour or effort. These factors can be thought of as making the output from a given amount of effort greater or smaller, with given land, type of worker, technique, etc. One such factor is the state of health of the worker, which in Africa can be of extreme importance, especially at periods of the season when the timing of labour is vital. Another is the size of the labour force (the' 'stock' of labour, rather than the 'flow' of labour): x hours of work done by two men will tend to be more productive than x hours done by one, since the two will be less tired and may work in co-operation.

Experience, motivation, managerial ability and the like will also affect the quality or productivity of the input of work. For example, it is probable that hired labour has less motivation to work carefully or hard than has family labour. Upton[11] found significant correlations between certain personal characteristics of farmers in south-western Nigeria and their farm incomes. Coefficients for these characteristics were measured using a scoring system and it was found that net income was significantly related to degrees of 'independence of thought', 'sophistication' and 'innovation', the correlations being derived after allowing for labour input, since that was found to be related to personal characteristics too. ('Independence of thought' refers to an absence of the tendency to reply 'yes' to all questions; 'sophistication' involves educational background, interest in affairs outside the village and membership of modern societies; 'innovation' refers to the extent of changes in farming practice and familiarity with extension advisers.) In a study of farmers in Zambia, it was found that returns, after the effects of physical inputs had been allowed for, were strongly related to an index of 'experience and knowledge of farming', rather than to attitudes as in Upton's study, or to formal education or even the adoption of good farming practices. Moreover it was found that marginal returns to 'experience and knowledge' were much higher for the lowest values of the index than for most of its range (see Table 4.5).

Table 4.5
Marginal returns in maize associated with a unit increase in the index of experience and knowledge of farming, Zambia

Index	Returns in kg of maize per unit increase in index
10	58
20	19
40	9·5
60	6·8
80	5·9
100	5

Source: Elliot *et al.*, *op. cit.* (metricated)

Factors affecting the input of effort through the year

In Chapter 2 we referred briefly to the influence of the rainfall regime on the time pattern of labour inputs. It was noted how particularly productive physical conditions – especially the initial moistness of the soil at the beginning of the rainy season – because they often last for only a short interval, make the application of labour to certain tasks rather urgent. This observation applies generally in that physical conditions make the labour applied to a given task *at any particular time* more or less productive.

Taking 'labour' to mean effort, perhaps measured in calories to allow for work rate as well as time, and effort applied to a particular task, say, sowing seed, we can think of all this in theoretical terms.

Each curve in Fig. 4.5 applies to a particular date, the labour applied to sowing on a given date affecting output with diminishing marginal returns. Here we have supposed that weather conditions and the conditions for plant growth have made 1st June the most productive day on which to sow; and delay makes labour progressively less productive. Sowing on 1st June therefore will tend to be a matter of some urgency. For each hour's work on that day (given the rate of energy use) the farmer knows from experience and from weather conditions that he is likely to get a better return than on another day.

It is worth noting too that where land for sowing is not limited, as is often – but not by any means always – the case in Africa, diminishing returns will not be very marked and will be determined largely by the growing tiredness and inefficiency of the workers. Also, it is very important to note that each of these curves implies an assumption that everything else remains fixed. Thus if, for example, some sowing is done on 20th May, *all the other curves will change their shapes and positions.* To see this, note that the curves as they stand, all start at the

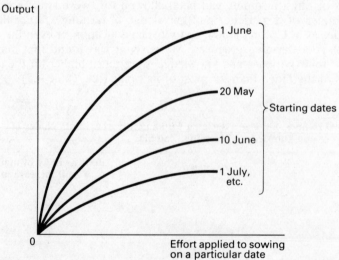

Fig. 4.5

origin, 0; which is reasonable, as there will be no output if no seeds are sown. Next suppose some sowing is done on 20th May. If we now take the '1st June' curve, this can no longer start from 0 since some output will be forthcoming even if sowing effort is zero on 1st June. Thus each date attached to each curve applies only to the starting date.

In practice, sowing or planting of the major crop is often done in a single day – as soon as the first rain has fallen – presumably because that day is very much more productive than other days, and because it is feasible to do so with the labour available. This may not always be the case, however. Weeding and other tasks are probably a good deal less sensitive to physical conditions, though they will be sensitive to some degree. Thus weeding effort will tend to be concentrated into a favourable period, with the input per day gradually increasing at the beginning of the period, and trailing off towards the end.

There is strong evidence to show that the productivity of planting is highly sensitive to the date of planting. Table 4.6 shows data obtained from a demonstration farm in northern Nigeria and illustrates the effect of planting date on the yield of groundnuts.

Table 4.6
The effect of planting date on groundnut yields

Date of planting (using decorticated seed)	Mean days from optimum	Yield kg/hectare	Per cent of maximum
May 6–9	−6	1 156	82
May 11–16	0	1 406	100
May 18–23	7	1 270	90
May 25–30	14	927	68
June 1–6	21	635	45
June 8–12	28	544	39
June 16–20	36	249	18
June 21–27	43	125	9
June 28 on		failure	0

Source: K.D.S. Baldwin, *The Niger Agricultural Project*, Basil Blackwell,1958.
Also printed in J.H. Cleave, *African Farmers* (metricated).

Similarly, Haswell's Gambian study[13] shows that yields of groundnuts are lower by about 2 per cent for each day's delay from the optimum planting date; Cleave[14] has graphs showing the effects of delay on cotton yields in Uganda and Tanzania, being roughly 0·5–1 per cent lower than the best for each day's delay from the optimum.

The urgency of work may be reinforced also by the fact that the same physical conditions can make work on several crops highly productive for a limited period; for example, cash crops may compete with staples in this way.

Thus far we have only considered one side of the phenomenon of varying labour inputs through the year, i.e. the returns and the timing of the returns. We have not yet discussed the costs. The input of effort on any given day, where we think of effort in terms of both hours and energy use per hour (or as total energy use), is determined partly by the productivity of that effort and the subjective valuation of the product. The production of the minimum amount of food needed for subsistence, for example, will have a high subjective valuation. It is also determined by how productive effort is on other days. Thus planting may result in failure if it is left too long, as we have seen. In other words the effort per day is determined by the urgency of the task, urgency being a function of two things: the productivity of labour at different times, and the subjective valuation of the product. On the costs side, the disutility of an extra unit of effort rises as more effort is put in. Thus even though work on a task is urgent on a particular day, the effort put in will be limited by the fact that another hour's toil, at a given rate of energy use, may be so disagreeable that the likely extra output resulting from it will be insufficient compensation. This will be all the more so if the work can be done the following day; even if it requires say two hours work tomorrow morning to get the same extra output as another hour's work today, that single extra hour may be so irksome on top of the rest of the day's work that it is worth doing the two hours tomorrow.

The relationship between the disutility (unpleasantness) of work and the amount of work (energy) done in a day depends on several factors. Firstly, some work is more unpleasant innately than other work, i.e., given the rate of energy use, x hours, say, transplanting rice in flooded fields is probably more unpleasant in itself than x hours spent, say, harvesting. It is important here not to become confused about the rate of energy use. Note that we have specified in the comparison that the relatively unpleasant and the relatively pleasant tasks are carried out equally energetically. We cannot say, for example, that transplanting is more unpleasant than harvesting because it is done rapidly, whereas harvesting is done at a leisurely pace. The pace of work, or rate of energy use, is not an innate characteristic of the task, but is controllable by the worker: transplanting *can* be done as slowly as one likes, while harvesting *can* be done at a frantic pace. So the degree of innate unpleasantness of a task is assessed independently of the pace of work. Another factor giving some work a higher or more rapidly increasing disutility than other work is the weather, hot sunshine versus cool, cloudy weather, for example. (It was mentioned earlier that there may be a decided attempt to make urgent work more pleasant – to lower the disutility – by means of music, beer, etc.)

The state of health of the worker at different times of the year will also affect the subjective costliness of a given amount of effort. If there is less food at one time of year than at others, people will find work more difficult, and they may also be prone to more illness. Haswell describes women in The Gambia fainting on the way back from the rice fields at certain periods owing to their physical state being inadequate for the demanding labour.[15]

The subjective cost of labour is also affected by what is sacrificed from time spent doing other things. These may be activities from which utility is directly derived – games, beer parties and so forth – or activities that generate utility indirectly, such as through the income earned from non-farm work, or from making utensils, constructing houses, etc. These alternatives to farm work, it should be noted, do not affect the disutility curve of farm work; they represent foregone utility. Fig. 4.6 may help to clarify this.

Points on the curves marked 'total subjective cost' are obtained

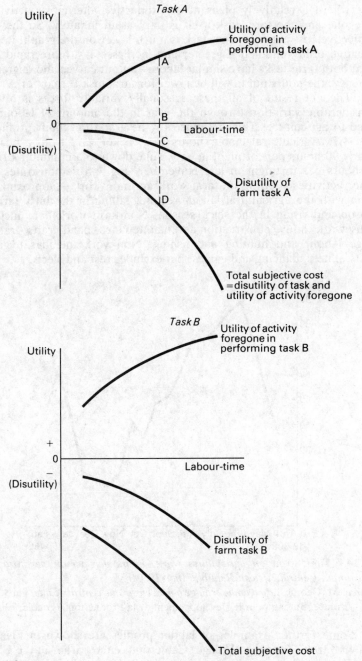

Fig. 4.6

from the vertical addition of heights on the 'activity foregone' curve to corresponding points on the middle curve; e.g. CD = BA, i.e. total subjective cost of *x* hours of work = disutility of *x* hours + utility of *x* hours foregone in alternative activity. The situation labelled Task B is one where a relatively pleasant or productive alternative activity is foregone and the farm task itself is unpleasant innately. So the total subjective cost curve for that task is much lower on the graph; i.e. the negative utility entailed is greater and increases at a more rapid rate. So if both farm tasks have similar labour–output curves and degrees of urgency, the hours put in will be lower for farm task B than for A.

The net result of all these seasonally variable forces is often a considerable variation through the year in the amount of labour applied to agriculture. This is typified by the graph (a labour profile) in Fig. 4.7. Agricultural labour hours per worker vary from a peak of nearly 90 hours per fortnight in early June down to a minimum of only 15 hours per fortnight in late November. Fig. 4.8 demonstrates how other activities – both non-farm work and non-work – approximately fit in with the agricultural labour regime, falling in the busy farming season and rising in the slack season. Non-farm work here includes housework, house construction and maintenance, hand crafts, trading, wage labour and hunting and fishing. Non-work includes hygiene, visits, illness, dancing and games, but excludes rest and sleep.

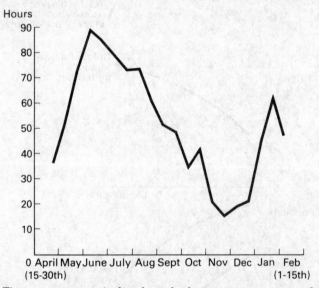

Fig. 4.7 Time spent on agricultural work, hours per person per fortnight, Pouyamba, Central African Republic (late 1950s)
Source: M. Georges, *Pouyamba: village banda en savane centrafricaine*, Paris, France, Bureau pour le Développement de la Production Agricole, 1960

Some further examples of labour profiles are shown in Figs 4.9 and 4.10 from Zengoaga Village, Cameroun, cited earlier in the Chapter. This time labour is broken down into male and female categories and a striking feature is the difference between the two. Most agricultural work for women is in food production, whereas men engage considerably in work on cocoa and coffee plantations. Also women do noticeably more non-agricultural work than men (Fig. 4.10) and their total work load is greater – a common feature throughout much of

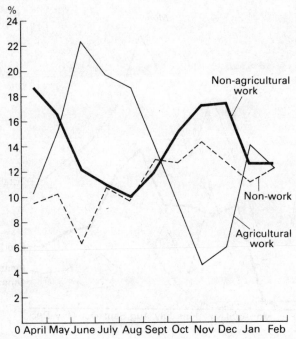

Fig. 4.8 Percentage of available time spent on agricultural work, non-agricultural work, and non-work (excluding sleep and rest), Pouyamba, Central African Republic (late 1950s)

Source: Georges, *op. cit.*

Africa (with the notable exception of some Islamic communities as in northern Nigeria where religious observance requires that married women be secluded).

Factors affecting the total input of effort in a year

Although we have emphasised the difficulties in exactly defining the term 'labour', in measuring it, and in aggregating different kinds of labour and labour performed by different classes of worker (males, females, adults, children), all is not completely lost. Firstly, we can say that some activities definitely are labour (e.g. weeding) and some are definitely not, even though there is a set of boundary activities that are difficult to categorise. Secondly, if we are consistent about what we include as labour, about how it is measured and about how it is aggregated, it is meaningful to compare and rank farms or groups of farms according to their total annual labour inputs, and to assess the variation in total labour input from year to year for individual farms, groups of farms or regions. We can thus expect to have some sort of meaningful answers to the question: 'In what way do annual labour inputs vary and why?' even though the answers may be a little imprecise.

We discussed earlier how in theory the position of the labour–output curve will affect the input of labour, given the indifference map, the height of the curve being determined by the other things that

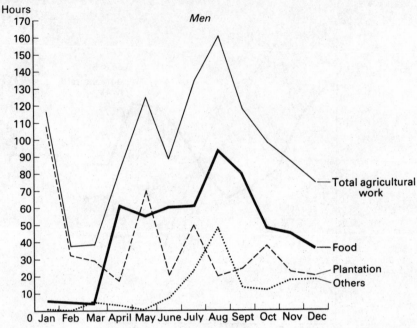

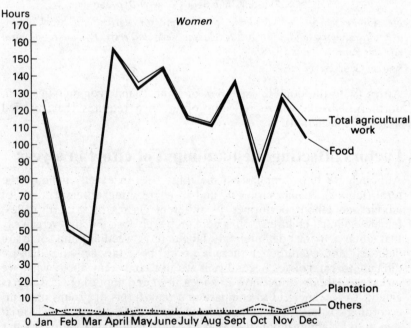

Fig. 4.9 Agricultural work by month, Zengoaga village, Cameroun, 1962; average hours per head
Source: Tissandier, *op. cit.* and cf. Table 4.1

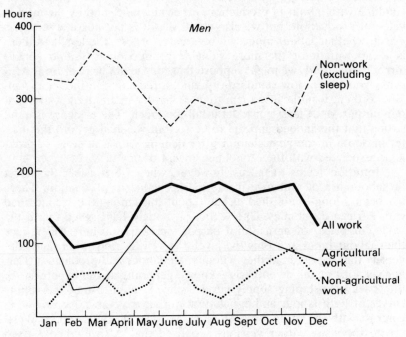

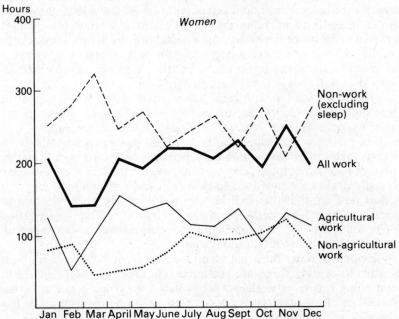

Fig. 4.10 Average hours per head, by month of agricultural work, non-agricultural work and non-work, Zengoaga village, Cameroun, 1962–64
Source: Tissandier, op. cit.

combine with labour in production, especially land, and by the market value of production; but we also noted that it is not possible to say, *a priori*, whether labour input will be greater or less, the less land there is to go with it or the more valuable production is. Intuitively, as already suggested, we might suppose that for the majority of rural Africans, who have a low standard of living, a reduction in the land available to them would cause them to work harder in an attempt to maintain output, or at least not to let it fall too much. The evidence is quite strong that this indeed appears to be so; but we shall go into the matter in depth in the next chapter after dealing with a number of problems associated with the economic concept of 'land'.

Intuition seems to fail us, however, when we consider the effect on labour use of a change in the market value of production. There has been a long-established dispute about this among those concerned with African economies. One school of thought has argued that if the value, or price, of agricultural output increases, farmers will reduce their labour input and thus the level of physical production; and conversely that if prices fall they will increase labour and production. Earlier versions of this hypothesis – known generally as the hypothesis of the 'backward-sloping supply curve', since it implies that the supply curves of both labour and agricultural output have negative slopes, in contrast with the orthodox positive slope found in the standard Western textbooks – earlier versions supposed that Africans had a fixed 'target' cash income, so that if prices fell, say, they would tend to work harder in order to maintain the 'target'. This is a crude assumption, however, and is not necessary, for the backward-sloping supply curve can be derived from our utility diagram with perfectly reasonable assumptions about the forms of the indifference map and the production – possibility curve (refer back to Fig. 4.4).

The other school of thought has pointed to the large amount of clear statistical evidence that when the prices of crops – especially the major export crops, for which a good deal of data are available – have risen or fallen, so have supplies. In fact this counter argument is fallacious if taken to prove the non-existence of a backward-sloping supply curve of *total* agricultural labour or output, for the statistical evidence typically deals with only a single cash crop and not with food crops. It is thus possible that the positive response of cash crop production to price results at least partly from the diversion of labour away from food production; nothing is concluded about the *total* labour supplied, i.e. in both cash and food production.

Evidence, other than that mentioned in the previous paragraph, is difficult to assess. There are scattered references in the literature to food crops becoming neglected when new cash crops begin to be exploited, or else to the type of food crops grown being changed to less labour-demanding ones.

The other type of influence on the total labour input can be summed up as the type that affects the indifference map; i.e. factors that determine preferences for agricultural activities. Perhaps the most important force in this direction is that of family structure; in particular the ratio of dependants to workers (the 'dependency ratio').[16] In diagrammatic terms we would expect the indifference curves to be tilted

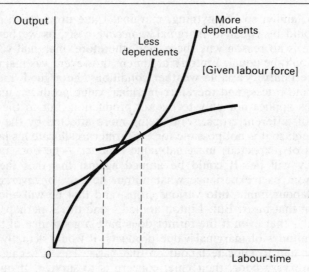

Fig. 4.11 Relationship between dependency ratio and labour input

revealing a greater preference for output as opposed to 'leisure' (see Fig. 4.11).

African evidence regarding this aspect of farm labour is scanty and not unambiguous. Guillard's study of a village in north Cameroun[17] indicates a fairly clear relationship between area cultivated per worker and consumers per worker (taking 'area cultivated' as representing the effort applied by the workers). Haswell's Gambian data are also broadly supportive.[18] Another implication of Fig. 4.11 is that for a given family size, families containing a higher proportion of workers would tend to work less; and the study of farming in Zaria Province, northern Nigeria, by Norman et al.,[19] showed that days worked per male adult (other things being equal) were smaller the greater the number of male adults in the family.

The allocation of labour

The orthodox theoretical view of the allocation of labour between different enterprises is that it will be carried out to the extent that the marginal value product of labour in each line of production is equal to the marginal cost of labour. Where there is a competitive environment for labour, the marginal cost of labour will be a constant, equal to the going wage rate, and so the marginal value products of labour applied to each enterprise will be equalised. T.W. Schultz, in his book *Transforming Traditional Agriculture*,[20] purported to demonstrate the economic efficiency of peasant farmers by some evidence from an Indian study, that marginal value products of labour did, in fact tend to be equalised. However Lipton[21] took issue with Schultz by arguing that the equalisation of marginal value products was not possible under the conditions typically faced by peasant farmers, and indeed was not rational even if it were possible. In any case, in Africa there is normally not a competitive market for labour, most of it being supplied by the farm family; so, if anything, marginal value products in different crops would be equal to marginal *subjective* costs, as we have seen, and there is no reason why these, and, therefore, marginal value products, should be equal. Lipton's argument, however, was mainly to do with uncertainty. Variable weather conditions, he argued, make production and prices, and therefore marginal value products, unpredictable. This applies not only to overall production, but to the relative outputs of different crops, some being more affected by the weather than others; so it is not possible for the farmer to allocate his labour on the basis of (expected) marginal value products – he does not know what they will be. It could be argued against this that the farmer knows from past experience what output he gets, *on average,* from various labour inputs into various crops, and that he will allocate his labour on that basis. But, Lipton argued – and this is perhaps his crucial point – that even if the farmer does have a good idea of the average magnitudes of marginal value products, it would actually be *irrational* for him to allocate labour on that basis. This is because, when people are very poor, their chief concern is to survive. If output fell below the average levels of the past, they might not survive to appreciate their attempts to 'optimise' over the long term. Farmers will therefore tend to operate an insurance strategy; they will work on the basis of what Lipton called a 'survival algorithm'. Production will be biased towards crops with a more certain, if less valued, output. For, example, *on average,* the marginal value product of labour-time applied to cassava might be lower than that of time applied to rice, implying under conditions of certainty, that too much work is being put into cassava and not enough into rice. But the cassava would be likely to have a much less variable yield than the rice (and can be left in the ground as an emergency store). The apparently excessive labour applied to it would be in order to ensure a basic supply of food.

In her study of a group of farms in Machakos District in Kenya, Judith Heyer[22] found that the cropping pattern was different from one dictated by a conventional economic analysis based on market valuation of crops. Three crops were not profitable enough to be included in the hypothetical farm plan; these were sorghum, millet and *wimbi.* But in practice, crop mixtures containing these made up 20 per cent of the total hectarage. The region is a dry one and rainfall not dependable, and it would seem that these crops were being included by way of insurance against famine; millet, for instance, can be stored for several years, and is very resistant to drought. Moreover, a hypothetical farm plan that included these crops turned out to be only slightly less 'profitable' than the one that did not.

The enactment of the survival approach is perhaps even more clearly demonstrated with regard to the growing of a combination of cash crops and food crops. In the cocoa belt of south-western Nigeria: '...even a very great difference between the amount of food [the cocoa farmer] can obtain for the proceeds of an extra acre planted with cocoa and the amount he can grow by devoting that acre to food crops will not induce him to abandon food farming altogether'.[23] At first sight it might be felt that in the event of a low food harvest, the farmer could easily buy enough with his cocoa proceeds, especially since some areas specialise in exporting food to the cocoa areas. But such a low harvest would tend to affect the entire region so that food prices would rise. The irrationality of what superficially looks like economically sensible specialisation in cash crops is so taken for granted in that area that most people in Upton's six villages thought of a farmer who buys his family's food as 'bad and foolish'.[24]

We have concentrated in the foregoing few paragraphs on the valuation – subjective versus market – of the various farm products, and the way this determines the allocation of labour. It is not only the valuation of output that is important, however; the (marginal) valuation of labour is important, too. This was something that went unconsidered by Lipton as well as by Schultz, who both seemed to assume implicitly that labour was homogeneous and its market competitive. But we have seen in previous sections that this is by no means so. If, for example, a crop can be planted at a time of year when there is not much else to do, the subjective valuation of the labour required will be relatively low. If also it can be harvested without critical attention to timing, this will make it even more useful as an insurance crop, even though there may be no great liking for it as food. This is perhaps what makes cassava (manioc) such an important crop in Africa: its attractive attributes are that it can be planted grown and harvested with ease and great flexibility, it can grow on the poorest soils and it produces plenty of calories to fill a hungry stomach if necessary. The low subjective costs of production may be just as important a consideration as the reliability of its output.

The low costs seem to be as influential as the insurance factor with regard to intercropping, at least in northern Nigeria. The comprehensive study by Norman et al.[25] found that returns per day of labour were lower under intercropping than with hypothetical pure stands. However, it was also found that if returns were divided not by total labour, but only by the labour-time put in at the busiest period, the comparison favoured intercropping. This suggests that if labour were appropriately valued, giving it a high average and marginal subjective cost during the busy period and relatively lower costs at other times, the 'profits' (returns minus subjective costs) from intercropping are greater than from pure stands. This is quite apart from giving insurance crops a higher valuation than the market value, which the survival plan should lead us to do.

References

1 J.H. Cleave, 'Decision-making on the African farm', *Papers on Current Agricultural Economic Issues*, No. 1, 1977, (Contributed Papers Read at the 16th International Conference of Agricultural Economists), pp 157–178.
2 D. Thorner, B. Kerblay and R.E.F. Smith (eds), *A.V. Chayanov on the Theory of Peasant Economy*, Richard D.Irwin, 1966.
3 J.W. Mellor, 'The use and productivity of farm family labour in early stages of agricultural development', *Journal of Farm Economics*, Vol. XLV, No. 3 1963.
4 C. Nakajima, 'Subsistence and commercial farms: some theore-

tical models of subjective equilibrium', in C.R. Wharton Jr. (ed.), *Subsistence Agriculture and Economic Development*, Cass, London 1970.

5 A.K. Sen, 'Peasants and dualism, with or without surplus labor', *Journal of Political Economy*, **74**, 5, 1966.

6 R. Galletti, K.D.S. Baldwin and I.O. Dina, *Nigerian Cocoa Farmers*, Oxford University Press, 1956, p. 292.

7 P.B. Hammond, 'Mossi technology and time allocation', in *Conference on competing demands for the time of labor in traditional African societies*, Holly Knoll, Virginia, USA: Joint Committee on African Studies of the American Council of Learned Societies, Social Science Research Council, Agricultural Development Council Inc., 1967.

8 J.H. Cleave, *African Farmers: Labor Use in the Development of Smallholder Agriculture*, Praeger, 1974.

9 M.R. Haswell, *Economics of Agriculture in a Savannah Village*, Colonial Research Studies, No. 8, HMSO, 1953.

10 J. Guillard, *Golonpoui: Analyse des Conditions de Modernisation d'un Village du Nord-Cameroun*, Mouton, The Hague, 1965.

11 M. Upton, *Agriculture in South-western Nigeria*, Development Study No. 3, Department of Agricultural Economics, Reading University, 1967.

12 C.M. Elliot, J.E. Bessell, R.A.J. Roberts and N. Vanzetti, *Some Determinants of Agricultural Labour Productivity in Zambia,* Universities of Nottingham and Zambia Agricultural Labour Productivity Investigation, Report No. 3, 1970.

13 Haswell, *op. cit.*, pp. 48–49.

14 Cleave, *op. cit.*, p. 232.

15 M.R. Haswell, *The Nature of Poverty: A Case History of the First Quarter-Century since World War II*, Macmillan, London, 1975.

16 Much was made of this factor by Chayanov, although he used the 'consumer-worker ratio', a variable which involves the refinement of different weights for different ages of consumers and workers. See Thorner *et al.*, *op. cit.*

17 Guillard, *op. cit.*

18 Haswell, 1953, *op. cit.*

19 D.W. Norman, *An Economic Study of Three Villages in Zaria Province. 1, Land and Labour Relationships*, Samaru Miscellaneous Papers, No. 19, Institute for Agricultural Research, Ahmadu Bello University, Zaria, Nigeria, 1967.

20 T.W. Schultz, *Transforming Traditional Agriculture*, Yale University Press, 1964.

21 M. Lipton, 'The theory of the optimising peasant', *Journal of Development Studies*, Vol. 4, No.3, April 1968.

22 J. Heyer, 'Agricultural Development and Peasant Farming in Kenya', Ph.D. (Econ.) thesis, University of London, 1966.

23 Galletti, *et al.*, *op. cit.*

24 Upton, *op. cit.*

25 Norman, *op. cit.*, Vol. 2 *Input-Output Study*.

5 Land

The nature of the land resource

Just as days or hours are not entirely adequate indicators of a quantity of labour, as we have seen, so hectares are an even less adequate measure of land because land is often very heterogeneous in quality, even within quite small areas. But let us be yet more precise: rather than use the vague term 'quality', let us define the term 'productivity' of land as the value of output per hectare for a given amount of labour applied using given techniques and with other inputs given.[1] To give a hypothetical example of how variable the productivity of land is likely to be – even when it appears at first sight to be constant – let us suppose there are two plots of one hectare each, giving identical yields of 1 000 kg of grain, both for 5 hours a day work in the field for 100 days a year. Now let one plot be next to the village and the other a kilometre away (not an unusual distance). If the farmer travels to and from the further plot in the morning and afternoon at 3 km per hour, he spends 1·33 hours a day walking, i.e. 6·33 hours labour altogether, or 633 hours per year.[2] His productivity (of labour) is 1 000 ÷ 633 = 1·58 kg per hour. If he cultivated the nearer plot his productivity would be 1 000 ÷ 500 = 2 kg per hour. To obtain the productivity per hectare for a given number of hours, let us assume for simplicity that there is a straight-line relationship between production and hours spent cultivating the plot (rather than the more realistic diminishing returns curve). Thus if the same 5 hours labour (*including* walking) is applied to the further plot as to the nearer plot, and the time spent walking is again 1·33 hours, the time spent cultivating is 5 − 1·33 = 3·67 hours and the output from the further hectare (the productivity per hectare) will be

$$\frac{3·67}{5} \times 1\ 000 = 734 \text{ kg}$$

compared with 1 000 kg from 5 hours applied to the near plot. The productivity of land of apparently identical quality is 36 per cent greater when it is next to the village than when it is a kilometre away! Of course, the productivity of land depends on many other things besides distance; for example, on how easy it is to clear, on the workability of the soil, the stone content, the slope, the degree of moisture, etc. Moreover, the quality of land is more than merely its productivity as defined above; the general desirability of land as a place to live is also an important consideration affecting its quality, or its value, either in subjective or in monetary terms. For instance, proximity to water, infestation by mosquitoes or tsetse fly, etc., affect the desirability of land as opposed to its productivity. Some of the many factors that can affect the quality of land are suggested in the following quotations selected from a passage in de Schlippe's book on Zande agriculture.[3]

> .... the Azande actually always settled on a very fertile step on the catena .... where they could find rich sandy loam, easy to cultivate ... The choice of a certain contour along a stream was also intimately linked with the desire to have the shortest distance for carrying water.
>
> Elephant grass formations, despite their fertility, were and still are, avoided. They are too difficult to clear with the small Zande hoe.
>
> Isolation from any 'territory' occupied by one of the natural enemies of crops is of importance. The neighbourhood of a hill inhabited by a herd of baboons, a quagmire favoured by a tribe of wild pigs, a wide humid grassland (*ndaurri*) full of waterbuck or an uninhabited forest (*ngbakingbo*) periodically visited by elephants are avoided.

Strictly all these other things should be measured or allowed for, as well as just the area, when the land input is measured.

We can conceive of two extreme situations in considering the influence of land on the equilibrium organisation of the African farm, and a range of possibilities between. At one extreme, cultivated land is not scarce; as much land is used as there is labour to work it, i.e. the land is always used to such an extent that its marginal product is zero – no more land could be combined with a given amount of labour to give any more product. In such a case, land is no more a factor of production than air. Unless there is some form of social discrimination regarding the allocation of land that prevents some people using as much as they want, land does not affect the productivity of labour. This extreme is common in African agriculture; it occurs where shifting cultivation is the norm and where population is sparse. In some instances people do not appear even to separate the concept of land from the concept of the occupiers and cultivators. Thus Bohannon says of the Tiv of Nigeria:

> The 'map' in terms of which Tiv see their land is a genealogical map and its association with specific pieces of ground is of only brief duration – a man or woman has precise rights to a farm during the time it is in cultivation, but once the farm returns to fallow, the rights lapse. However, a man always has rights in the 'genealogical map' of his agnatic lineage, wherever that lineage may happen to be in space.[4]

At the other extreme, all land is under permanent cultivation and cultivated land is scarce with a positive marginal value product generally. This type of situation is relatively uncommon in tropical Africa, in contrast to more heavily populated regions, where it is the norm. But here we must be careful, because although permanent cultivation systems do not take up a high proportion of the total land *area*, the prop-

ortion of rural Africans they support is bound to be considerably greater as discussed in Chapter 2. For example, recall that 5 per cent of the
area of Tanzania, accounted for by what could be called intensive
farming, supports at least 30 per cent of the population.

Between these extremes is the situation where some types of land
are scarce but others are freely available. A common occurrence, for
instance, is the scarcity of moist land along rivers and streams, while
the drier land at a higher level is used for bush-fallow cultivation and is
surplus. In such a case the quantity of moist land used by farmers will
affect the marginal product of labour, even though the quantity of high
land will not,[5] and the moist-land endowments of farmers, however
determined – socially or economically – will affect their equilibrium
positions. Again, land close at hand may be scarce while more distant
land is not. Moreover, settlements will tend to be established near to
the innately best-quality land, reinforcing this tendency. This is of
course why the concentric-ring form of land use is so very common. A
greater endowment of scarce land, *ceteris paribus* will raise the labour–
output curve, tending thereby to increase both consumption and leisure. Furthermore, once zero marginal product no longer holds for
land of a given quality, it becomes worthwhile *paying* for the privilege
of cultivating that land and increasing the area paid for as long as its
marginal value product is greater than the rent per hectare. There is a
tendency for a price to be set upon land once it becomes scarce, but in
practice this tendency may not be realised. One problem, for instance,
is that land is often communally owned. Who, therefore, does one pay
for the use of land? Even if individuals own land, or at least have
control over its use, there are often varying degrees of social inhibition
against renting it to other people, let alone selling the land, which may
be out of the question. These inhibitions have a tendency to break
down as necessity intervenes but, in fact the market for land services
may take a covert form. Payment may be in terms of gifts in kind for
example, or there may be no payment in cash or kind, but an increase
in social dependence in the form of a commitment to render services
or support to the lender of the land. In a study of the Rungwe District
of Tanzania,[6] for instance, where some kinds of land are scarce, there
is no mention of any form of rent being paid: the motivation for lend-
ing lands appears to be largely in terms of social power, while labour
services form an important means of 'payment'.

Land as an economic commodity

Land is, of course, not simply an economic commodity, just as labour
is not. In areas where it is abundant, there seems to be a marked
tendency for people to think of it only as a place where people live and
as the ground where ancestors are buried: it has a sacred quality. It
may indeed be the case in sparsely populated areas, whether pastoral
or agricultural, that land is not scarce and is thus not a true economic
resource in the usual meaning of the term; and these conditions were
probably the norm, say, a century ago. G.K.Helleiner used the term
'land-surplus' in referring to these circumstances;[7] this was intended to
contrast with the term 'labour-surplus', which in the fifties and sixties

frequently was applied to the rural areas of relatively densely populated parts of the Third World, such as India, Egypt and Java.[8] 'Land-surplus was thought to convey more realistically the conditions found in tropical Africa, especially, and more so, in recent history. This way of classifying economies can be expressed more clearly by using theoretical diagrams, as employed by Helleiner.[9]

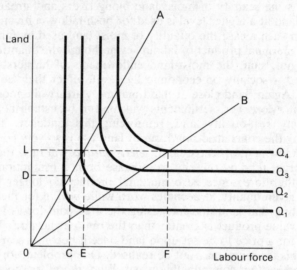

Fig. 5.1

In Fig. 5.1, the curves Q_1 to Q_4 are isoquants, each one showing how different combinations of land and labour can be used to generate the same output. OA and OB are ridge lines. Above OA, any further combination of land with labour adds nothing to output, i.e. land has a marginal product of zero along OA. Similarly, below OB, labour has a marginal product of zero. We assume that the size of the labour force is in proportion to the total population, so that as population grows so does the size of the labour force. OL is the fixed supply of land. When population is sparse and the labour force is relatively small, some of the land will remain unused. For example, at labour force OC, only OD land will be used and DL will be in surplus, because any further use of land with OC labour will not produce any more output. Indeed at any labour force less than OE, some land will remain unused – the economy is 'land-surplus'. Up to OE, too, the amount of land used is in direct proportion to the size of the labour force, and there are constant returns to labour and land. When land is being fully used, however – after the labour force has reached OE – more and more labour is applied to the same amount of land, OL, and the marginal product of labour declines until at OF it becomes zero. When the population has grown to that point, i.e. such that the labour force is equal to or greater than OF, the economy is said to be 'labour-surplus'. Furthermore, just as there are diminishing returns to labour from OE onwards, so there are *increasing* returns to land – the marginal product of land increases, i.e. land becomes more and more *scarce*. When we say that land has become scarce, it is the same thing as saying that land has a positive marginal product when fully used. Thus it becomes worthwhile buying if it is possible to do so, and paying any amount which is less than the value of its marginal product. Moreover since the marginal product – the scarcity – increases as population and labour grow, the price it is worth paying for land rises. In other words, the value of land goes up as population grows, and goes up more rapidly the more rapidly the population grows. This obviously has important implications for the relationship between the individual land-owner and the rest of society, for the more rapid the growth of population, the better land is as an investment for the individual who can afford to buy it. We shall come back to this phenomenon later on, after some further complications have been gone into; it is mentioned simply to give an insight into some of the implications of population growth in its relationship to land.

The above theoretical exposition needs some qualifying. First of all the idea of a zero marginal product of land may be a little artificial. Even if a rural economy is using forest-fallow cultivation, with fallow periods that are much longer than is necessary for fertility to be regenerated, forests can be used productively in other ways than mere cultivation: in particular they can be used for hunting and gathering. Indeed that is the major technique of 'producing' food among, for example, the pygmy people of the Congo and Zaïre rain forests. With more forest land a greater amount of game could live and hunting would be that much easier, for example. Thus even under extremely land-intensive conditions, land may have a positive, though probably slight, marginal product. However, the Helleiner exposition presented above is probably near enough to the truth to serve as useful abstraction.

Another important point to notice in this context is the distinction between cultivated land and fallow land in shifting cultivation. Even if land as a whole under shifting cultivation has a positive marginal product in that more land would allow a longer fallow period and thus higher production, the land actually cultivated is likely to be used up to the point where it has a zero marginal product. Thus land as a whole is scarce, but cultivated land is not. Another diagram may help to clarify this. Figure 5.2 shows two relationships between the input of cultivated land (of a given innate quality) and output, given a fixed labour input. The upper curve represents the relationship for land that has had a long fallow period, so that x hectares combined with y labour units gives a relatively high output. The lower curve is for land that has been left fallow for a relatively short period and gives a relatively low output when x hectares are combined with y units of labour.

In both cases, cultivated land is used up to the point of zero marginal product, because under the usual tenure arrangements with shifting cultivation, (a) there is no charge for cultivated land, and (b) if more land is needed it is simply cleared from the land that is lying fallow. Supposing now the two curves represent the situations in two neighbouring regions, S and L of a country, the inhabitants of S would dearly like to get some of the L land because it is fallowed longer, is therefore more fertile and gives a greater output for a given amount of labour. In other words if S were to annexe land from L, that land

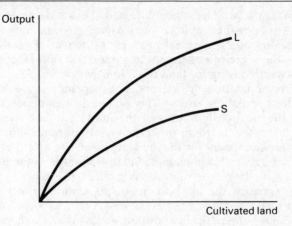

Fig. 5.2

would have a positive marginal product for the inhabitants of S; but still each farmer would continue to cultivate an area up to the point of zero marginal product in any particular year. (Of course, cultivation beyond zero marginal product is irrational because, by definition, nothing further is added to output.)

Let us return now to Helleiner's diagram and the land-surplus rural economy. We have been talking so far about 'labour' in the sense of the labour force, or stock. But how hard does that labour force work? Figure 5.3 shows the relationship between the stock of labour only and output, land being fixed. On OF are the points that represent the potential output of any given labour force, i.e. the output obtainable if labour were to work to full capacity. As we saw in the last chapter, however, labour tends not to work to full capacity, but to devote time to other, 'non-labour', activities. Actual output is thus lower than potential output and OD shows the actual output produced by each level of the labour force. At level A, for instance, AB is produced, while BC is foregone in order to devote time to other activities. At the portions of these curves near to the origin (where they are straight

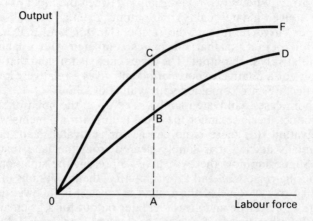

Fig. 5.3

lines) there are constant returns to labour because land is supposed to be in surplus (with the possible qualification mentioned above), and it is in this region, Helleiner suggests, that Nigeria, as an exemplary African economy, moved during the years up to about the middle of this century, but especially up to the end of the nineteenth century, when slave raids, wars and disease vied with human fertility to make the population and labour force fluctuate in essentially land-surplus conditions.

We shall come back to this useful diagram in following chapters, but it is worth noting a couple of points in advance here. One is that in modern times, population is no longer going up and down, but only up – and rather rapidly at that. It can be seen from Figure 5.3 that as this happens, production, moving along OD, comes closer and closer to productive potential on OF – the 'pressure' on the resources of the land increases. Another point is that at any particular point on OD, if a market opens up for the agricultural produce of a region, OD may rotate upwards towards OF, because it becomes worthwhile devoting more time to, the now more profitable, farm production.

The distribution of land between farmers

In the last section, we were concerned with the overall availability of land to the rural populace as a whole; here we are concerned with differences between farmers in the endowment of land.

Many writers on agriculture in developing countries have noted that there is an inverse, or negative, relationship between

1 output per hectare and size of farm in hectares;
2 value added (value of output less value of purchased inputs) per hectare and size of farm;
3 labour input per hectare and size of farm.[10]

A number of studies show that these relationships seem to hold in African agriculture as much as in other developing areas. If we assume that land is approximately homogeneous in quality this seems to imply that farmers who control relatively small amounts of land substitute labour for land. Such an implication does not seem too unreasonable when considering a geographically restricted group of farmers where land is scarce, as, for example, in much of India; but in shifting cultivation with communal types of ownership (see the next section) this does not seem to make much sense. Farmers are not faced with a fixed endowment of land that they have to do the best they can with, but rather an amount of cultivable land is available to them in proportion to their needs: there seems to be no need for labour to substitute land. With regard to African agriculture, however, we must remember two important points. Firstly, there are major regions where land is very scarce and where farmers are faced in the short run with fixed land endowments (they may be able to buy more land, but that will only be a solution in the longer term – and is not possible for all farmers). Examples are parts of Kenya, where in some cases there is registered individual title to land in the Western mode; Ethiopia,

Rwanda and Burundi; Zimbabwe and the Kano close-settled zone in northern Nigeria. In these circumstances we might well expect sub- stitution of labour for land and the inverse relationships mentioned above.

The second point is that land is not at all homogeneous, as we have already emphasised – even its distance from the dwelling affects its quality. Thus, even in relatively land-abundant conditions, if the head of a farming-family thinks he needs a higher output than hither- to, he is likely to obtain it only partly by extending the area cultivated, because new land is likely at least to be further away and so of lower quality; it is also likely to be poorer because settlements will tend to be close to the best land (easiest worked, close to water, etc.). Land is 'not scarce' only in a rather imprecise sense. Economically, new land of quality equal to what is already being farmed is likely to be scarce even where land – in the broad sense – is abundant, so that to some extent at least there will tend to be *some* substitution of labour.

Examples of these phenomena are shown in Tables 5.1 and 5.2.[11]

Table 5.1
Farm size, output and labour per hectare on settlement schemes, Kenya, 1967/68

Farm size group, hectares	Average farm size, hectares	Gross output, K.Sh. per hectare	No. of labourers per hectare
Less than 4	3	1 587	2 020
4–7·9	5·5	625	997
8–11·9	9·5	390	585
12–15·9	14	403	397
16–19·9	18	283	310
20–23·9	21	245	277
24–31·9	26	245	272
32 or more	50·5	278	175

Source: Judith Heyer, J.K. Maitha and W.M. Senga (eds), *Agricultural Development in Kenya. An Economic Assessment*, Oxford University Press, 1976 (metricated).

Table 5.2
Size of farm and labour input per hectare, shifting cultivation, Sierra Leone, 1970

Village	Number of farms	Average size, hectares	Workdays[1] per hectare
Njala	18	0·7	78
		1·5	60
		3·0	40
Ngesehun	13	0·75	80
		1·6	65
		4·3	50
Sogbale	4	0·7	98
		1·6	65
		2·4	53

[1] Workdays were on brushing, felling and hoeing.

Source: A.O. Njoku and G.L. Karr, 'Labour and upland rice production', *Journal of Agricultural Economics*, Vol. 24, No. 2, May 1973, Table 4 (metricated).

Land tenure

The system of land tenure in a rural community is the system of rights and duties of the people with regard to the use of land. This is an area about which it is extremely difficult to generalise safely; as Bohannon, in a classic article, has put it:

> It is probable that no single topic has exercised so many students and men of affairs concerned with Africa as that of land. It is equally probable that no single topic concerning Africa has produced so large a poor literature. We are still abysmally ignorant of African land practices. That ignorance derives less from want of 'facts' than that we do not know what to do with the 'facts' or how to interpret them. The reason for this state of affairs is close at hand: there exists no good analysis of the concepts habitually used in land-tenure studies, and certainly no detailed critique of their applicability to cross-cultural study.[12]

Nevertheless, one can perhaps discern the following broad pattern.

The 'basic' system of tenure, which is associated with the 'basic' system of agriculture – shifting cultivation – has a communal character. Individual farmers, and the family or other units under their authority, obtain the right to cultivate a piece of land from the head of the community (chief, village headman, lineage head, elders, etc.). Where land is abundant, this right lasts only as long as the piece of land is being cultivated and is relinquished when the plot is left to lie fallow. A fresh plot of land that has been fallow for some time is then requested from the community's head. In some circumstances where land is relatively scarce, but fire–fallow is still practised, it is recognised that a family's rights to a piece of land are maintained even when it is fallow. Land may revert to the community if it is considered that it has been left uncultivated for too long; but as long as it is being 'used', in whatever sense, rights to cultivate tend to be secure. Furthermore, it is usual that every member of the community has the right to cultivate some land.

Often there is more than one kind of tenure in operation, corresponding to different types of land use. Thus, permanently cultivated and manured compound land may have permanent individual tenure, while more distant land under shifting cultivation is still subject to communal rules. In reality, though, the difference between permanent tenure and communal tenure is only one of degree. The right of a farming unit to cultivate a piece of land exists as long as they are in fact cultivating it or using it, where 'use' may sometimes also cover the practice of leaving the land fallow for what is generally accepted as a reasonable period. As land becomes scarcer with the increasing demands of population or of external markets for crops, cultivation ceases being regularly transferred from plot to plot and remains on a single plot, while the fertility of the land is maintained by more laborious methods than simply allowing natural regeneration.

Even when there are permanent rights of individual cultivation, though, there can be a good deal of variation in the precise nature of those rights. Most importantly, rights may be constrained as regards inheritance, gifts and sale or rent of land. In other words, while there may be permanent individual tenure, this does not necessarily mean 'ownership' in the full sense. In particular, even when land is very scarce, there is often a strong view that the land still belongs to the community (perhaps including those who are dead and those yet unborn), so that alienation of land is inhibited at least or even prohibited. In addition rights to graze cattle on common land or on crop residue are often maintained. Nevertheless, possibly because the rules of land tenure are unwritten, markets in land do tend to develop as land becomes scarce; the traditional mores and sanctions are not strong or clear enough to overcome the powerful influence of economic needs and desires. As we would expect, land markets are most evident in areas where the density of population relative to the productivity of the land is high, as in the Kano close-settled zone in northern Nigeria, for example, or where commercial agriculture has become important, as in the cocoa areas of Ghana and western Nigeria.

In some parts of Africa, the above general picture has been overlain or removed by various extraneous factors, such as the past subjection of one people by another, but especially by the influence of colonial governments. This is particularly true of Kenya, Buganda and Zimbabwe. In Ethiopia, land tenure resembled more the Asian, or European feudal, pattern than the African, but since the revolution there, it is not clear what will be the final outcome (although, *de jure*, the land has been nationalised, and in the south at least there has probably been a takeover of land rights by tenant farmers). The same applies of course to the former Portuguese countries, Guinea-Bissau, Mozambique and Angola. (In Mozambique, large, former Portuguese, land-holdings were initially collectivised, but more recently, policy has been to revert to something like the old capitalist system.)

In Kenya, large areas of land, in the highlands especially, were taken over by Europeans during the colonial period, forcing many farming and pastoral people into parts of the country where the land was inadequate to maintain their numbers at even minimal standards of living. The unrest caused essentially by this distortion of land use came to a head in the Mau Mau uprising in the early fifties. The initial solution to the problem was embodied in the 'Swynnerton plan',[13] which sought, not to return the European lands – the 'scheduled areas' – to Africans, but to set about improving agriculture in the existing African areas. One principal ingredient of the plan was, in some of the more densely populated areas, to consolidate fragmented holdings and to grant full individual ownership in the European sense, of farms, together with the formal registration of title. By this means, it was thought, African farmers would achieve their full potential through the greater incentive to invest, supposedly generated by full title and by the greater ability to obtain credit using their land titles as collateral.

With the coming of Independence, many of the European settlers departed of their own volition. Also, the new government embarked on a policy of purchasing European farms, dividing them up into small-holdings and resettling Africans on them. But by no means all the European lands were dealt with in this way. Many have been maintained as large-scale farms, owned by individual Africans, by companies or by co-operatives, and it is thus felt by some observers that the old distortions have to a large extent been preserved, except that Africans have replaced Europeans.[14]

Buganda is another region on which the colonial regime imposed a completely alien system of land tenure, beginning in the 1900s. Under this system persons who had previously held power over land balanced by political duties, such as the *Kabaka* (king) and chiefs, were given full ownership of the land within their areas of rule, so that the ordinary farmers became tenants. Such land is known as *mailo* land. However, the inequality thus engendered soon broke down under laws that fixed the rent paid by tenants in money terms (and which became insignificant in real terms as the years passed) and prevented eviction. The huge estates gradually shrank and a new class of farmers grew up consisting of former tenants or their heirs who had bought their own and other holdings.[15]

Another major example of a land tenure system imposed by Europeans was that found in Zimbabwe (at least until it ceased to be Rhodesia in 1980), where it was different only in degree from those of colonial Kenya and South Africa. About half the land was restricted to the white farmers, and that the best land with the kindest climate. African areas were divided into 'tribal trust lands' and 'purchase areas'. The latter took up a relatively small proportion of the land, and were set up to allow Africans to buy land in areas that were not in close proximity to European land. There were also 'irrigation schemes' which were operated under a European type of tenure and production system.[16] In the tribal trust lands land allocation was controlled by tribal land authorities (chiefs) and there was provision for the establishment of individual tenure if it was desired. Previously an attempt had been made to enforce registered individual tenure and restricted common grazing, but by the early seventies this had been abandoned.

The land reform controversy

There has been a good deal of argument about what constitutes an efficient system of tenure, from the points of view of general economic development and of social justice. Many have claimed that full ownership in the European sense, together with registered title, is a prerequisite for rural development, for only under those conditions, it is asserted, will there be any significant incentive for the farmer to invest in land improvements, buildings, tree crops and the like and to take any care about conserving the soil. A further spur to investment would be the possibility of using land titles as collateral for loans. Without the clearness and certainty of title engendered by registration it is held that much time and effort will be wasted in law suits; and many instances can be cited where this indeed appears to be the case. Some would further argue that the development of a free market in land consequent on the establishment of full ownership would be economically beneficial since it would allow the transference of land to those who can use it most efficiently from the less productive farmers, through the market mechanism. This would also make labour available for non-agricultural development;[17] as Swynnerton put it in a telling remark:

> ... able, energetic or rich Africans will be able to acquire more land and bad or poor farmers less, creating a landed and a landless class .... a normal step in the evolution of a country.[18]

Associated with these views is the idea that larger farms are more efficient, in some sense, and more economically desirable; and this is also held to be true with regard to consolidated, as opposed to fragmented, holdings. Under farming systems which support cattle, communal grazing rights tend to be the norm, and these appear to result in over-grazing, because the individual does not have to bear the cost of grazing an extra animal; the position is made worse by the continuous pressure, from a growing population, to extend the cultivated area. Individually-owned plots of grazing land have been seen as a possible solution to the problem.

There are several counter-arguments to these tenets. Firstly, in conditions where land is fairly abundant, communal types of tenure provide a form of social-security system, for one is secure in the right to cultivate and every member of the community has the right to cultivate some of its land. The latter feature would be lost under a system of individual ownership, while the former would simply be maintained. Secondly, as regards investment, there are very many cases of considerable rural investment under customary tenure rules (see Chapter 6, below). It is true that one can cite particular instances where investment may be inhibited – especially investment by a farmer who is not a member of the native community – but it is totally untrue to say that there has been little investment. The planting and tending of economic trees, such as cocoa, coffee, oil palms, etc., which bear fruit for many years, is the major example of such investment, most of which has been on land subject to the rules of customary tenure. Usually, economic trees can be individually owned even on land which is communally owned, but in practice such a distinction tends to fade, especially where the trees are closely planted, so that cultivating the trees means the same thing as cultivating the land. In such circumstances, either investment in trees is inhibited or else individual ownership develops: both outcomes have in fact occurred, but probably the latter has tended to prevail. There is clearly a conflict here between the desire to retain the good features of communal rights and the general reverence in which land – or perhaps 'ground' is a slightly better word in this context – is often held, and the need to reward someone for the investment of their labour in trees or other improvements.[19]

The notion that credit would be significantly more forthcoming if land titles were available as security is belied by experience in the Kenyan reform. In Nyeri District:

> The original hope that the commercial banks would become an ever-larger source of credit for African farmers has not, by and large, been realized ..... The possibility of getting a mortage has not .... significantly enhanced the security of a loan.[20]

Individual tenure (without formal registration), and markets in land, tend to evolve naturally under pressure from growing populations and commercial demands. There may be some case for the government to assist the process because, for example, there is the tendency for legal disputes about boundaries to increase, some formal settlement of boundaries may thus be of value, but not necessarily to the extreme of formal registration. In Kigezi, Uganda, where plots were demarcated and surveyed, farmers apparently felt sufficiently secure, and the amount of land litigation fell, without the need for an actual title deed.[21]

However, there is one great danger involved in a change towards individual tenure and a land market, whether it is a naturally evolving, or an imposed change, and that is the greater tendency for inequality to develop and accumulate. The farmer who has more land than others tends to be wealthier and better able to buy still more land, become still more wealthy, and so on. The poorer farmer tends to get into debt (to the wealthier members of the community) and to lose his land. Evidence for the occurrence of such a process is found in Polly Hill's work among the Hausa of northern Nigeria, in the village of Batagarawa where there is a great deal of continuously cultivated land (Table 5.3).[22] As mentioned earlier, there are those who think this a good thing in the long run and part of the 'normal process' of development. But, that it occurred in Europe does not necessarily imply that it is a 'normal' thing (quite apart from the obvious 'problems' of the short run, clearly seen in Table 5.3, and of how long the 'short run' lasts). It did not happen in Japan or Taiwan, for instance (if anything, the reverse), and many economists argue that governments should make positive efforts to reverse the process through various controls over land distribution.

Table 5.3 Acquisition of land by socio-economic group, Batagarawa, northern Nigeria

	Socio-economic group**			
	1	**2**	**3**	**4**
Average farm area in hectares	1·4	0·96	0·68	0·68
Estimated per cent of mapped farm area inherited*	46	60	67	68
Estimated per cent of mapped farm area bought*	31	23	10	3

* Likely to be underestimated

** 'Group 1 consisted of units which were so far from suffering that they were in a position to render help to others, by gift or loan; in Group 2 were those farming units which were not short of basic foodstuffs, either because they still had stocks or because they had cash with which to buy them; in Group 3 were the units the members of which were known to be suffering seasonal hardship over food consumption; and Group 4 . . . consisted of those who were suffering very severely, often because they were considered so "hopeless" that no one would lend to them.'

Source: G.K. Helleiner, 'The typology of development theory: the "land surplus" economy (Nigeria)', *Food Research Institute Studies*, Vol 6, 1966, p. 249.

This leads on to the question as to whether large or small farms are more economically efficient, for it is often implied by writers on African land reform, especially those who favour individual ownership, that larger farms are assumed to be more economically efficient. Larger farms undoubtedly tend to generate a higher productivity of labour than smaller farms and thus a higher standard of living for the fortunate farmers, and the conclusion has often been drawn from this observation that larger farms are thus a good thing since it is a major goal of economic development to attain higher labour productivity. Thus, the argument goes, those enterprises that appear to be achieving that goal best – the larger farms – should be encouraged. An important point is missed here, however, for the goal of economic development should surely be a widespread increase in labour productivity and standards of living. Because larger farms have high productivity themselves, it does not at all follow that their encouragement will lead to a widespread increase in productivity: there is no *a priori* reason why it should. It may well also be the case that public investment in larger farms gives the best and least risky financial rates of return (i.e. returns to capital); and this has been seen as another reason why development efforts should be directed towards them, for it is capital that is perhaps *the* scarce resource in developing countries (although see the next chapter for some qualification of this notion). But again, it is not just the rate of return, on the individual farm, of a development project that is relevant to general development, but the returns that include the economic repercussions of the initial investment through the second, and further, rounds of income generated and through the encouragement of further enterprise.[23] Johnston and Kilby have argued that the returns to investment, when these include secondary repercussions are likely to be greater under a development strategy that is oriented towards smaller farms rather than larger.[24]

Although larger farms may be 'efficient' in one sense – that of achieving relatively high returns to labour – that is not the only sense in which the term can be used. They tend to be less efficient at using the nation's resources in accordance with their relative scarcities. For most developing countries, the extensive use of 'modern' purchased inputs, such as tractors, is inefficient, since those countries are poorly endowed with resources of that nature. In contrast, labour is more abundant, and so farms that use relatively more labour and less purchased capital resources would tend to be more efficient users of the nation's resources (given the returns to purchased capital). Furthermore, land tends to be scarce or becoming scarcer, so that farms that achieve a relatively high productivity of land tend also to be more efficient from a national point of view. We have seen from the section on the distribution of land, above, that output per hectare and labour input per hectare tend to be greater on smaller farms, and so there is an important sense in which smaller farms are more efficient.[25]

References

1 Clearly we are landing ourselves in trouble here, by assuming what we have shown to be untrue, viz., that labour is homogeneous and

that we are sure what labour is. This is done for simplicity. Purists may substitute the word 'time' for 'labour'.

2 We are here assuming for simplicity that x hours walking can be lumped together with y hours cultivating, calling both types of activity 'labour', which can be measured as $x + y$ hours.

3 P. de Schlippe, *Shifting Cultivation in Africa. The Zande System of Agriculture*, Routledge and Kegan Paul, London 1956, pp. 194– 195. The Azande (plural of Zande) occupy an area that straddles the borders of Zaïre, Sudan and the Central African Republic.

4 P. Bohannon, ' "Land", "tenure" and "land tenure" ', in D. Biebuyck, (ed.), *African Agrarian Systems*, OUP, 1963.

5 Note that with shifting cultivation land *including fallow* may be scarce to a community – a longer fallow would add to output – at the same time as *cultivated* land (excluding fallow) is not scarce to the individual farmer; more of the latter does not add to the individual's output, even if more is available.

6 P.M. van Hekken and H.V.E. Thoden van Velzen, *Land Scarcity and Rural Inequality in Tanzania*, Afrika-Studiecentrum, Leiden, 1972.

7 G.K. Helleiner, 'The typology of development theory: the "land-surplus" economy (Nigeria)', *Food Research Institute Studies*, Vol.6, 1966, pp. 181–194.

8 'Labour surplus' was used by the early post-war writers on economic development, as for example in W.A. Lewis's classic article: 'Economic development with unlimited supplies of labour', *Manchester School*, May, 1954.

9 Helleiner, *op. cit.*

10 See especially R.A. Berry and W.R. Chine, *Agrarian Structure and Productivity in Developing Countries*, Johns Hopkins University Press, 1979. See also, for example, D. Mazumdar, 'Size of farm and productivity: a problem of Indian peasant agriculture', *Economica*, N.S., Vol. 32, 1964.

11 Data from several other studies provide further supporting evidence: R. Galletti, K.D.S. Baldwin and I.O. Dina, *Nigerian Cocoa Farmers*, Oxford University Press, 1956; R.W.M. Johnson, 'The labour economy of the reserve', Occasional Paper No. 4, Department of Economics, University College of Rhodesia and Nyasaland, Salisbury; D.W. Norman, *An Economic Study of Three Villages in Zaria Province. 1. Land and Labour Relationships*, Samaru Miscellaneous Papers, No.19, Institute for Agricultural Research, Ahmadu Bello University, Zaria, Nigeria, 1967; H.A. Luning, 'Economic aspects of low labour-income farming', Agricultural Research Report, Centre for Agricultural Publications and Documentation, Wageningen, Netherlands; M.R. Haswell, *Economics of Agriculture in a Savannah Village*, Colonial Research Studies, No. 8, HMSO, 1953; J. Guillard, *Golonpoui: Analyse des Conditions de Modernisation d'un Village du Nord-Cameroun*, Mouton, The Hague, 1965.

12 Bohannon, *op. cit.*

13 R.M.J. Swynnerton, *A Plan to Intensify the Development of African Agriculture in Kenya*, Government Printer, Nairobi, 1954.

14 L.D. Smith, 'An overview of agricultural development policy', in Judith Heyer, J.K. Maitha and W.M. Senga (eds), *Agricultural Development in Kenya. An Economic Assessment*, Oxford University Press, 1976.

15 See A.I. Richards, F. Sturrock and J.M. Fort, (eds), *Subsistence to Commercial Farming in Present-day Buganda*, Cambridge University Press, 1973.

16 See A.K.H. Weinrich, *African Farmers in Rhodesia*, Oxford University Press, 1975 and M. Yudelman, *Africans on the Land*, Harvard University Press, 1964.

17 A document that had much influence, and that favoured full ownership, was the East African Royal Commission 1953–1955, *Report*, HMSO, Cmd. 9475, 1955.

18 Swynnerton, *op. cit.*, p. 10.

19 See C.K. Meek, *Land Tenure and Land Administration in Nigeria and the Cameroons*, Colonial Research Studies No. 22, London, HMSO, 1957, p. 116, and Galletti *et al.*, *op. cit.*, pp. 107–131. An oft-quoted statement made by a Nigerian chief in 1912 is referred to in Meek's book (p. 113): 'I conceive that land belongs to a vast family of which many are dead, few are living and countless members are still unborn'. Again: 'The ground is sacred to the Ifes, we came from the ground and we have to go back to the ground, and it is altogether out of place for anyone to think of selling the ground' (*loc. cit.*).

20 J.C. de Wilde *et al.*, *Experiences with Agricultural Development in Tropical Africa, Vol.II, The Case Studies,* Johns Hopkins University Press, 1967, pp. 63, 64.

21 Beverley Brock, 'Customary land tenure, "individualization" and agricultural development in Uganda', *East African Journal of Rural Development*, Vol.2, No.2, 1969.

22 Polly Hill, 'The myth of the amorphous peasantry: a northern Nigerian case study', *Nigerian Journal of Economic and Social Studies*, Vol. X, No. 2, July 1968.

23 A.O. Hirschman, *The Strategy of Economic Development*, Yale University Press, 1958.

24 B.F. Johnston and P. Kilby, *Agriculture and Structural Transformation*, Oxford University Press, 1975.

25 There is evidence, too, from other countries that capital stock per hectare tends to be greater on smaller farms. See J. Levi, 'Traditional agricultural capital formation', *World Development*, Vol. 7, No. 11/12, Nov./Dec., 1979, pp. 1053–1063.

6   Capital and change

The causes of agricultural change

In the last two chapters we were concerned with the nature of the two most fundamental factors of production, labour and land, and with what determines the ways in which they are used. We now return to the theme of change, as in Chapter 3, and look at the forces that can make optimal behaviour become sub-optimal – at the things that can make a given mode of farming no longer as good as another mode –, and at the ways in which African farmers respond to these forces.

We can consider three major kinds of factor that can induce agricultural change. The first of these is the product market, its effects arising from changes in the profitability of different agricultural products. These may involve, say, a rise in the price of a commodity that is already being produced or the appearance of an entirely new and profitable crop. Changes in profitability may also occur because of changes in the costs of production or marketing, the latter being probably more important, especially through improvements in transport facilities.

The second class of factor inducing change is the population factor. Clearly with a fixed supply of land and with population growing, the land must be made to yield more and more if hunger and general poverty are to be averted. But there is another important way in which the population factor operates in Africa, and that is by migration from the land. It is not so much that the total number of mouths to feed is lessened by migration, but rather that, usually, the demographic structure is altered because the migrant population often contains a relatively high proportion of active workers, who leave behind a rural population with much the same number of non-working, or less active, dependants, but with fewer labourers to sustain them.

The influence of both types of force for change can be seen more clearly with the aid of Fig. 6.1. Again, OF shows the potential output which can be produced by a given stock of labour, while OD shows the actual output produced by the stock of labour. The vertical distance between the curves at any particular size of the labour force represents the production sacrificed for the sake of activities other than labour (ignoring problems of definition for the sake of simplicity). As was mentioned in the last chapter, Helleiner used a similar diagram to show how Nigeria, in particular, and implicitly other African economies, reacted to the new-found profitability of the export crops; OD rotated anticlockwise to come closer to OF. In other words, the rural labour force worked harder to obtain a higher level of agricultural pro-

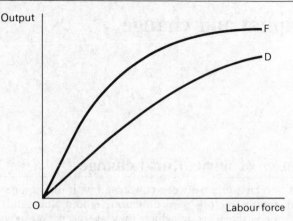

Fig. 6.1 Relationship between labour force and actual and potential output

duction and forewent more of the alternative activities such as construction work, craft work, festivities and so on. We can also think of this phenomenon in money terms by replacing the physical output on the vertical axis with the value of output. In that case the rise of the new market for the export crops is represented by an anticlockwise rotation of OF as well as OD; agricultural production became more valuable potentially, and the labour force responded to the attractions of profit by exploiting the new potential.

In the case of the population factor, it can be seen that as population and the labour force grow, OD, the actual level of agricultural output, comes closer and closer to the potential output curve. Here, the declining slope of OD implies that the rural population allows the level of output per head to decline (assuming that the ratio of total population to labour force remains constant). The assumption underlying this is that people will not try to maintain output per head at all costs, i.e. at the cost of a rather rapid decline in non-labour activity. Rather they will tend to forego output per head little by little so as to prevent the alternative activities to labour from disappearing too quickly. In practice, judging from the statistics of food production per head (Chapter 2, Table 2.1 and Fig. 2.1), there does seem to be a definite long-term decline.

The other type of population factor, migration, can have an effect similar to that of the product market factor. Here, we suppose that the labour force is reduced and, at the same time, that the proportion of dependants in the population increases. Thus, although the position of the rural economy moves further to the left on the diagram, thereby tending to reduce the pressure on the productive potential of the land, OD will also rotate somewhat, because at each level of labour stock the dependency ratio – the proportion of non-working mouths to feed – rises. This may more than offset the reduction in pressure due to emigration, and indeed experience seems to show that the people left behind by migrants often have to work harder than otherwise and have a lower general standard of living. This, of course, is not the case if the demographic structure of the emigrating population is similar to that of the whole population, and such emigration has happened, especially when the restoration of peaceful conditions has allowed people to abandon congested zones of refuge.

The third major factor that influences agricultural change is the activity of external agencies, and in particular, of government, but we shall discuss this at length in Chapter 9.

Investment and intensification

It is worth distinguishing broadly between two types of modification of production methods that occur in response to the major influences. The first type involves an increase in the costs – including subjective labour costs – of production in every production cycle, or what we can call an *intensification* of production. The second type involves a single, once-for-all cost in order that a new method of production can be embarked upon; this is investment or capital formation. Brief examples should help to clarify what is meant. Usually, intensification involves more and harder work, for example, by hoeing manure and compost into the soil, by regularly applying purchased night-soil as in the area around the city of Kano in northern Nigeria, by paying more attention to weeding, by changing to a crop-rotation system, and so on. Examples of capital formation are: the planting of cocoa trees, the clearing of swamps for permanent cultivation, making or purchasing ploughs, rearing draught animals, building cultivation terraces. Some of these things can be done gradually, a little each year, and when they are completed they are likely to involve some intensification and, of course, maintenance. But the act of creating the capital itself is a once-for-all activity in the sense that it does not become a permanent annual feature of production. Another point to note about intensification is that it may on the one hand involve simply applying more labour to an unchanged production method; for instance, the area cultivated may be extended, a higher seed rate used, or more weeding may be carried out. On the other hand it may involve a reorganisation of production. For example, intercropping might be reduced and intensive garden or compound production of vegetables substituted; manure and compost may be applied where that was not done previously; a crop rotation pattern may be introduced and, of course, the mixture of crops grown may be changed.

The distinction we have made here, between investment and intensification, is intended as a conceptual aid. In practice, the distinction is less clear, for investment and intensification may be complementary: the keeping of livestock along with manure application, for example. So, as always, the realities of economic life need to be borne in mind while thinking about the rural economy in the abstract. But broadly speaking we can think of intensification as a movement along OD in our diagram, as would occur under the normal process of population growth, or else a rotation of OD upwards towards the potential product curve, OF, as in response to new markets or better market prices for agricultural produce. Investment, on the other hand, represents an attempt to rotate the potential product curve OF upwards, usually in response to 'pressure' from actual production on the

OD curve, either because the rural economy is far to the right on it, or because of its anticlockwise rotation. This 'pressure' makes itself felt through the need to do more work to keep up living standards, or by a falling level of output per head, or, most likely, through a combination of the two. Investment or capital formation is an attempt to create or establish more productive assets – terraces, cleared land, livestock, irrigation works, etc. – that can be combined with labour and land to give a higher level of productive capacity.

Capital formation: its nature and extent

It is important to be very clear about what exactly is meant by the economic concept of capital, because a great deal of confusion arises over the use of the term. Moreover, the concept we use in the context of the rural economy is rather different from, because more general than, the orthodox concept found in Western economic writings. One source of confusion that needs to be cleared up immediately is the difference between 'capital' used to denote an amount of money or financial assets such as stocks and shares, and the economist's meaning of the term. The latter is the meaning we are concerned with herein. This is physical capital; that is to say, goods produced by man, and used over more than one year in the production of goods for consumption. Similarly, 'investment', which in common language may refer to the purchase or acquisition of financial assets, is restricted in economics to the creation or purchase of physical assets which are productive: thus investment here means an increase in the stock of capital goods.

Note that capital goods are *assets*; i.e. they are something which stays in existence for some time, conventionally, for two or more 'production periods' (years, in agriculture). But there are other physical assets which are not capital; for example, furniture, jewellery, carvings and houses. These are generally referred to as durable consumer goods; they are not used to produce other consumer goods. Also, productive inputs like manure and fertiliser would not usually be referred to as capital goods – even though they are plainly not consumer goods – because they do not last for more than one production period.

Next, we introduce some more of the rather confusing realities of capital. Some commodities possess both the attributes of capital and of consumer goods. Cattle are a good example. They may help to produce other commodities, such as milk and blood, or through their use for ploughing, transport and the conversion of unwanted vegetation into manure; but they may also be killed and eaten and are thus consumer goods, too. Similarly, farm buildings may be used partly for human residence and are thus consumer durables, but partly also for animal shelter and food storage, thereby acting as capital goods. Furthermore, there exist what are known as 'human investments', such as education, which can have a role in the production of goods and may also be considered a desirable commodity in itself.

It was mentioned above that the concept of capital used here is more general than that conventionally employed in the standard Western texts. The usual assumption is that consumption must be foregone in order to create capital goods which will add to the flows of consumption in future years. For instance, suppose we have a one-man business producing carved wooden elephants for the tourist trade. Suppose, for the sake of simplicity, that all the elephants are the same and sell at a fixed price. A salesman visits the carver to demonstrate a machine that will put a shine on the carvings much more rapidly than by the carver's hand-polishing method. By investing in the machine he could produce and sell a lot more elephants per day and make more money. He buys the machine, thereby temporarily foregoing consumption; and foregone consumption we refer to as 'savings'. This present sacrifice is supposedly more than made up by the extra money he makes in the future from the sale of the increased output of carvings. Alternatively, he may borrow the money for the machine, so that not he, but someone else, foregoes consumption – does the saving – and of course he will have to pay interest to compensate the saver.

In rural Africa, however, it is quite possible, indeed quite common, for people to create capital without actually foregoing any consumption, but by devoting non-productive time to it. For example, time during the slack season may be used in planting cocoa trees. Thus it is more general to say that *utility* is foregone – consumption or time or a combination – in return for the extra production and consumption made possible by the capital created. It should be noted, though, that even if capital is formed with unpaid family labour, it does not necessarily mean that no consumption is foregone, since the labour may be diverted to some extent from production. For example, in Heyer's study of farms in Machakos, Kenya,[1] it was noted that work on land improvements such as terracing and fencing clashed with productive time. This was because the earth was too hard to work during the slack, dry, season, so that earth-moving had to be done after the rain had moistened the ground, i.e. just at the time when work on cultivation was most productive.

But we can be more general still. Take the case of investment in a water-tank and other requisites for collecting water from a tin roof. The principle benefit may be in saving the womenfolk large amounts of time spent in fetching water from a distant source. If no more water were used than hitherto (admittedly unlikely, but we are being hypothetical), there would be no future gain in terms of extra *output*, but only in terms of disutility reduced. There are thus in principle two extreme cases with regard to capital formation. The one involves purely the foregoing of consumption in return for extra consumption in the future; the other requires only foregone non-productive time offset by a future gain in the availability of non-productive time or a reduction in work and its disutility. The former, which embodies the conventional Western view of investment is just as much a special case as the latter. It may be fairly realistic in a Western context, in fact, but it is not so in application to African agriculture. The general case – which is much more realistic for our purposes – is that utility is foregone in return for extra utility in the future; the net utility, both that sacrificed and that gained, being generated by a combination of consumption and the disutility of work and the utility of non-working time.

Types of physical capital

The number of different kinds of rural physical capital found in Africa is not great, but the variation from region to region in the mixture of capital items and their incidence is very great. In some areas there is probably very little capital of any sort to be found, apart from hoes, cutlasses and the like, and perhaps food stores and some livestock. These are the most sparsely populated areas, such as the Zaïre basin, most of central Tanzania, and the Sahel. In the drier parts, like the last two, cattle, and camels towards the Sahara, are important. It is often said that in pastoral societies, livestock are not really a form of productive capital at all, but largely act as a store of value, convertible into food or income in emergencies; but this view is misleading. The animals represent an efficient way of converting widespread and unpalatable vegetation into food and manure. The food is usually 'tapped' as milk or blood, and only occasionally do the animals become consumer goods when their meat is eaten. In fully pastoral societies, the dung is often used as fuel, a thing of vital importance in any society in the production of the final food product, and especially where there are few trees to supply wood as an alternative. Also, of course, livestock are a source of hides and other useful materials. In effect, the vegetable matter that can grow on the land in the drier zones, is so poor that it would be impossibly laborious for men to try and cultivate it; livestock are in a sense partly necessary tools, used to exploit the exiguous produce of the land. They are reared and maintained by man and thus fit in at least partially, with our definition of capital.

In semi-pastoral societies, where some agriculture is practised, cattle often complement the agricultural part of the system, even when they are not used to draw ploughs or carts. Again they are used to exploit relatively poor land or to 'recycle' weeds, crop residues, kitchen waste and similar vegetable matter which is not directly usable, into milk, blood and manure; and here the manure tends to be used to make crop land more fertile, rather than as fuel. We shall look at the complex economic issues involved in the keeping of cattle, along with those of ploughing, in greater depth later on; at present the concern is just to introduce the major types of capital and give some idea of their implications.

In the sparsely populated forest zones, large livestock are far less in evidence, although small livestock such as goats and even poultry perform a similar function in using up vegetable matter that would otherwise go to waste. Tsetse flies, carrying trypanosomiasis (sleeping sickness), are of course a major factor inhibiting the keeping of cattle in these areas. In intermediate areas – mainly wooded savannahs – cattle are more common, but again are much restricted by tsetse fly, which needs the shade of trees or bush to survive.

Far-fetched though it might seem at first sight, tree crops actually also carry out something of the same role as do livestock in the drier zones. The fertility of the soil in a forest environment is often extremely poor and tends to be leached by the heavy rainfall. The roots of economic trees or perennials bring fertility upwards from deep in the ground, so that, for example, in densely populated eastern Nigeria agricultural systems are coming to be based more and more on tree foods and cash products, like palm oil especially, but also breadfruit, coconuts, plantains and bananas. Also, of course, trees are a source of fuel and of material for building, utensils, furniture, fabric, etc. (just as cattle are in the dry regions). Trees that are wild are not part of the capital stock but part of the stock of natural resources (land); trees that are planted or nurtured by man are, however, unquestionably part of the stock of productive capital, even though, like livestock, they may be 'consumed', as fuel, for construction, for palm wine (sometimes obtained by felling the palm), etc.

The export tree and perennial crops – coffee, cocoa, tea, oil palm, rubber, sisal, etc. – are the best known form of investment in rural Africa, but some perennials are important sources of food, too: oil palm, and bananas and plantains in particular. Trees are also exploited as timber but these are predominantly wild as yet and do not therefore represent true capital by the present definition. It is also often said that most oil palms are wild or semi-wild, but there is some evidence against this view.[2] We shall return to the problems of export tree crops below, however, and in the next chapter.

Terracing and similar kinds of soil-conservation works are significant in certain upland areas, especially in Ethiopia and some of the highland areas of the Lake Victoria region, and Floyd cites examples of terracing found in Nigeria and Cameroun.[3]

Water control and irrigation works, such as bunding, drainage, irrigation channels, ponds, wells, etc. are variable in incidence. One such form of investment is the clearance and bunding of swamps for the permanent cultivation of rice, which is becoming increasingly common in West Africa; we shall deal with this more fully, using data from Sierra Leone, in following sections. The irrigation system constructed by the Chagga on the Tanzanian slopes of Mount Kilimanjaro is remarkable by any standards. Allan has this to say of it:

> The construction of the furrow system through which water is distributed to homesteads throughout the mountain, over many miles of difficult country, represents an engineering feet of no mean order, and the successful operation of the delicate machinery required to maintain the works and to administer rights and easements must be regarded as a social achievement no less remarkable. Users of furrows formed what was in effect a 'water users association' which met to decide on the equitable division of water and to arrange a programme of maintenance by communal effort.[4]

The rights and duties of the 'owners' of the different segments of the system – canals, furrows, springs, streams and ponds – were carefully balanced and rights could be lost on failure in duty, while a pecking order of water use was maintained, modified by urgency of need and discussion of special cases.

Apart from the above types of rural capital there are also hoes, axes, ploughs, fishing nets, winnowing baskets and other equipment, and farm structures such as food stores, animal shelters and fences and walls. These structures may be surprisingly 'productive' in that they reduce attacks by pests of many kinds. The high stockades built, for example, in Botswana are very necessary for the protection of cattle from lions in particular. At the other extreme, granaries may be designed to reduce bacterial, fungal and insect damage. The humble fence keeps crops and livestock separate.

It should be noted at this point, that some have sought to include land clearance as part of capital formation.[5] This can only be the case, though, if the clearance can be considered an initial and permanent improvement to the land, as with the establishment of swamps as rice paddy; it is *not* true of the cyclical clearance of land under shifting cultivation except for the original clearance of virgin bush. Thereafter the regular regrowth and reclearance of natural vegetation simply *maintains*, more or less, the land in a cultivable state and no new productive capacity is created.

The above gives some idea of the nature of rural capital formation in Africa and of the various kinds that occur. Further examples will appear in the following paragraphs where we discuss the major causes and effects of investment, and, to a lesser extent, of intensification.

Benefits and costs, and their distribution

Quantitative information regarding rates of return to traditional types of capital formation are scarce, not merely for Africa, but for the whole of the Third World. However, qualitative information is slightly more available, and may indeed be of greater use. This is because ordinary market valuations of costs and returns are likely to be rather misleading when one is concerned with an economic sector characterised by widespread poverty and by production using mainly unpaid family labour to grow predominantly food for home consumption rather than for market. Market prices, whether of commodities or of factors of production (chiefly labour), result from the interacting decisions and behaviour of those who happen to be buying and selling in the market. There is no reason why they should reflect necessarily those economic forces occurring outside the market. The obvious case is that of food. Clearly it is rather meaningless to apply, as a valuation, the market price of food to the quantity of food produced by people who are going hungry or starving. Their valuation of food will be very high indeed.

Similarly social valuation of costs and returns may differ from private ones. For example, a government may attach a good deal of importance to preventing economic inequality. Thus a type of investment that yielded apparently high rates of return might be of benefit mainly to those farmers who are already relatively wealthy. The government in question would then tend to put a lower weight on the net benefits than that obtained using market prices: the social rate of return would be lower than the private rate.

So for these reasons, quantitative data may be of limited, though not necessarily zero, usefulness. A few examples should help to clarify this.

One instance where we do have the figures to derive conventional rates of return clearly demonstrates the hazards involved in doing so. This is the investment of labour in the clearance and bunding of swamps in Sierra Leone for the permanent, or near-permanent, cultivation of rice. Shifting cultivation of rice is the norm in Sierra Leone, made possible by the very heavy rainfall. But swamp cultivation is gradually displacing it as population grows, fallow periods shorten and thus yields under shifting, or upland, cultivation fall. The process is far advanced in some parts of the country, swamp cultivation having become the principle technique. There is an inclination to believe that swamp cultivation is economically superior to shifting cultivation, but this is not necessarily so. Certainly swamp yields tend to be higher than upland yields, but the labour requirements per hectare of swamp tend to be greater, so that the advantage over upland in terms of output per day of labour may not be there. This is most likely to be so where upland yields are highest, i.e. where fallow periods are longest. In 1970/71 a national agricultural survey was conducted which found that inland swamps (as opposed to tidal swamps and deep-flooding grasslands) yielded 1 600 kg of rice per hectare on average, while shifting cultivation was averaging 1 350 kg per hectare. Labour inputs have been estimated at 195 workdays per swamp hectare and 155 workdays per upland hectare.[6] From these figures we derive the labour productivities as 8·2 kg per workday from swamp cultivation and 8·7 kg per workday from shifting cultivation. On this basis, then, swamp cultivation is on average actually inferior to shifting cultivation. However, the survey's yields are probably unrepresentative; other sources give a much wider differential. An earlier and larger-scale national survey in 1965/6, for example, estimates the average yield from swamps at 2 032 kg per hectare, and that from upland at about 1 383 kg per hectare. The productivities are then 10·4 kg per workday from swamp and 8·2 kg per workday from upland.

The question that now needs to be asked is whether this differential in labour productivities is enough to compensate for the initial investment of labour in clearing a hectare of swamp, which has been estimated at 235 workdays.[7] The conventional approach of economics towards supplying an answer is to estimate the rate of return to investment in a hectare of swamp. If we assume that the returns will accrue far into the future and that they will not vary significantly from year to year, the rate of return is approximately the increase in the annual net return expressed as a percentage of the initial cost.

The annual labour applied to a hectare of swamp is 195 workdays. The opportunity cost of that labour in terms of foregone upland rice is 195 times the productivity of upland cultivation per workday, i.e. 195 × 8·2 = 1 439 kg. The output from the hectare of swamp is 2 032 kg as above. Thus the extra output from the swamp, i.e. over and above what would have been obtained by applying the same labour to upland, is 593 kg (2 032 − 1 439). Valued at the market price in recent years of about 100 Leones per tonne, this is worth 59.3 Leones.[8]

Using a hired labour wage of Le0.63 per workday,[9] the investment labour of 235 workdays used to clear the swamp is valued at Le148.05, and the conventional rate of return is 40 per cent (100 × 59.3/148.05). This apparently fairly attractive rate of return, however, is misleading, because of the way in which we value the net return (as mentioned above), which consists of more food, and the capital, which is extra labour. Extra food may reasonably be valued much more highly than the market price if food is in short supply. Also 235 workdays of investment labour is a considerable additional burden on top of the normal annual workload and it is doubtful whether it would in fact be forthcoming, given the size of the net return. In other words, the average hiring wage probably understates the subjective valuation put on that labour, especially at the margin. Given the other figures, it is probable that the amount of investment-labour that would be worth the farmer's while would only be a fraction of 235 workdays. Thus it is easy to see from this exercise why a single – even approximate – figure for a rate of return is inadequate as a measure of the net benefit to society from a particular item of physical capital. The figure obtained will be very sensitive to the assumptions one makes. Nevertheless some indication of the likely effects of an investment is worthwhile even though one may not wish to venture a valuation of those effects. A valuation must depend on one's own set of values.

Two other studies give some notion of the economic effects of agricultural capital formation. The first is Heyer's study of 16 farmers in Machakos, a fairly dry part of Kenya.[10] In her statistical analysis of the data she found a good deal of variation from farmer to farmer in crop production, that was not accounted for simply by the variation in measured inputs of land and labour. Although this element of unexplained variation could be due to a number of factors – not least the difficulties we have emphasised associated with the definition and measurement of land and labour – some of it was probably due to variations in the endowments of productive capital, which is much in evidence. The major types of capital are stores, fencing, soil-conservation works, ploughs and oxen (not all the farmers possessed ploughs, and some of them shared).

While admitting that there are other unquantified factors at work, Heyer allocates the unexplained residual variation in outputs to the catch-all factor, 'management'. She concludes, regarding this rather arbitrarily-named variable: 'Variations in managerial skills led to better farmers being able to make about four times as much as poorer farmers with the same labour and land resources'.[11] This is a very big variation, especially considering its 'residual' nature, and it seems difficult to believe that it could be due largely to such a nebulous factor as 'managerial ability' (though Heyer simply uses that as an arbitrary term). On the other hand this does not help us disentangle the effects of other factors; the evidence is tantalisingly vague.

In the Darwin Purchase Area of Zimbabwe, Massell and Johnson found that a considerable amount of labour during the slack season was being devoted to contouring, ridging, building dams, etc.[12] They attempted to estimate a production function which included capital equipment but did not include any variable or indicator representing the labour-capital. Like Heyer, they attributed to 'management' any variation in output not attributable to the inputs included, but admitted that this could be a catch-all for land improvements, selection of seeds and use of pesticides as well as pure managerial ability. The effect of these residual factors was apparently quite significant: '. . . . . the best farm could, *with given inputs* [i.e. those measured and included], obtain just twice as much output as the worst farm' (p. 64). They carried out a similar exercise for another part of the country – Chiweshe Reserve – but this time used the government's rating as an indicator of a farmer's management ability, which they classed in one of three broad categories for inclusion in the production function. They found that the 'semi-skilled' farmer got a return \$4.2 higher than the 'unskilled' farmer, after allowing for the effects of all other measured inputs, and that the 'skilled' farmer's return was \$10 higher than the 'unskilled'. (The average return per farm was \$83, which gives an idea of the proportionate effect.) The telling point, though, is that the government rating used to assess managerial class was 'according to certain objective criteria – in particular according to their *willingness to adopt soil conservation measures*' (p. 24, emphasis added).

Livestock and ploughing

We have already touched on the nature of capital in the form of livestock, especially, but not only, cattle. The use of livestock for ploughing is perhaps rather a special case, and is discussed below, but aside from ploughing, the animals are a form of productive capital in themselves. They not only supply food in the form of milk and blood, but they also concentrate fertility, via manure, on home fields if they are grazed on more distant and relatively infertile land.[13] More laborious variants of such a system have evolved, entailing the carrying of fodder, such as grass and weeds, from the land to the housed animals, which convert it to manure to be applied – with still more labour – to crop land. Also, animals convert kitchen waste and crop residue into manure. They may be used for transport, too, as is common in the vicinity of Kano in northern Nigeria where donkeys act as pack animals. Animal-drawn carts seem to be uncommon in black Africa, though, perhaps because they need proper roads or tracks; according to Haswell an animal can transport, pulling a cart, four times as much as it can carry on its back.[14]

Turning next to ploughing – usually with oxen, but sometimes with donkeys, or even camels – the major benefits and costs may be broadly listed as follows (although they depend on particular circumstances). The first advantage is that a larger area can be planted than by hand-hoeing. Thus, though planting labour is usually a bottleneck with hand-hoeing, because special weather conditions make it urgent (see Chapter 4), ploughing overcomes that constraint. But weeding seems to become a new bottleneck and sometimes such a large area is ploughed for planting, that some of it has to be left unweeded for want of labour.[15] Planting of the larger areas made possible by ploughing can only happen, of course, if land is initially abundant. But the general adoption of ploughing under such circumstances will itself make land more scarce and perhaps unevenly distributed among farmers – the latter depending on rules of tenure and how they change. This seems to have happened in The Gambia, where the official encouragement of ploughing combined with very high world prices of groundnuts were probably the major factors behind a rapid spread of ploughing in the early seventies, in an area where hand-hoe, fire-fallow cultivation had predominated hitherto.[16]

Another example of such an occurrence is found in Tiffen's penetrating study of farming in Gombe Emirate, in north-eastern Nigeria.[17] Again, the introduction of the plough, in 1946, combined with a rise, during the forties and fifties in the price of the major cash crop – in this case, cotton – led to a rapid expansion of ploughing at the expense of hoed fire-fallow cultivation. Initially land was very abundant and an individual farmer could plough more land simply by clearing it without cost except in labour. This process, in quite a short time, made land scarcer, not just for those ploughing, but for those still hoeing, too.

> When I interviewed in 1967, the expansion of farmland in southern Gombe was such that in some village areas there was no longer any cultivable bush. Farmers were conscious of falling fertility levels, and the option of shifting to new fields was no longer available. They were obliged, therefore, to conserve the fertility of their existing fields by better cultivation methods.[18]

These methods consisted of planting in ridges instead of on the flat, paying more attention to spacing and weeding, rotation of crops and use of fertiliser and manure.

A second advantage of ploughing is that draught animals have greater power (i.e. rate of doing work) then men. Thus the, often critical, timing of planting can be more accurate. We have seen in Chapter 4, that with hoeing, planting labour properly timed, especially in relation to early rainfall, is highly productive, but that the productivity quickly decreases after the optimum date. Ploughing, by getting the work done faster, breaks this constraint.

What of ploughing in conditions where land is scarce? Under such circumstances it appears that for only a minority is it economically possible to possess ploughs and draught animals, although others may well hire them. Such is the case in Machakos, Kenya[19] and in the Kano close-settled zone, Nigeria.[20] In the latter region, which lies roughly within a radius of 20 km from Kano city, most of the land is permanently cultivated, so that maintaining oxen is expensive, as there is little readily available pasture land. Very rough figures from Hill's study and from another by Nicolas et al.,[21] referred to by Hill, of Hausa farmers across the border in Niger, give some indication of the private rate of return to the individual farmer who invests in a plough and ox-team. The cost of these items is put at about £70. The sample of Niger farmers leased out their ploughs to an average extent of about 24 plough-days per season at about £0.75 per day. The return from leasing was thus about £18 per season. There is also some return to the farmer, which is unknown, but let us say not more than £2, making £20 gross return. Costs of feeding in the farming season are roughly £0.1 per day (the animals have to be grazed on distant bush-land as there is virtually none available in the vicinity, until crop residue is available after harvest). We are not informed how many days there are in the farming season or what the costs of feeding are outside it, but if we suppose the former to be 200 days, then the total costs are at least £20, and the net return and rate of return are zero at most. Not unexpectedly, only 13 out of 171 farming units in the village studied by Hill, possessed ploughs, and Nicholas *et al.* conclude that prestige is the principal factor motivating the ownership of ploughs and ox-teams.

This leads us on to a general consideration of the costs associated with ploughing. Feed costs depend on the nature of the land, being high where there is a high proportion of cultivated land and relatively low where there is grazing land. If there are common rights to grazing the costs of feed to the individual farmer will be very low, although time spent driving cattle to and from pastures and guarding them from predators may be considerable; this may be done communally, however. Further, although the individual does not bear all the costs of grazing the marginal animal, the society as a whole does, so that over-grazing is very likely. This seems to be the case in Lesotho[22] and the Transkei[23] for instance, and there could well be a vicious circle, for, as land becomes more scarce with population growth, families may try to substitute cattle for land, especially if there are grazing rights.
valued at £5 per hectare, an arbitrary figure, but presumably some-

In naturally wooded areas, much time and effort may be devoted to removing tree stumps from the land so as to increase the cultivatable area and to make ploughing easier. Morgan Rees and Howard valued the various kinds of capital on a sample of farms among the Sala of Mumbwa District, Zambia.[24] (These farms received subsidies and were more highly capitalised than usual.) Destumped land was thing approaching the true order of magnitude. It accounted for 22 per cent of total capital value on 'improved' farms and 14 per cent on 'unimproved'. (Over 40 per cent of the value of capital was in cattle.)

The effects of population change

We have already discussed in the opening paragraphs, the theoretical basis for the effects of population change on agricultural systems; so we shall now look briefly at the empirical side.[25]

One piece of evidence relates to a case we have already referred to: that of the clearance of swamps for permanent rice cultivation in Sierra Leone. Figure 6.2 shows observations for each of the twelve administrative Districts of the country and clearly depicts a high correlation between the degree of adoption of swamp cultivation on the one hand and the shortness of the fallow period under shifting cultivation on the other.

Another, more qualitative, kind of evidence is the occurrence of intensive systems of agriculture, with traditional forms of productive capital, in regions where the population density is 'artificially' high, i.e. where the density is greater than would have freely occurred in the absence of special circumstances. The most important instance is that of the refuge from surrounding hostility – generally upland areas which are easier to defend, or occasionally islands. The outstanding case of the latter is Ukara on Lake Victoria, where each field yields on an average two crops per year and and is well-manured. Cattle are kept in sheds and fed on specially grown fodder crops, all this requiring a

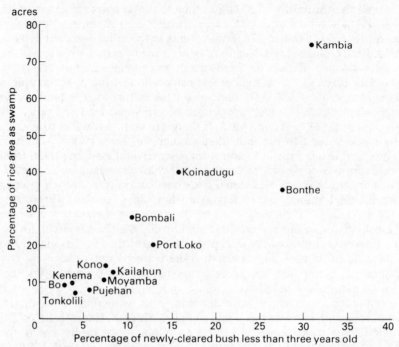

Fig. 6.2 Relationship between degree of swamp cultivation and length of fallow period under shifting cultivation, Sierra Leone

great deal of labour. The inhabitants of the island, however, once peaceful conditions were restored, were glad to go back to the more extensive and less laborious techniques of fire-fallow cultivation on the shores of the lake.

Another example of such a refuge is that of the Mandara Mountains of Cameroun where the pagans of Dikwa Emirate[26] practised mixed farming on manured terraces, rotation of crops and the planting and tending of trees for building timber, firewood and forage leaves. Many other similar cases are cited in Gourou's *The Tropical World*,[27] such as the Dogon of Bandiagara Plateau, Mali; the Tura, Ivory Coast; and in swamp 'refuges', the Diola of Lower Casamance, Senegal and the Severes, also of southern Senegal.

More generally, population densities may become comparatively high in modern times because a populace becomes 'trapped' within boundaries – *de facto* or *de jure*, tribal or political. This may partly explain the considerably uneven distribution of population in Nigeria, for example. Otherwise it is difficult to see why people in the very densely populated parts of the south choose to intensify cultivation rather than move out to more land-abundant areas.

Another interesting example of intensification in response to population growth is contained in a study of Abakaliki in eastern Nigeria.[28] Welsch calculated that the income per hectare from growing yams was about four times that from growing rice (costing labour at 1 shilling per man-day), and yet rice had expanded from zero to 36 420 hectares in 20 years. On the face of it, this is the reverse of what one would expect to happen when land was becoming scarcer with a steadily rising population: one expects people to try and get more and more income per hectare. The essential reason for the paradox apparently lies in the effects of rotating crops: the allocation of resources to one crop affects the output of the crop that follows on the same land and the productivity of labour applied to it. Yams cannot be grown continuously without a reduction in yield, but the highest yam-yields occur after fallow. Rice-yields, on the other hand, are about the same after yams as after fallow, and the labour required is less after yams because the yam mounds make the soil easier to work after the yams have been harvested. Welsch found that when land was limited, the best income per farm was obtained with a rotation: fallow, yams, rice, yams, rice, rice. With land unlimited, a combination of yams alone and a long fallow was best. It was a rising population density that had caused the increase in rice production, through a contraction in the amount of land per farm and a change in the optimum rotation of crops.

References

1 J. Heyer, 'Agricultural Development and Peasant Farming in Kenya', Ph.D. (Econ.) thesis, University of London, 1966.

2 See G.K. Helleiner 'Smallholder decision making: tropical African evidence', in L.G. Reynolds (ed.), *Agriculture in Development Theory*, Yale University Press, 1975, p. 38, fn. 34; J. Levi *et al.*, *African Agriculture: Economic Action and Reaction in Sierra Leone*, Farnham, Commonwealth Agricultural Bureaux, 1976, p. 50; S.La-Anyane, 'The Oil Palm Industries of Western Tropical Africa', unpub. Ph.D. dissertation, Stanford University, 1966.

3 B. Floyd, 'Terrace agriculture in Eastern Nigeria', *Nigerian Geographical Journal*, **7**, 1964, pp. 91–108.

4 W. Allan *The African Husbandman*, Oliver and Boyd, Edinburgh, 1965.

5 For example, M. Yudelman, *Africans on the Land*, Harvard University Press, 1964.

6 These labour figures exclude pest-scaring and harvesting, which are here assumed to be about the same under both production methods. Swamp figure: G.L. Karr, A.O. Njoku and M.F. Kahlon, 'Economics of the upland and inland-valley swamp rice production systems in Sierra Leone', *Illinois Agricultural Economics*, Vol. 12, No. 1, 1972. Upland figure: A.O. Njoku, 'Labor utilization in traditional agriculture: the case of Sierra Leone rice farmers', unpub. Ph.D. dissertation, University of Illinois, 1974.

7 Karr, *et al.*, *op. cit.*

8 1 Leone = £0.50 Sterling.

9 From the 1970/71 Agricultural Survey.

10 Heyer, *op. cit.*

11 *ibid.* p. iii.

12 B.F. Massell and R.W.M. Johnson, 'Economics of smallholder farming in Rhodesia: a cross-sectional analysis of two areas', *Food Research Institute Studies*, VIII, Supplement, 1968.

13 This technique may take the form of a comparatively sedentary, agricultural, people-reaching agreement with a more pastoral people that the latter should graze their animals on crop residue – grazing in exchange for manure. The pastoral Fulani of West Africa, for example, are known to enter such agreements.

14 M.R. Haswell, *The Nature of Poverty. A Case-History of the First Quarter-Century since World War II*, Macmillan, 1975.

15 See, for instance, W.I. Jones, 'The food economy of the Ba Dugu Djoliba, Mali', in P. McLoughlin (ed.), *African Food Production Systems*, Johns Hopkins University Press, 1970.

16 Haswell, *op. cit.*

17 Mary Tiffen, *The Enterprising Peasant. Economic Development in Gombe Emirate, North-Eastern State, Nigeria, 1900–1968*. Ministry of Overseas Development, Overseas Research Publication, No. 21 HMSO, 1976.

18 *ibid.*, p. 115.

19 Heyer, *op. cit.*

20 Polly Hill *Rural Hausa. A Village and a Setting*, Cambridge University Press, 1972.

21 G. Nicolas, H. Magaji and M. Dan Mouche, '*Problèmes posées par l'introduction de techniques agricoles modernes au sein société africaine: Vallée de Maradi, Niger*', University of Bordeaux (cyclostyled), 1968.

22 Sandra Wallman, *Take Out Hunger: Two Case Studies of Rural Development in Basutoland*, The Athlone Press, London, 1969.

23 G.L. Rutman and D.J. Werner, 'A test of the "Uneconomic Culture" thesis: an economic rationale for the "sacred cow"', *Journal of Development Studies*, Vol. 9, No. 4, 1973.

24 A.M. Morgan Rees and R.H. Howard, 'An economic survey of commercial African farming among the Sala of Mumbwa District of Northern Rhodesia', N. Rhodesia Dept. of Agriculture, Lusaka, 1955.

25 The pioneer work concerning the effects of population change on agricultural systems is the remarkable book by Ester Boserup: *The Conditions of Agricultural Growth. The Economics of Agrarian Change under Population Pressure*, George Allen and Unwin, London, 1965.

26 S. White, 'Agricultural economy of the hill pagans of Dikwa Emirate', *Farm and Forest*, 5, 1944, pp. 130–134. See also Allan, *op. cit.*, and K.M. Buchanan and J.C. Pugh, *Land and People in Nigeria*, London, 1955.

27 P. Gourou, *The Tropical World*, Longman, London, 1966.

28 D.E. Welsch, 'Response to economic incentive by Abakaliki rice farmers in Eastern Nigeria', *Journal of Farm Economics*, Nov. 1965.

7 Exports

Contribution to economic development

Until about the late sixties agricultural exports received a good deal of attention in the literature, as compared with the food economy. And indeed most of this attention was directed at the more external aspects of trade. Presumably the apparent lack of concern for the food economy was mainly due to a shortage of reliable information: there were very few good micro-economic studies. This lack of information resulted from the great physical difficulty of carrying out such work.[1] It contrasted with the greater 'visibility' of the export trade, the statistics of production and prices being good and the structures of marketing being relatively easy to cope with. Furthermore, the trade in agricultural exports was of more immediate concern to the richer importing countries, and to the colonial powers – up to independence, of Britain and France, C. 1960 – whose local administrations derived revenue from the taxation of traded goods.

First we look at the general economic benefits of agricultural exports, and some of the possible costs. There is in fact a whole spectrum of opinion in the literature about the good or harm they do to Africa, ranging from the extremely pessimistic to the rather enthusiastic, and depending in part on which countries, which products and which periods of time one is considering. For what it is worth, the writers consider that in general the benefits are real but limited, and that there are more important aspects of the economy for governments to devote their thought and energy to; but all the questions are by no means answered nor all the problems solved, for they are quite complex.

Secondly, we consider the economics of the production of agricultural exports: the chief influences on supply at the micro-economic and at the national level. Finally there is a section on the centralised marketing arrangements and in particular on the effects of their use as taxing agencies, as well as the effects of more explicit taxation; this continues to be an area of major concern, as it has been since the late forties.

One way in which to assess the economic contribution of agricultural exports is to look at the proportion of total exports taken up by agricultural products. In Table 7.1, it is clear that some countries have a particularly low reliance on agriculture for their export earnings, such as Zambia, Gabon and Nigeria. This is mainly because certain minerals are particularly important, for instance, copper in Zambia and oil in Gabon and Nigeria.

Table 7.1 Statistics of Agricultural Exports (1976 except where otherwise indicated)

	$m. US Major agricultural exports	All Agricultural exports	Agricultural exports as percentage of total exports
Angola	Coffee: 247·1	247*	20
Benin	Cotton: 6·8; palm kernel oil: 2·1; cocoa: 1·3	17	43
Botswana		40	
Burundi	Coffee: 48·8	66	89*
Cameroun	Coffee: 162·0; cocoa: 128·5; cotton: 17·6	364	52
Central African Republic	Coffee: 19·7; cotton: 9·7	38	46
Chad	Cotton: 26·2 (1975)	87	c.100
Congo		130	71
Equatorial Guinea		20	
Ethiopia	Coffee: 155·7; hides and skins: 26·2	267	4
Gabon		48	
The Gambia	Groundnuts: 27·1 (1975)	41	85
Ghana	Cocoa: 515·8	533	66
Guinea		13	
Guinea-Bissau		4	
Ivory Coast	Coffee: 562·1; cocoa: 381·3	1 125	69
Kenya	Coffee: 223·1; tea: 75·9	468	57
Lesotho		10	
Liberia	Rubber: 46·2	67	15
Malawi	Tobacco: 70·1; tea: 28·9; sugar: 25·6	154	93
Mali	Cotton: 42·6	81	95
Mauritania		20	11
Mozambique	Preserved fruit etc.: 31·4; sugar: 25·7; Fresh fruit, nuts: 20·9; cotton: 17·6	107	71

Country			
Namibia	Vegetable oils: 4··8	97	28
Niger		38	5
Nigeria	Cocoa: 70·4; groundnuts, palm kernels, etc.: 39·5	532	90
Rwanda	Coffee: 62·1; tea: 5·5	73	62
Senegal	Groundnut oil: 126·5	294	30
Sierra Leone		33	75
Somalia	Fresh fruit and nuts: 10·3	64	28
South Africa		1 360	96
Sudan	Cotton: 191·8; oil seeds, nuts, kernels: 140·5	531	
Swaziland		86	
Tanzania	Coffee: 153·1; cotton: 73·2; spices: 31·0, Sisal: 28·8; tobacco: 22·4	408	83
Togo	Cocoa: 21·8; coffee: 8·2	39	37
Uganda	Coffee: 310·7; cotton: 21·8; tea: 10·7	338	96
Upper Volta		49	91
Zaïre	Coffee: 104·4	353	38
Zambia		10	1
Zimbabwe		239	c.50

Sources: FAO Trade Yearbook, UN Yearbook of International Trade Statistics, and Monthly Bulletin of Statistics.

* Coffee exports only.

Even though these statistics are likely to be reasonably accurate, however, they can be misleading in that they can well understate the economic contribution of agricultural exports. The reason for this is that the non-agricultural exports often generate quite large import bills, directly or indirectly. For example, mineral extraction requires the importing of expensive machinery and the use of foreign personnel who have the appropriate expertise. The firms involved may be wholly or partly foreign-owned so that profits will be remitted overseas. Also, the employees will often be paid relatively high wages and salaries and will thus tend to spend a high proportion of their incomes on imported products, more suited to their pockets than domestic products. All this means that figures of *gross* export earnings from the non-agricultural sector tend to overstate the net contribution that they make to the balance of payments and indeed to a country's income. An example of how large the overstatement can be is found in a study of the economic impact of mineral extraction – mainly diamonds and iron – in Sierra Leone.[2] Although the authors are cautious about the precise levels of the figures they obtain, the orders of magnitude are considered plausible; they conclude that the net contribution of the mining companies to the balance of payments is only about 12 per cent of the gross value of the companies' exports.

So we can conclude that the economic contribution of agricultural exports – the value added that is retained in the country – generally tends to be a good deal higher than that of non-agricultural exports, per unit of gross export earnings. Value added is the value of the output less the value of purchased material inputs and is equal to the income accruing to the factors of production; in the case of agricultural exports, the retained value added will tend to be equal to, or nearly equal to, the gross earnings since purchased inputs are relatively unimportant except for fairly small amounts of insecticide, fertiliser, etc.

Linkages with other industries are not very significant, although there may be some forward linkages in so far as produce is processed internally; for example palm kernels or groundnuts may be turned into oil and by-products before exporting. There will also be multiplier effects in that a rise in income earned from agricultural exports will raise spending power. If some of the goods or services demanded by those who have become richer are not produced domestically, however, imports will increase so that the multiplier effect will be dampened by leakage from the economy. Furthermore even those products that are available domestically will have a supply response to the extra demand that is not completely elastic, especially in the short term; thus there will tend to be an upward pressure on prices and on imports. However, all this is not to say that there will be *no* domestic response to the greater money demand generated by export earnings, and in the longer term it could be considerable. In the Ivory Coast and Ghana, for example, specialist food-producing zones have developed which supply the major export-crop regions to the south.

The nature of the extra demands arising from export earnings will depend a good deal on the new distribution of income between people. A big rise in earnings, but one which accrues to only a small proportion of the rural population will bring about a new pattern of demand quite different from that arising from a more widespread improvement in incomes. In Ghana, about 80 per cent of cocoa production comes from about 30 000 plantations, covering about 1·4 million hectares; i.e. averaging 45·3 hectares, though they vary in size considerably. Any increases in cocoa earnings will therefore tend to be fairly concentrated, and the demand pattern somewhat specialised. Similarly, in the Ivory Coast, in 1965, about 20 000 planters owned nearly a quarter of the land in the main export-crop areas, and they tended to spend their earnings on conspicuous consumption and to invest in such urban enterprises as housing, and lorry and taxi businesses.[3]

Supply

Conditions of production

It is conventional in the literature to make the distinction between 'plantation' and 'smallholder' systems of production. This is a useful simplification provided one is fully aware of its limitations. The difficulty is that there is no true dividing line, but rather a whole spectrum, the extremes of which acceptably can be termed plantation and smallholder production, while the centre is vague: there are 'large smallholdings' or 'small plantations', and they are not uncommon in Africa.

The literature of economic development shows a tendency to conceive of plantations as being essentially exploitative of labour and typified by, for example, sugar production in the Caribbean region, and coconut and rubber production in Southeast Asia. In the past at least they were largely foreign-owned and there is still a good deal of foreign involvement. To give perhaps an extreme example, the operations of the Booker McConnell company (mainly sugar production) in Guyana come about as close as it is possible to be for a single company to control an entire economy.[4] Like mines they have been seen as economic 'enclaves', operating with modern, imported, technology, remitting profits to the overseas parent companies, paying high salaries to expatriate personnel and low wages to local employees, and thus having a relatively small impact on general development. Furthermore, capital equipment – for processing, transport, etc. – is often highly specific to a particular commodity. Thus, for example, if the profitability of banana supply falls, production will not switch to other enterprises, because plant and equipment can to a large extent only be used for bananas. But perhaps the main point of criticism is that large plantations have a high degree of market power – in labour and land markets and even in the product markets.[5] This grip on the land market is particularly acute in island economies, such as Jamaica, where almost half the land is taken up by the sugar estates. This would be less of a problem in Africa, generally, because of relative land abundance, except in certain areas. The very hold over land itself creates greater power over labour, since the latter is squeezed by land scarcity into seeking wage employment. Such an effect has undoubtedly been of significance in some parts of Africa, notably Kenya and Zimbabwe where white appropriation of land (not necessarily as plantations only) combined with strict and discriminatory labour laws effectively created a captive labour force. Probably much the same circumstances occurred too in Angola and Mozambique before the Portuguese withdrawal. Plantations proper, growing export crops, have been most important in Zaïre and Liberia, and less so in Cameroun, Angola, Kenya, Tanzania and Mozambique. Zaïre nationalised its oil palm plantations after independence, but has been attempting to sell them off again to private concerns. Other countries have, since independence, attempted to establish or promote plantations in the belief that they would advance the cause of development; but they have tended to be very unprofitable. The plantation in the classic 'colonial' mould, with a high degree of foreign resources, has remained most firmly entrenched, ironically enough, in the one African country that has never been a colony: Liberia. There has been an expansion in rubber production by smallholders in recent years, but the way in which land and labour resources have been utilised in the plantation sector (mainly rubber) is worth noting, as it clearly demonstrates the major elements of plantation economies.

The original land concession was granted to the American Firestone Company in 1928, and measured 363 km^2 in area. Since then smaller, independent estates, many owned by government officials, have developed, along with concessions to other companies. In the early sixties at least, wages were kept low officially, despite the fact that Firestone was willing to pay higher rates and experienced shortages.[6] These shortages were eased by an open and official policy of involuntary labour recruitment under which paramount chiefs were assigned quotas and were paid for sending labourers to the plantations.

> .... there is no denying the coercive features of recruitment; the chiefs respond to the carrot of per head payments by Firestone, as well as to the stick of governmental power. They exert pressure by levying fines (and, we are told, more drastic penalties) on their recalcitrant subjects.[7]

In a land-abundant economy, the device of restricting the availability of land so as to stimulate labour supply is not effective, so other measures are resorted to.

Even without coercion of labour, which in colonial times in other countries included forced labour, poll (head) taxes and hut taxes, the market power of a plantation in the labour market ensures that it will be exploitative of labour (provided we suppose that the plantation operator will try to increase its profit, given the opportunity to do so). The term 'market power' simply means that a firm has some influence on the market price through its own operations – in this case, in the market for labour. In the extreme, there may be only a single buyer – a monopsonist. The equilibrium employment position of the plantation is shown in Fig. 7.1. Here we suppose that labour has a diminishing marginal product, while the price of the commodity is determined on the world market and is unaffected by the operations of the plantation. Thus the marginal revenue product curve (MRP) is the same shape as the marginal physical product curve. The supply curve of labour to the plantation is assumed linear for simplicity. This is also the average cost

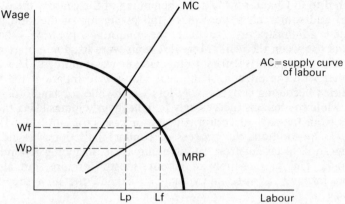

Fig. 7.1 Relationships of market, price and labour in plantation production

curve, to the plantation, of employing labour, and its marginal labour cost curve will be steeper as shown (the slope of MC being twice that of AC). It can be seen that both the wage, W_p, and employment, L_p, are lower than under competitive conditions, W_f and L_f. Coercion of labour exacerbates this difference by pushing AC to the right and downwards.

At the other end of the spectrum, the 'true' smallholder export crop grower might be considered as the head of a nuclear, or perhaps extended, family who farms only with unpaid family labour, coping with a fairly small farm not much different from the farms of his neighbours. He has fitted his export crop into the food-production system, so that labour applied to the one does not clash with the other. Sometimes, too, it is evident that food-production systems have been modified so as to allow better integration of food and cash crops. This is perhaps the stereotype picture of the African smallholder export producer, although it is difficult to get any quantitative indication of the relative importance of this type of farmer. Very often there is a great deal of hired labour used in smallholders systems and, as has already been said, individually-owned farms can become quite large,[8] while producers may have a very commercial or 'capitalist' attitude to land, contrary to the more traditional attitudes outlined in Chapter 5. For example, in the early fifties, in the important Yoruba cocoa lands of western Nigeria:

> It would perhaps be too much to say that Yoruba villages are now dominated by a class of landed gentry surrounded by an impoverished peasantry. But there seems to be little doubt that an aristocracy of warriors and hunters has in part survived in the form of a group of families asserting control over large extents of land and has in part been replaced by a group of other families which have succeeded in acquiring or at least obtaining possession of equally large extents.[9]

Another interesting and important case is that of the coffee growers of Buganda, on the northern shores of Lake Victoria, this has been referred to in Chapter 5.[10] At the beginning of the century the *Kabaka* (king) and some chiefs were given full ownership of the land by the colonial administrators, so that the majority of farmers became tenants. Between the wars, however, rents were fixed in money terms, and later, complete security from eviction was enforced. The latter, together with the erosion of the real rent due to inflation, led to the tenancies becoming progressively less worthwhile for landlords to retain, while the tenants increasingly bought their holdings using the proceeds from the sale of cotton, the major cash crop until after World War II. In addition, the process of commercialisation was aided by immigration of labour from surrounding areas, including Rwanda and Burundi. This extra supply of labour, mostly for hire, but also for tenant farming, allowed individuals to expand the area they could manage.

A similar, highly commercial, approach to farming is described in Polly Hill's famous study of Ghanaian cocoa farmers.[11] Initially, these farmers accumulated cash from the sale of oil palm produce. They used this to buy land outside their home territory, for the purpose of growing cocoa, and they formed 'companies' each cultivating a block divided into strips managed by individuals.

Supply functions

Quite a volume of literature has developed to do with the statistical estimation of supply functions for African export crops, and because of the importance, of the question 'What determines the supply of export crops?', we need to look at the subject, at least briefly, even though we cannot go into the technical econometric details. We shall see in the next section one reason why the question is of importance.

Firstly, the early literature was much concerned with the question whether or not supply response to price was actually positive or negative. The orthodoxy of economics said that it should be positive, but a counter argument was that African farmers tended to aim for a more-or-less constant, or 'target', cash income. Thus, the argument went, if the price of an export crop rose, less of it would need to be supplied to meet the cash target, i.e. there would be a negative relationship between price and quantity supplied. In fact, the 'target income' assumption is not necessary to deduce the possibility of such a negative relationship. It can easily be shown that, given certain preferences regarding leisure and other non-labour activities versus labour, a farmer may both take a higher cash income and reduce his labour input and quantity supplied (see Chapter 4). In other words, when price rises there may be some substitution of 'leisure' for cash income, but not necessarily so much as to keep cash income the same as before.

However, there was a view that if it were true that farmers did respond negatively to price, then they were in some sense irrational.[12] (This, as we have just pointed out, does not follow.) Early work on African supply response seemed to be overly concerned with this aspect, and preoccupied with establishing that response was positive.[13] Indeed the statistical evidence shows overwhelmingly that this is indeed so. On the other hand, most of that evidence is concerned with the response of a single crop to price: it says nothing about the total response of agricultural output, whether marketed or overall. Even with the unlikely 'target income' assumption, it is not just likely, but must be the case that if more than one product is sold and the price of a single crop rises, farmers will switch their efforts into that crop and thus respond positively. Furthermore, the statistics used were aggregate, so even if a single farmer might react negatively, others – and the sum total – might not. Also, the aggregate response is to some extent the response of *traders* seeking to buy more produce if the price they get goes up, as well as the response of farmers. In a sense then, much of this empirical work seemed to be answering, but was not, a question that did not really need to be asked. In principle a negative response of total marketed supply to price on the part of an individual farmer is quite possible and even likely. But the empirical evidence based on aggregative statistics for single crops, showing positive supply responses, says nothing one way or the other about that individual response, and in particular does not contradict the possibility that it may be negative.

Having disposed of this rather empty controversy, let us look at supply functions as they are in fact. An important distinction needs to be made between annual crops, such as groundnuts, on the one hand, and perennials, such as cocoa, coffee, rubber, etc., on the other. Provided the statistics are available, the estimation of supply functions for annual crops does not present much difficulty. Hectares planted will be related positively to the expected price, while the harvest will depend mainly on weather conditions. Thus supply should be related statistically to the price prevailing at planting time and to some indicator of weather conditions during the growing period. One particular crop that has an even simpler supply function is palm kernels. These are supplied in parts of Western Africa mainly as a by-product of palm oil extraction. The palm fruits are processed by boiling, etc., to extract the nutritious red palm oil from the flesh. This leaves the nut, inside which is the palm kernel, and from this another type of oil can be extracted. In many cases, the fruits are harvested primarily for the palm oil, either for consumption or sale, while the effort put into the cracking of nuts depends on the price being offered for them. Thus unlike the vast majority of agricultural products there is no significant time lag between deciding how much to sell and the sale itself.[14] An example of a palm kernel supply function for Sierra Leone is shown in Fig. 7.2. The statistics used to construct the diagram are mainly from the Sierra Leone Produce Marketing Board, which fixes the buying price for the season and is the sole buyer. (It is as well to remember, however, that few farmers sell directly to the Board but to traders who are the ones to receive the official price from the Board.) The 'price' in the diagram is the 'real' price; i.e. the money price is deflated by the Consumer Price Index. A straight line is fitted to the scatter by least-squares regression.

Supply functions for perennials present greater conceptual and statistical difficulties. This is mainly because of the delay of some years – generally 5 to 10 – between planting and first harvest. Also the yield usually continues, barring disease or destruction by pests, for several years; for example, cocoa trees yield for 30 years or more. The leading

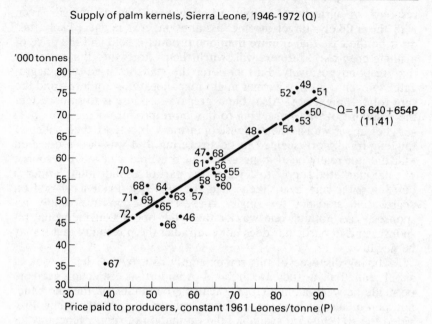

Fig. 7.2 *Supply of palm kernels, Sierra Leone, 1946–1972*

question is, that given there will be no returns for a few years, on what do farmers base their decision to plant perennials? One possible answer is that farmers react to an approximate expected future price level, and that the latter is based on current, or recent, price levels. Superficially, it may seem a little far-fetched that farmers will hazard any such prediction of prices so far in advance. (Remember that it is not merely the price that prevails at the time of the *first* harvest that determines the profitability of perennials, but also the prices that prevail for perhaps 30 years thereafter.) But there is quite a lot of statistical evidence that is consistent with such behaviour. If we accept for the moment that farmers do decide to plant to a greater or lesser extent depending on the levels of recent prices, we should expect the area, or more strictly the number, of bearing trees in any year to be positively correlated with the price levels of say, five to ten years earlier (the lag depending on the crop in question). One influential study which appears to support this is Stern's article on West African cocoa supply.[15] For example, using five-year moving averages for hectares of cocoa planted and cocoa prices in Nigeria, 1919/20–1944/45, he found a high degree of correlation ($R^2 = 0.86$). However, Sara S. Berry has recently challenged the standard interpretation of these results and others like them.[16] Using more and better Nigerian data than did Stern, she arrives at the conclusion that it is farmers' *incomes* that determine the extent of new planting, rather than prices, although of course the two variables are related. As she puts it: 'Given the uncertainty of future crop prices, it seems more likely that farmers plant more trees when they can afford to do so, so long as opportunity costs are not prohibitive'.[17]

Marketing boards and export taxes

During the 1940s most of the British African countries established Marketing Boards which operated as sole buyers of the export crops in each country, and sold them on world markets. These boards were of greatest significance in the four British West African countries and in Uganda. They were really a continuation of the special marketing arrangements that had been set up by the British during World War II to secure supplies. Later, in the early fifties, the French established rather similar institutions in the territories they governed. They were termed '*Caisses de Stabilisation des Prix*' (Price Stabilisation Funds). Both of these types of institution were continued after independence. We shall return to a discussion of the French arrangements later and concentrate for the moment on the British Marketing Boards, which have been the subject of much contentious debate in the English literature.

The stated purpose of the Boards was mainly to stabilise prices received by producers, by means of an official price fixed for a crop season. Price instability, both seasonal and year-to-year which was thought to occur under a free market system, was held to be undesirable because it supposedly led to unpredictable farm incomes and was a disincentive to productive farm investment and planning. It was also felt that the middlemen, who operated the marketing system tended to have too strong and monopolistic a hold over domestic commodity markets. The Marketing Boards by offering 'fair', publicly declared and fixed prices, would, it was believed, do much to remove the exploitation of farmers by traders. The Boards also began operations by stating their intention to reduce inter-year price variation, and this they were to do by paying below the free world price in relatively high-price years and above the world price in years when it was relatively low. In the event, the early life of the Boards, in the late forties and early fifties, saw an unprecedented world boom in commodity prices (known as the Korean war boom), peaking in the early fifties. They duly paid official prices well below world levels (partly to avoid inflation, as well as for the reasons already stated) and thus accumulated very substantial surpluses during this period. For example, by 1951 the Gold Coast Cocoa Board had built up the huge sum of £81 million, while the Nigeria Cocoa Board had £37 million and the Nigeria Oil Palm Produce Board, £31 million; by 1953 the Uganda 'Price Assistance Funds' had amassed about £30 million, but about another £50 million had already been diverted to a hydro-electric scheme.

There were many critics of this whole policy, typified perhaps by P.T. Bauer whose book *West African Trade* was published in 1954.[18] Bauer argued that domestic marketing systems were actually very competitive and that middlemen could not have made excessive profits. He also maintained – as have other economists – that stabilising prices does not stabilise farmers' incomes, and worse, tends to reduce them. Furthermore, the payment of low producer-prices inhibits the expansion of production by making it less profitable than otherwise.

After the early, profitable years, the Boards failed on the whole to

115

offset the surpluses by subsidising farmers during the following leaner years, except to a small extent. Furthermore a good deal of the surpluses were used by central government as sources of general finance, so that in effect the Boards became little more than collectors of taxes on agricultural exports. On top of the Board surpluses, however, there were also imposed quite overt export taxes which went directly to government.

Helleiner[19] defended the Marketing Boards – specifically the Nigerian ones, but implicitly the system in general of taxing agricultural exports by paying low producer-prices. He put the core of his argument as follows:

> The disposition of Marketing Board surpluses may not have been perfect, but the rates of return from their investments in research, roads, agricultural schemes, universities, modern manufacturing plants and so forth are unlikely to have been any lower than those on housing, sewing-machines, land clearing and other small-scale outlets for peasant funds discussed above, let alone so much lower as to offset the difference between consumption ratios. It can, therefore, unambiguously be stated that Nigerian development has been aided through the device of channelling a portion of its export earnings via the Marketing Boards away from the producer to other (governmental) decision-makers.[20]

He then went on to the internally logical conclusion that the central authorities should actually try to maximise export tax revenue.

But are Helleiner's basic premises correct? Would it have been quite so economically unfruitful as he assumes to have left the money with the export-crop growers? To answer such questions we need to be able to estimate what would have been the likely result of farmers receiving the free-market, untaxed, price. This is not an easy thing to do with any confidence for most crops, especially perennials, in the major countries, because as we have seen, the supply functions tend to be rather complex and the statistics inadequate. But there is one case for which estimation of the supply-inhibiting effects of low pricing is relatively straightforward, namely, palm kernels. Sierra Leone happens to have good statistics of palm kernel export supplies and prices (largely from the records kept by the Marketing Board) as we have seen. It also has the advantage that it only accounts for a small proportion of the total world supply, unlike, say, Ghanaian cocoa, the production of which itself affects the world market price significantly, thereby complicating the problems of estimating the response of production to price changes.

We refer again here to the graph of deliveries of palm kernels each year to the Sierra Leone Produce Marketing Board against the annual deflated price paid by the Board for kernels, shown in Fig. 7.2. As can be seen a straight line is fitted to the observations by simple least-squares regression, and this line can be used to estimate what the supply in each year would have been if there had been a free-market price without export duties or Marketing Board surpluses (or, occasionally, deficits). The calculation is very simple. We take the export duty per tonne of palm kernels and the Board surplus per tonne and add these to the actual producer price per tonne. The total is then what the free price would have been. This is then deflated (by a Consumer Price Index) and substituted for 'P' in the formula for the supply function obtained by regression: $Q = 16\,640 + 654P$. We thus obtain an estimate of what Q would have been had there been free and untaxed producer prices. The results are set out in Tables 7.2 and 7.3 where it can be seen that the dampening effect on supply has been very considerable and the financial loss to producers much greater than the mere value of the funds taken from them by low pricing.

As we have mentioned, though, Sierra Leone can be considered a 'price-taker' with regard to her palm kernel exports. This is not so of Ghanaian and Nigerian cocoa, Nigerian oil palm products, Ugandan coffee, etc. The levels of production in these cases being a significant proportion of world production, affect world prices, so that the reduction in supplies resulting from low pricing in these other countries must have served to keep world prices higher than they otherwise would have been. It is possible therefore that these higher prices might have offset, at least to some extent, the reduced supplies, so that there may even have been a gain in money terms.[21] Gains of this nature, however, can only be short-term in highly competitive world markets. Other countries can profit from the high world prices engendered by export taxation through expanding their own production. Thus in the longer term, the advantages of taxing exports accrue not to the countries that indulge in such a policy, but to their competitors.

This is where we consider the policies of the French-speaking countries, for although they appear superficially the same as those of the English-speaking countries, there is a very important respect in which they have differed.[22] Unitl 1964, when the rules of the European Economic Community under the Yaoundé Convention began to come into force, France offered to her former colonies prices higher than world prices, particularly for coffee, groundnuts and bananas. The financial advantage of this policy of price support was considerable, especially in the cases of Senegal and Ivory Coast. For example, it has been estimated that for the period 1960–1966, the effective subsidy of Ivory Coast exports by France was about $100 million.[23] This is likely to be an underestimate of the true figure, for it is obtained simply by multiplying the quantities exported to France by the difference between French and world prices, and thus makes no allowance for the fact that supplies would probably have been smaller had only the world prices been received. Even so it is a very large amount for a country whose population was then less than four million.[24]

Apart from French price support there were other sources of trading advantage in favour of the Francophone countries. For example, although there was no support for cocoa prices, there was an intervention price and loans were made available to the Stabilisation Funds to moderate the effects of price fluctuations. The Yaoundé Convention also made provision for loans to the Funds and for direct aid to increase productivity. Another device used to enable the payment of high producer-prices is suggested by Dumont in his account of dealings in Brazzaville (Congo):

Table 7.2
Estimation of the supply-inhibiting effects of taxing palm kernels, *Sierra Leone*, 1950–1972

	(a) Marketing Board profit or loss[1] (Le/tonne)	(b) Export duties (Le/tonne)	(c) Actual producer price (Le/tonne)	(d) 'Free' producer price (a + b + c) (Le/tonne)	(e) F.P.P. deflated ('61 Le/tonne)	(f) 'Free' supply response (tonnes)	(g) Deflated actual producer price ('61 Le/tonne)	(h) Actual supply response (tonnes)
1950	18·54	5·00	42·43	65·99	134·94	104 890	86·81	71 269
1951	30·82	6·82	57·80	95·44	145·93	112 078	88·38	75 854
1952	6·84	22·70	63·25	92·79	122·57	97 455	83·55	75 870
1953	1·72	18·20	63·25	83·17	111·04	89 260	84·45	69 525
1954	−2·68	15·48	63·25	76·05	96·38	79 673	80·16	68 562
1955	−3·26	12·18	57·80	66·72	77·85	67 554	67·44	57 445
1956	−0·94	11·26	57·80	68·12	75·94	66 305	64·44	58 100
1957	0·44	7·98	57·80	66·22	67·98	61 099	59·34	52 899
1958	4·82	8·00	60·80	73·62	78·48	67 966	61·62	53 694
1959	27·82	8·30	63·20	99·32	105·88	85 886	64·82	57 444
1960	11·58	13·16	63·20	87·94	91·60	76 546	65·83	54 442
1961	(−7·74)[2]	10·80	63·20	n.a.	n.a.	n.a.	63·20	59 558
1962	−5·34	2·36	63·20	60·22	60·77	56 382	63·77	60 633
1963	8·90	4·10	54·20[4]	67·20	67·26	60 628	54·25	51 540[6]
1964	11·56	6·76	59·62	77·94	69·96	62 394	53·52	52 000
1965	24·34	11·52	59·62	95·48	81·96	70 242	51·18	49 300
1966	20·25	11·36	63·62	95·23	78·31	67 855	52·32	44 900
1967	−42·44[3]	3·08	50·00[5]	10·64	8·35	22 098	39·22	35 700
1968	62·18	15·94	63·22	141·34	109·40	88 188	48·93	54 000
1969	9·81	10·30	65·00	85·11	63·71	58 306	48·65	52 200
1970	27·16	12·24	65·00	104·40	72·65	64 153	45·23	57 200
1971	20·75	11·60	65·00	97·35	69·34	61 988	46·30	51 000
1972	−33·21	32·69	65·00	64·48	44·19	45 540	44·55	46 000

[1] 1964 onwards are estimates. These are obtained as follows: Board revenue is assumed to be the same as f.o.b. export value. Costs consist of: (a) payments for produce, which are obtained by multiplying producer prices by quantities purchased, (b) buying agents' allowances, or estimates based on actual figures, (c) export duty revenue (from Trade Reports and Trade Journal), (d) marketing costs (transport, storing, etc.) obtained by estimating a cost function using marketing cost and quantity data from SLPMB Reports, 1949–1963. (This function fitted the data quite well.) The estimates are most sensitive to errors in estimated sales and purchases whose values are big enough to outweigh the other components of the calculation.

[2] Figures for the first half only of 1961 are available.

[3] It may be that the loss per tonne in 1967 was smaller than shown. Different sources, purporting to give the same statistics in fact show different figures, and for 1967 those differences are quite large (especially for Board purchases), although in other years they were not big enough to have a significant effect on the estimates.

[4] First six months only.

[5] This is a rough average figure for the year as the actual price varied.

[6] Obtained by doubling the tonnage for the first six months.

Sources: Sierra Leone Produce Marketing Board Annual Reports, 1949–63; Sierra Leone Trade Reports; Sierra Leone Trade Journal; Bank of Sierra Leone Economic Review; Tropical Products Quarterly; and Sierra Leone Statistical Bulletin.

Note: In the article, J. Levi, 'African Agriculture Misunderstood: Policy in Sierra Leone', *Food Research Institute Studies* (1974), footnote 'd' Table 4 states that producer price and quantity in 1961 are available only for the first six months. This in fact applies to 1963, as does the doubling of tonnage. The Marketing Board loss correctly refers to 1961, however. The blame for this error lies with the author.

Note: The data in Tables 7.2 and 7.3 are based on the long ton (2240 lbs). Since this is very close to the metric tonne (2200 lbs) the figures have not been altered. Nominal metrication retains consistency with the rest of the book.

Table 7.3
Estimated producer loss due to tax on palm kernels, Sierra Leone (constant 1961 Leones)

	(a) Free producer receipts	(b) Actual producer receipts	(c) Loss in producer's income	(d) PMB Surplus and Export Duty
1950	14 153 856	6 200 403	7 953 454	3 184 016
1951	16 355 543	6 675 152	9 680 391	4 361 361
1952	11 945 059	6 373 080	5 571 979	2 712 396
1953	9 911 430	5 840 100	4 071 330	2 142 109
1954	7 678 884	5 484 960	2 193 924	1 106 365
1955	5 259 079	3 848 815	1 410 264	600 714
1956	5 035 202	3 718 400	1 316 802	668 033
1957	4 153 510	3 121 041	1 032 469	458 495
1958	5 333 972	3 329 028	2 004 944	758 232
1959	9 093 610	3 733 860	5 359 750	2 170 913
1960	7 011 614	3 593 172	3 418 442	1 416 267
1961	n.a.	n.a.	–	–
1962	3 426 334	3 880 512	−454 178(gain)	−181 899
1963	4 077 839	2 783 160	1 294 679	810 585
1964	4 365 084	2 783 040	1 582 044	855 081
1965	5 757 034	2 523 174	3 233 860	1 517 454
1966	5 313 725	2 349 168	2 964 557	1 167 403
1967	184 518	1 400 154[1]	−1 215 636(gain)	−1 102 039
1968	9 647 767	2 642 220	7 005 547	3 265 263
1969	3 714 675	2 539 530	1 175 145	786 078
1970	4 660 715	2 587 156	2 073 559	1 568 546
1971	4 298 248	2 361 300	1 936 948	1 650 200
1972	2 012 424	2 049 300	−36 876(gain)	123 800

[1] Estimate

Source: Table 7.2 and J. Levi, *et al.*, op. cit..

In the summer of 1961 the peasant in Souanke received 85 CFA francs for a kilogram of cocoa, which came to 104 francs delivered to Pointe-Noire. The world price there would have been 66 francs. The Congolese budget paid the difference, but because it had an increased deficit, was unable to make investments, and 'held out its hand' for foreign aid to balance the budget, instead of 'rolling up its sleeves'.[25]

The gain from this kind of special treatment by France, and later the European Economic Community (EEC), did not of course accrue directly to export-crop cultivators but to the Funds, which were thus able to accumulate surpluses and export duties while paying producers' prices that were, in general, much closer to (or even above) the prices they would have received in the free market. The Funds and governments accumulated surpluses and taxes, therefore, through European subsidies much more than by effective taxation of indigenous cultivators and in complete contrast to the situation in the Anglophone countries. In Togo, for example, Fund surpluses during the early sixties were about the same order of magnitude as the financial advantage from French support.[26] We have seen what these arrangements can mean in terms of economic effects: the French-speaking countries did not inflict economic losses upon themselves through interventionist policy to anything like the extent that the English-speaking countries did; moreover, the Anglophone loss was a Francophone gain, for it involved a unilateral supply restriction and kept up world prices to the benefit of all countries, including competing ones.

The above analysis of the economic effects of taxing versus subsidising exports in the two African blocs omits any discussion of the dynamic effects. We have seen the evidence for the influence of current prices on current supplies, but there was probably also an effect on the level of investment in the same direction. High producer-prices for perennials would tend to stimulate additional planting and low prices would hold such investment back. Thus, for example, these pricing policies we have described must have dampened investment in coffee trees in Uganda while encouraging it in Ivory Coast, although any attempt at quantifying this effect can only be speculative. Even high prices for annual crops have evidently induced capital formation, as we have seen (Chapter 6) in the case of ploughing in Gombe Emirate, Nigeria (cotton) and in The Gambia (groundnuts).

References

1 Margaret Haswell's classic study of a Gambian village, in the late forties, is still unsurpassed in standard. M.R. Haswell, *Economics of Agriculture in a Savannah Village*, Colonial Research Studies, No. 8, HMSO, 1953.
2 A. Killick and R.W. During, 'A structural approach to the balance of payments of a low-income country', *Journal of Development Studies*, July 1969.
3 S. Amin, *Neo-Colonialism in West Africa*, Penguin, Harmondsworth, 1973.
4 G.L. Beckford, 'The economics of agricultural resource use and development in plantation economies', *Social and Economic Studies*, Vol. 18, 1969, pp. 321–47; also in H. Bernstein (ed.), *Underdevelopment and Development*, Penguin, Harmondsworth, 1973.
5 '.....most bananas sold in Britain and other Western countries are marketed by two companies, which buy the crop from plantations (which may themselves not be independent) in a number of developing countries. The companies are virtually monopoly purchasers who can set "world" prices at a level to suit their own interests', K. Morton and P. Tullock, *Trade and Developing Countries*, Croom Helm, London, 1977, p. 98.
6 R.W. Clower, G. Dalton, M. Harwitz and A.A. Walters, *Growth Without Development. An Economic Survey of Liberia*, Evanston, Illinois, North Western University Press, 1966.
7 *ibid.* p. 158.
8 Recall that in Ghana about 80 per cent of cocoa production comes from about 30 000 farms averaging 45·3 hectares, and in the Ivory Coast in 1965, about 20 000 planters owned nearly a quarter of the land in the main export crop areas.
9 R. Galletti, K.D.S. Baldwin and I.O. Dina, *Nigerian Cocoa Farmers,* Oxford University Press, 1956, p. 145.

10 See A.I. Richards, F. Sturrock and J.M. Fortt, *Subsistence to Commercial Farming in Present Day Buganda*, Cambridge University Press, 1973.

11 Polly Hill, *Migrant Cocoa Farmers of Southern Ghana*, Cambridge University Press, 1963.

12 The same sort of argument had been applied to the supply of labour in response to changes in the wage rate.

13 e.g. W.O. Jones, 'Economic man in Africa', *Food Research Institute Studies*, Vol. 1, May 1960.

14 Strictly speaking oil palms are of course perennials, but, in the case of Sierra Leone at least, the evidence is that most of the planting and nurturing of the palms occurred from about the early 1900s to about the 1920s and that thereafter the number of bearing palms was far in excess of that warranted by actual palm oil and kernel production. See J. Levi, M. Havinden, O. Johnson and G. Karr, *African Agriculture: Economic Action and Reaction in Sierra Leone*, Commonwealth Agricultural Bureaux, Farnham, 1976, Chapters 2 and 4.

15 R.M. Stern, 'Determinants of cocoa supply in West Africa', in H. Ord and I.G. Stewart, (eds), *African Primary Products and International Trade*, Edinburgh University Press, 1965.

16 Sara S. Berry, 'Supply response reconsidered: cocoa in western Nigeria, 1909–44', *Journal of Development Studies*, Vol. 13, No. 1, October 1976.

17 Further evidence supporting Berry's conclusion is found in Polly Hill, *op. cit.* See also G.K. Helleiner, 'Smallholder decision-making: tropical African evidence', (p. 43) in L.G. Reynolds (ed.), *Agriculture in Development Theory*, Yale University Press, 1975.

18 P.T. Bauer, *West African Trade. A Study of Competition, Oligopoly and Monopoly in a Changing Economy*, Cambridge University Press, 1954 (re-issued 1963).

19 G.K. Helleiner, 'The fiscal role of the Marketing Boards in Nigerian economic development', *Economic Journal*, Vol. 74, 1964, pp. 582–610.

20 *ibid.*, p. 603.

21 Whether the way in which such gains were distributed domestically was desirable, is another matter, though.

22 One difference which is not of much economic significance is that the *Caisses de Stabilisation des Prix* did not actually perform any of the marketing functions themselves, but left these to private companies and simply dictated the official prices, duties, etc., unlike the Marketing Boards, which did take over a large part, but not all, of the marketing operations.

23 International Monetary Fund, Africa Department Study Group, 'Financial arrangements of the CFA Franc Zone', *I.M.F. Staff Papers*, July 1969.

24 In the mid-sixties, the annual *per capita* cash income of coffee-growers in lower Ivory Coast was approximately $80, about four times the figure for the Central Department See J.C. de Wilde *et al.*, *Experiences with Agricultural Development in Tropical*

Africa, Vol. II, Johns Hopkins University Press, Baltimore, 1967, p. 395.

25 R. Dumont, *False Start in Africa*, Sphere Books and Andre Deutsch, 1966, p. 179.

26 U. Tun Wai, E.L. Bornemann, M.M. Martin and P.E. Berthe, 'The economy of Togo', *I.M.F. Staff Papers*, November 1965.

8 Agricultural policy: history

Inevitably past decisions influence present and future courses of action, in agricultural policy as in other fields of government activity. Past investments in trained manpower and in physical plant (research stations, experimental farms, training colleges, etc.) often determine what is currently possible. More important, perhaps, are the intellectual traditions and habits of thought of the past. They often live on and continue to have an influence on politicians, officials, and other policy-makers when the conditions to which they were relevant no longer exist. This intellectual 'drag effect' of the past is well-known to economists and was amusingly highlighted by Keynes in his famous aphorism about self-styled 'practical' men being slaves to the out-dated ideas of long-dead economists. There is, of course, much in the history of past policies which is useful and constructive; but one needs to bear in mind the need for constant re-evaluation to ensure that policies remain fully relevant to current needs and are not continued merely through force of habit.

The development of agricultural policy in Africa may be approached from many points of view, such as changes over time, distinctions between regions, distinctions between colonial and non-colonial policies, or between export and domestic food-production policies, and many others. There is, however, one broad distinction which cuts across all the others, namely whether government policy was fundamentally concerned with stimulating and helping indigenous farmers (as it was broadly in West and Central Africa) or whether it was attempting to establish a white-settler community in addition to, and frequently in competition with, local farmers (as classically in South Africa and Zimbabwe, but also in many parts of East and Central Africa).[1] Clearly where government policy was concerned primarily with the establishment and development of settler communities it had very little relevance for African farmers (except of a negative kind, such as the packing of farmers into 'native reserves' or restrictions on the crops which could be grown, as with coffee in Kenya before 1937).[2]

In most African countries, though, policy was not so simple as suggested by the extreme cases listed above. Even in nations like Kenya, where the non-indigenous settlers were very important, they were still restricted to certain relatively small areas of the country, and government policy had to concern itself positively with the large areas where increased production could only come from the efforts of the African population. It goes without saying, however, that in countries where the main thrust of policy was to establish and encourage immigrant settlers (primarily Zimbabwe and Angola, but Kenya, Zambia, Malawi, Mozambique and Tanzania to a lesser extent) the long-term effects on indigenous farming were mainly harmful; though in some cases Africans later benefited by being able to take over the farms created by former settlers, as in Kenya. In view of the lack of future relevance for this type of policy, it is not proposed to investigate its history any further, except where the effects of past decisions still exercise a continuing influence. The same may be said also for the related policy of establishing non-indigenous plantations. This had some importance in a few countries, like Zaïre, Mozambique and Ivory Coast; but in general this phase also is now passed.

Again at a very general level it is probably true that there was a major shift in agricultural policy in nearly all African countries during the 1930s. Basically this was a shift from the encouragement of export crops to concentration on food production for the local market. Obviously there were many regional and local variations to this general pattern. For instance, some countries like Zambia and Tanganyika had never been so export-orientated as others, like Nigeria and Zaïre; but despite such variations a general swing in policy is noticeable in the 1930s, although it did not become operative in some countries until somewhat later. The causes of the change of emphasis were no doubt manifold and complex, but two main factors were probably dominant: first, the dramatic fall of export prices during the slump of 1929–34 damaged faith in export crop production as a route to prosperity (see Chapter 3 for some details). Secondly the population of most countries was steadily growing, and with it the demand for food. The estimated population of Africa nearly doubled between 1920 and 1960 (from 141 to 254 millions) and the rate of increase probably accelerated throughout this period.[3]

More significantly, the urban component (whether commercial, professional, or industrial) was growing much more dramatically, as can be seen in Table 8.1, which shows population changes in eight major African cities between the 1930s and the 1970s. Between the 1930s and the 1950s they all more than doubled, four of them grew by over 400 per cent, and one (Abidjan, capital of the Ivory Coast) by no less than 1 180 per cent! Between the 1950s and the 1970s, the rate of increase of most of them slowed down slightly (Abidjan again leading with 603 per cent), but the absolute size was of a completely different order of magnitude, and presented severe problems of food supply, amongst a host of other difficulties. In the 1930s only two of these cities had a population of more than 100 000 (Addis Ababa and Lagos). By the 1950s, four were already between 300 000 and 400 000, whereas by the 1970s, the smallest had 475 000 (Luanda), five had over 700 000, and three had over a million, with Kinshasa, capital of Zaïre leaping into the lead with 2 008 000 people.

Thus even in the 1930s and 1940s, these expanding urban markets for foods enabled many farmers to leave export production and to concentrate on serving these local markets. Not only basic cereals like millet, sorghum, maize and rice were needed; but also a wide range of perishable products such as fruit, vegetables, eggs, cheese and meat. Agricultural policy shifted accordingly and usually with benefit.

Table 8.1
Urban growth in selected cities (c. 1930 – c. 1970)

City	Population 1930s	Population 1950s	Percentage increase since 1930s	Population 1970s	Percentage increase since 1950s
Kinshasa Zaïre	36 000 (1938)	300 000 (1955)	733	2 008 000 (1974)	569
Lagos Nigeria	126 000 (1931)	312 000 (1956)	148	1 477 000 (1975)	373
Addis Ababa Ethiopia	150 000 (1936)	400 000 (1952)	167	1 161 000 (1975)	190
Abidjan Ivory Coast	10 000 (1931)	128 000 (1955)	1 180	900 000 (1976)	603
Accra Ghana	70 000 (1931)	388 000 (1960)	454	738 000 (1970)	90
Nairobi Kenya	65 000 (1939)	210 000 (1956)	223	630 000 (1973)	200
Salisbury Zimbabwe	33 000 (1936)	168 000 (1956)	409	502 000 (1973)	199
Luanda Angola	40 000 (1934)	190 000 (1955)	375	475 000 (1970)	150

Sources: Adapted from Table 8.1 in M.J. Herskovits and M. Harwitz (eds), *Economic Transition in Africa* (1964) p. 161 (The 1936 estimate for Addis Ababa is taken from the *Encyclopaedia Britannica* article on Abyssinia); *UN Demographic Yearbook*, 1975, pp. 253–5; and *Africa South of the Sahara, 1979–80* (Europa Pubs., London, 1979).

Whereas previously, taxation policy, transport development and advisory (extension) services had concentrated on trying to boost exports, this had had the effect of favouring a minority of farmers, for the great majority were usually more concerned with food production than with export crops. More seriously where the export crop was non-edible, such as cotton, sisal or tobacco, it could actually endanger food supplies by pre-empting land at the expense of food crops. It might be thought that if food was in short supply it would fetch a higher price than the export crops, and so such pre-emption would not arise. This was not necessarily so. Export-crop prices were determined by overseas (not local) markets. Similarly imported food might keep local prices down, and even undercut local farmers who were unable to switch to export crop production by reason of poor soil, lack of capital, etc. This situation was particularly serious in the Zambian copper belt, where it encouraged the movement of men out of farming and into migrant labour in mining. By 1956, 86 per cent of male wage earners in Zambia were already outside agriculture and forestry.[4] This increased the dependency on imported food. In years of high prices for copper exports this was not too serious, but in years of low copper prices, it led to severe strains on the balance of payments, because the supply of imported food could not be suddenly cut off.

For reasons of this kind, the governments of African countries were beginning to place their primary emphasis on food production for their own domestic markets in the 1930s. This trend was strengthened by the events of World War II (1939–45) when both export markets and supplies of imports were cut off by military action or its associated transport shortages. In the immediate postwar period (1945–51) with its shortages of raw materials and foods (and consequent high prices) there was a natural revival of interest in exports, but governmental policies in general, did not swing back to their former almost exclusive obsession with them.

From a logical point of view it would be desirable to survey the development of agricultural policy on a regional basis, since geographical variation is such an important factor; but owing to the fact that agricultural policies have their roots in colonial organisations and services which ignored regional economies, this approach makes for difficulties. The integrated and centralised nature of colonial agricultural services imposed a common pattern on countries in widely separated regions. This common tradition therefore provides the most convenient approach to the evolution of agricultural policy.

Agricultural policy in Anglophone countries

As with so much else in British administration, the early stages of agricultural policy evolved out of the day-to-day needs of the different colonies, and it was only in the 1920s and the 1930s, that these experiences began to be distilled into an integrated approach towards common problems. This common approach was facilitated by the constant movement of British officials from one country to another (and this was not only in Africa but amongst other tropical areas such as the West Indies, Malaya, Sri Lanka and Polynesia). Thus the advantages of comparability and flexibility were maximised; but the cost was often an inadequate knowledge and experience of particular areas.[5]

At first, however, this centralising tendency was weak. In fact the agricultural branch of the colonial administration was not separately organised as a specialist service until 1935 and it did not produce an official policy statement until 1945.[6] Nevertheless most of the African countries had Agricultural Departments before 1914, although a few had to wait until the 1920s. These Departments were very small and were always under-staffed and under-financed, but they provided the government with some sort of professional advice in formulating policy.

Since the economy of all tropical African countries was overwhelmingly agricultural this relative neglect of the subject seems surprising. It has to be remembered though that Britain itself was a highly industrialised country in which farming was relatively insignificant, so that British officials were not accustomed to treating the subject as an important one. More important still all British officials were imbued with the *laissez-faire* view that governments should concern themselves with economic affairs as little as possible. As a corollary to this was the Treasury doctrine that all colonies should be financially self-supporting (except in special cases like Sierra Leone where the British government had been responsible for settling the slaves rescued at sea, and where it felt a sense of moral responsibility – albeit rather a limited one).[7]

In fact, had it not been for financial pressures, it is doubtful whether British colonial administrations would have had any agricultural policy at all. But the colonial administrations had to be paid for, which meant that revenue had to be raised. There were not many ways in which this could be done. By far the easiest was by customs duties, and this was the preferred method where foreign trade was sufficiently large to raise the desired sums. Where it was not it was necessary to fall back on some form of poll-tax or house-tax, always unpopular, and sometimes difficult and expensive to collect.[8]

In either case the effect on agriculture was similar. It meant greater emphasis on products which could be sold for cash to pay the taxes, and the British naturally preferred export crops for which there was a demand in Britain, such as cotton, palm oil, cocoa, groundnuts, etc. Generally speaking in West Africa the main response to the need for a cash income was an increase in agricultural exports (although this was of course not the only – or even the main – reason for such an increase) but in East and southern Africa the response was often different – driving workers out of farming into the new mines of South Africa or Zimbabwe to pay the taxes. Occasionally this also happened in West Africa where the supply of labour for the gold mines in Ghana was stimulated by poll taxes in neighbouring French colonies.[9]

In this situation the main task of agricultural policy became to facilitate the introduction of export crops. Sometimes this could be done fairly simply by allowing traders and railways to 'open-up' the country so that the production of some of its natural plants could be increased for export. Palm oil in Nigeria and groundnuts in The Gambia are obvious examples.[10] The next step was the introduction of a new crop from another tropical environment. Here Britain's long experience of tropical agriculture in other parts of the world proved most useful. The Royal Botanic Gardens at Kew had been founded as early as 1759 and had been exchanging plants with Botanical Gardens in India, Asia, the West Indies and South America for a very long time. Notable successes had been the introduction of tea into Sri Lanka in the 1860s and rubber to Malaya in 1877.[11]

This process was continued with the new African colonies. The Aburi Botanical Garden in Ghana (established in 1890) played a part in the introduction of cocoa to the country (though the role of Tetteh Quarshie in smuggling in seeds from Fernando Po may have been more important). The introduction of American cotton to Uganda and the Sudan and of pyrethrum to Kenya are other examples of this first phase of agricultural policy. The task was relatively easy, and where conditions were right, as in the case of Ghanaian cocoa and Ugandan cotton, results could be not only rapid, but almost sensational.

Although the establishment of new crops has never stopped, it has long ceased to provide the easy successes of the early years, and from about 1920 onwards agricultural policy began to shift towards new approaches. Here the lack of clearly-defined objectives had a negative effect. Colonial governments could never really make up their minds about what they wanted to do. They were hampered by paternalistic conceptions of trusteeship and protecting their 'wards' from the possibly undesirable influence of contacts with commercial 'civilisation' which would undermine the social stability and political cohesion of traditional societies. Hence by implication the traditional farming systems on which these were based should be preserved. Yet governments were also conscious of the need for increased productivity as the population rose. Moreover they were further hampered by a commitment to 'indirect rule' which made it very difficult to propose changes in any branches of traditional social organisation without the consent of the chiefs. By the nature of things the chiefs were the people with the strongest vested interest in the *status quo*. This aspect of British policy is one which contrasted most strongly with French and Portuguese policy. Neither of these powers hesitated to upset traditional arrangements, and yet the practical results of this difference were negligible. The French and the Portuguese had the ability to act more positively than the British, but they seldom used it constructively. It was political control, not agricultural improvement, that they were primarily interested in.

This inability to work out a coherent long-term strategy for agricultural development meant that policy was unduly subject to passing fashions (often imported from abroad) or to pressures from powerful individuals (usually Directors of Agriculture) who pursued particular enthusiasms. Examples of the influence of fashions were the campaign for soil conservation in the 1930s, the brief enthusiasm for group farming schemes in the 1940s, and the passion for grandiose, mechanical projects in the same decade. The influence of powerful individuals can be seen in Kenya where R.J.M. Swynnerton's 1954 *Plan to Intensify the Development of African Agriculture in Kenya* had an important effect, especially on the reorganisation of farm layouts. Swynnerton's plan, in fact, was part of a not-fully-formulated British policy in East Africa, which had been smouldering for a long time – namely to encourage the break-up of traditional farming and tenurial relationships and to replace them by individually-owned, and commercially-run, farms producing for the market. The political and social implications of this policy were so far reaching that the East African colonial governments could never finally decide whether they wished to implement it or not; but partial programmes, mainly in Kenya and Uganda, went some way towards breaking up the indigenous peasant societies, and towards the creation of new classes in the rural areas. The political tensions which sprang from these moves, during the growth of nationalism in the 1950s, were powerful deterrents against further action.[12]

In Nigeria, a powerful Director of Agriculture, O.J. Faulkner, had a deep influence in the 1930s. He insisted that useful agricultural advice could not be given unless it was based on research carried out in local conditions, and tested and verified by experiment. As a result his Department became very research orientated, and extension work, which was considered more important elsewhere (especially in East Africa), was rather soft-pedalled.[13] Faulkner's emphasis on research was very important and the unified research stations which were set up in West Africa provide an early example of the co-operative way in which research should be carried on, even though they were under-financed and rather late in being established. It was not until 1944 that the Cocoa Research Station of the Gold Coast at Tafo became the West African Cocoa Research Institute; not until 1949 that the Sierra Leone Experimental Rice station at Rokupr (founded 1934) likewise had its functions broadened; and not till 1951 that the Nigerian Oil Palm Research Station at Benin was similarly reorganised. A weakness was the failure to link up with related institutions in the Francophone countries (although there were some contacts, as when an Anglo-French conference on livestock was held at Jos in Nigeria just after World War II, and an international conference on African soils was held at Goma in Zaïre in 1948 at which representatives from Anglophone countries in East and West Africa were present). But such contacts were rather informal and spasmodic. In 1950 the United Nations established the Commission for Technical Co-operation in Africa South of the Sahara (CCTA) with headquarters in Paris, to try to improve contacts, but the task is by its nature a difficult one.[14]

Unfortunately the unified research stations of Anglophone West Africa reverted to a purely national basis after their component countries became independent, and it is only recently that efforts have been made to re-establish them – but this time on a wider regional basis. Since fundamental research can be expensive and its results long-term, it makes good sense to share the costs – especially as successful research, as with locust control, or the suppression of coffee mealybug parasites, can have enormous economic benefits. What would Ghana save if a method for controlling swollen-shoot disease in cocoa could be discovered; and how much more would this have been if it had happened thirty years ago?

It is quite possible that Faulkner was right to believe that the encouragement of research is the most important way in which governmental policy can help agriculture; but it is a slow method, and the results are useless unless they can be communicated to the farming population in a form which enables improved methods to be voluntarily and enthusiastically integrated into the farming system. This is the role of an extension service and it is one which can pay high dividends provided that certain predisposing conditions exist. The most important of these are that the farming population perceive the need for new methods or new techniques and that the innovations offered by the extension service are ones which can be integrated into the farming system without causing pressures or tensions in other parts of that delicate mechanism. In African farming systems, where the amount of labour available *at critical times of the year* (such as bush-burning, sowing and harvesting) is often the most important constraint with regard to increasing production, it follows that the extension workers must have a thorough knowledge of the system in all its parts, and particularly of the economic and social implications of any proposed changes. It was in this area that the colonial agricultural extension services were at their weakest. Inevitably with all senior posts held by expatriates (this began to change in the late 1950s) and with Departments seriously understaffed (there were only 20 agricultural officers in the whole of Nigeria in 1920, though their number had increased to 82 by 1938) the detailed knowledge necessary for an effective extension service was lacking.[15] This weakness was increased by the almost total neglect of agricultural economics – a weakness which was still very noticeable in the 1960s.[16]

With the knowledge of hindsight it is clear that certain crucial decisions of the 1920s about the organisation of extension services, although inspired by the desire for reform, were unfortunate in their results.

The first of these relates to staffing and sprang from the report of the committee set up in 1919 to investigate recruitment problems under the chairmanship of Sir Herbert Read. The Read report (1920) rightly recognised that there would be a need 'for skilled scientific assistance on a scale much larger than heretofore' and it placed strong emphasis on the need for highly trained recruits.

> Second-rate officers are worse than useless where scientific aid is in question; the service of any but first-rate men is not only uneconomical, but may be expected to lead to disaster . . . . The type of man required to make a good agricultural officer is of a very high order. Not merely must he be a highly qualified technical expert, fitted by his scientific training to grapple with and overcome the problems that will arise in the work of his department, or to carry out independent research work that will lead to valuable improvements in the methods of planting and raising tropical crops, but he must also be endowed by his general education and upbringing with the tact and administrative ability necessary for dealing with the native mind.[17]

Despite the quaint phrasing of the final sentence these criteria are mainly admirable, but they carried certain implications which may not have been fully apparent at the time. The fact that the higher branches of the service were to be confined to expatriates was regrettably an implicit assumption of the political thinking of that period, which only partly can be excused by the fact that there were hardly any colonial universities capable of teaching agricultural science; especially since training in extension work could have been provided.

Equally serious was the implication that entry to the service was to be limited to those who had undergone some form of university training (either at degree or certificate level). The effect of this was to ensure, that although the service would contain high quality personnel, recruitment would always be small and the staffing problem would be almost insoluble. In fact average entry was around 25 officers a year in the inter-war period and rose to a peak of 57 in 1956. During its whole history the entire senior staff barely topped 1 000. In 1925 there were only 150 Agricultural Officers serving 51 million people in 38 territories at an average of one for every 333 000 people.[18] The logical solution to the educational problem would have been to found agricultural colleges in the more populous colonies for the purpose of training indigenous extension workers. This would have been more economical than using expatriates, with their expensive foreign-leave requirements and constant health problems; and also more efficient since the local students would have had a fuller understanding of the farming systems they were trying to improve, and fewer language problems. Unfortunately such a solution would have been inconceivable to British colonial policy-makers before 1945 for a complex of reasons which are too well known to merit further discussion. Instead a compromise was arrived at by establishing the Imperial College of Tropical Agriculture in Trinidad (during 1921–24). To this college the Colonial office sent 20 postgraduates each year for a one-year course to be followed by a second year at Cambridge University in England.[19] This compromise solution was far better than nothing (and the Trinidad College benefited from some excellent staff) but from an African point of view, this was still very much a second-best solution. The provision of adequate agricultural training within Africa was still neglected, and some of the few University Colleges which then existed, such as Fourah Bay College in Sierra Leone, had no faculties of agriculture. It was not until the 1950s that the newly-formed University Colleges of tropical Africa were able to offer degrees in agriculture and related sciences, and not until the 1960s that their graduates were ready to occupy senior positions in their national agricultural research and extension services.[20]

One of the biggest weaknesses of agricultural policy in the past, and one which is only now being remedied, was the lack of detailed and reliable knowledge of the rural economy in all its facets. When one considers that governments of the pre-independence period did not even have adequate censuses of their populations it is perhaps not very surprising that they also lacked knowledge of the agrarian structure and production processes. When there was ignorance about such fundamental matters as the pattern of land tenure, the size of farms, the products produced, the labour supply, marketing networks and the whole vast field of farm economics, it is not really surprising that poli-cy-makers floundered. Apart from export-crop statistics they had very little hard knowledge on which to base their policies; although, in fair-ness, it should be acknowledged that Agricultural Departments built up quite large files of basic information from the annual reports of their field staff. What they lacked were systematic, published surveys and statistics of a comprehensive nature. This failure did not spring from shortcomings on the part of the Departments, but from their chronic neglect by colonial governments. Thus it was the long-continued and fundamental failure to rectify this situation, which lies at the root of the ineffectiveness of early agricultural policy rather than the failure of any specific projects or programmes.

Agricultural policy in Francophone countries

This section includes not only former French and Belgian colonies, but also the mandated territories which had been German colonies until 1918. These were Cameroun and Togo (French mandates) and Rwan-da and Burundi (Belgian mandates). For all practical purposes these mandates were treated as if they were colonies, and their agricultural policy (such as it was) did not differ materially from that in neighbour-ing territories.

Basically agricultural policy was rather negative in all these coun-tries in the pre-independence period. Indigenous farming was generally neglected (although there were some important exceptions) or more seriously was positively harmed by policies designed to facilitate the spread of foreign-owned plantations or concession companies.

On the question of concessions there was considerable regional variation. In general in former French West Africa, (*Afrique Occi-dentale Française*, subsequently referred to as AOF) where indige-nous agriculture was fairly developed and was capable of a spon-taneous response to export market opportunities (as most noticeably with Senegalese groundnuts) the granting of concessions was fairly li-mited. The main exception to this was in the Ivory Coast where about 90 500 hectares had been alienated to French plantation owners by 1938.[21] They concentrated on coffee and cocoa, but only provided about 5 per cent of Ivory Coast's exports of these crops. In the same year Governor Boisson of Cameroun announced that European colonisa-tion had reached its fill and that he had stopped it in Cameroun. Short-ly after he became Governor-General of the AOF and had an oppor-tunity to extend his policy, though he hardly needed it since the war, and France's defeat in 1940, put a stop to French colonisation for the time being. The new French policy was however confirmed at the Brazzaville conference of 1944 where General de Gaulle rallied the French African colonies to the Free French cause by offering them a much more prominent role in a new French Union. Nevertheless, it was not until 1955 that the land law was changed and France finally abandoned the concessions policy.[22]

In the lands of the Zaïre basin (both those under French and Bel-gian rule) the policy of alienating land was pursued much more vigor-ously and generally with unfortunate (and at times vicious) results. In these lands the population density was lower than in the AOF, and people were less inclined to enter the export trade without compulsion. During the world rubber boom (*c.* 1890–1910) the concession companies licensed by King Leopold of Belgium in his so-called Congo 'Free' state, became notorious for their cruelty and rapacity. Recent research has shown that, not only did they oppress the people, but their greed was self-defeating: by 1906 the rubber supplies had become so depleted that there was no longer any profit to be obtained.[23] Yet, even after Belgium took over the Congo 'Free' State in 1908, and suppressed the more notorious companies, the policy of granting concessions was continued. In 1911, Lever Brothers, having failed to obtain land for oil palm plantations from the French and British administrations, secured an enormous concession from the Belgians. This consisted of a lease (until 1945) of 5 circles, each of 120 km (75 miles) in diameter, and containing some of the richest palm forest in central Africa. Levers established highly successful plantations on these sites, but in so doing restricted the opportunities for the indigenous population to engage in the trade, except as labourers on the plantations. This in its turn reduced the labour supply for local food production.[24]

In former French Equatorial Africa (*Afrique Equatoriale Française*, or AEF) the concessions policy was also initially pushed on a massive scale. During 1899, 40 companies, containing Belgian as well as French interests secured 30-year monopoly leases on 665 000 km², distributed as shown in Table 8.2.

Table 8.2   Land owned by concession companies

Concessions area	km²
Lower Oubangui	202 000
Songha basin	152 000
Upper Oubangui	140 000
Gabon	82 000
Lower Congo	79 000
Chad basin	10 000
	665 000

Practically the whole of Gabon and Congo/Brazzaville were included in these leases, and much of the Central African Republic. Each company had monopoly rights (other than mining) for all natural products in its territory, which were at that date mainly wild rubber, ivory and timber. The companies were empowered to levy a head-tax on the population, which was collected by means of contributions in kind of these and other products required by the companies. In this way the inhabitants were diverted from their own agricultural (or collecting) activities, into providing tribute for the concessionaires. The intention was that on the expiry of the leases (in 1929) the companies would have been able to retain as freehold property any land which they had improved and cultivated, and any forest from which wild rubber had been regularly collected.

In the event there was so much criticism of the companies' methods of extorting produce from their territories, that the French government changed its policies (*c.* 1914) and decided that they would limit concessions after 1929, and greatly reduce the area to be allotted as freeholds. However, this policy was not fully implemented. Several large concessions survived beyond 1929, and more seriously, policy continued to confine the production of export crops to European-owned plantations.[25] As a result agriculture stagnated throughout the AEF until 1945. Only after that date when the *Fonds d'Investissement pour le Développement Economique et Social* (FIDES) were set up was more rapid progress possible, and even then achievements were not dramatic.

An equally important reform of the post-war period was the abolition of forced labour throughout Francophone Africa. It was appropriate that the AEF, where this burden had been most severe, should have been largely responsible for this reform, as a reward for being the only part of the former French Empire to support General de Gaulle and his Free French movement after the fall of France in 1940. That forced labour should have survived so long in French (as well as in Belgian and Portuguese) Africa was a primary reason why so many plans for improvement were unsuccessful.[26] Governmental policies for agriculture which have to be forced on the people are almost always bound to fail.

The well-known French agronomist, René Dumont, emphasised this point strongly when criticising Belgian policy in Zaïre. The Belgians had believed in the slogan 'no elites, no problems'. As a result they had refused to allow any higher education in Zaïre (until 1955) and also refused to allow anyone to go abroad for study. Their whole emphasis had been on automatic obedience to orders from above. Dumont tells how in 1953 a Belgian colleague had rebuked him for writing that in Zaïre,

> The peasant springs to attention before the agronomist; those not fulfilling the directives of the Plan ran the risk of going to prison, eight days if they have not cleared the land, fifteen days if they have not harvested, up to a month if they have not burned the stalks after the harvest to prevent the spread of parasitic insects.

He comments that as a result of his Belgian colleague's remonstrances he had later toned down his remarks, but after the disastrous effects of such policies had become more apparent he wished he had kept to his original version.[27] His point is that it is useless to attempt to *coerce* farmers into obeying instructions from extension workers. The farmers must understand the purpose of any proposed changes, and incorporate them voluntarily, if new systems or methods are to have any long-term effect. It is amazing that it took so long for this simple, self-evident, proposition to sink in.

The long-term effects of such policies can lead to a loss of confidence in extension services or other government-backed organisations which may take years to overcome. Another example comes from the history of co-operative marketing societies in the AOF. The formation of such societies was a sensible idea, and so was official encouragement; but when encouragement turned to coercion and control, people were turned against the co-operative idea. These societies were called *Sociétés Indigenes de Prévoyances* (SIP). Their origins go back to before 1910 in the Sine Saloum area of southern Senegal where a *Commandant de Cercle* founded one to lend seed to farmers. Private traders had been making loans for this purpose at interest rates of 200 to 300 per cent. The SIP charged only 5 per cent and repayment was in seed for the following year. The idea spread, and in 1910 the Societies were recognised by a government decree. It was decided to charge a membership fee and raise the rate of interest to 25 per cent. In 1915 membership was made compulsory in Senegal (in direct contravention of the principles of the co-operative movement generally). By 1923 the *Commandants de Cercles* had become Presidents *ex officio*, replacing the Senegalese farmers who had originally held the position.

During the depression of 1930–33 the SIPs spread widely throughout the AOF and *compulsory* grain storage was added to their functions in 1935. Again, the storage of grain as an insurance against a bad harvest was a sensible idea in principle, but farmers were often ordered to bring in more than they could really spare. The normal quota was 100–150 kilos of grain for everyone except children. This caused hardship, which was sometimes aggravated when poor storage facilities ruined much of the grain.[28] Governments would be well advised to encourage genuine co-operative societies, but organisations like the SIPs can only bring the whole idea into disrepute. Unfortunately the harm resulting from such past mistakes can be remembered for a long time and can make the work of future extension workers much more difficult than it need be.

Francophone countries also suffered from the same tendency as Anglophone ones to place excessive reliance on large-scale, mechanised schemes, aimed at bringing dramatic improvements in a short period. The most famous of these was the irrigation scheme for the inland-Niger delta in Mali, known as the *Office du Niger*. This scheme has been analysed in detail by a World Bank study, which revealed it as yet another example of governments' regrettable tendency to plunge into complex situations, and to invest huge sums of money before they have obtained the basic ecological, economic and social data which are the absolutely essential prerequisites for all such schemes.[29]

In sum, the history of governmental policies in the Francophone countries was characterised by an unfortunate mixture of overall neglect of agricultural development at the village level combined with a rigidly autocratic approach when intervention did occur. This is not to say that individual extension workers did not on occasion provide valuable advice and encouragement. In particular government research stations did useful work, such as the groundnut experiment station at M'Bambey in Senegal, which bred and distributed improved seed over a wide area. There was a marked improvement in all aspects of governmental policies after about 1955, and much larger investments; but the earlier traditions of agricultural policy had not left a very well-cultivated seed-bed for these new plants to grow in.

Policy in Portuguese-speaking countries

Portuguese colonial policy was in some ways similar to French, but much more rigid and authoritarian and much less well financed. The similarity came from the shared attitude that the overseas parts of their empires were not colonies, but were integral parts of the metropole. Thus Portugal pretended that Angola, Mozambique and Guinea–Bissau were all parts of Portugal – from which it followed that Portuguese citizens should be allowed (and encouraged) to settle there. Agricultural policy in these territories, therefore was concerned almost exclusively with setting-up Portuguese planters in the export-trade for such products as coffee, cocoa, palm oil, sugar and sisal. This involved ensuring that the local inhabitants were not enabled to compete in the production of these products; and that the colonists were always kept well supplied with cheap and docile labour.[30] Of course, it was not possible to keep export production entirely in foreign hands, and in 1965 it was estimated that some 60 000 Angolans were growing coffee, and that almost all the cotton for export was indigenously produced. In Mozambique, local farmers produced cotton and cashew nuts for export, although, again, the major share of all export crops was reserved by law to foreign-owned monopoly companies, who were empowered to force the farmers within their concession areas to produce particular crops. The producers were only allowed to sell to the monopoly companies who could thus pay prices well below what the products would have fetched on a free market.

From all this it can be seen that Portuguese governmental policies were, in general, harmful in those areas where they were effective. A mitigating factor was that Portuguese colonial administration was thinly stretched over vast areas and hence its influence was limited. However, even in the food-producing sector, where government policy left the people a freer hand, its effects were sometimes negative. For instance between 1935 and 1962 there seems to have been a sharp fall in the cattle population of Angola if the regional figures in Table 8.3 are indicative of national trends.[31]

Table 8.3 Numbers of cattle in Angola

Year	Huila District	Mocamedes District
1935	over 1 million	300 000
1962	705 000	87 000

By the 1960s Portuguese misrule had generated armed nationalist opposition, first in Angola (1961), then in Guinea–Bissau (1963) and finally Mozambique (1964). It is clear that discontent in the rural areas, caused by progressive impoverishment, was an important causal factor, exacerbated by the Portuguese policy of sending people from Angola and Mozambique to work as contract labourers in the mines of Zambia and South Africa – a policy which was itself necessitated by the economic stagnation in the countryside.[32]

After the outbreak of rebellion, agricultural policy became much more active and grandiose plans of rural regroupment were announced. It was declared that subsistence agriculture, based on shifting cultivation, should give place to more modern methods based on production for the market. The rural population was to be re-settled in new villages with private ownership of land. This would also enable services such as housing, health, education, and agricultural extension to be improved. However, compulsion was not to be used, the local population was to be consulted, and the traditional infrastructure was to be assimilated into the national structure. Most of this was simply rhetoric. It is doubtful if the colonial governments ever gave any serious thought to the probable effects of giving up shifting cultivation in environments to which it was naturally adapted and in which it had been worked out over long periods of time. Thus the independent governments of Portuguese-speaking Africa will not, unfortunately, be able to derive many positive advantages from past agricultural policy.

Ethiopia and Liberia

Although in many ways very different, these two countries share the distinction of being the only ones in Africa to have avoided colonial rule (if the short-lived Italian occupation of Ethiopia, 1935–41, be discounted). They thus provide an interesting opportunity to analyse the development of agricultural policies undistorted by colonial influences, and in widely differing geographical environments. This gave them the advantage that they were not obliged to tailor their agricultural policies to suit foreign interests (although both did so to some extent for differing reasons) but it also meant that there were no outside pressures on their governments to give priority to agricultural affairs. The result was that prior to the 1960s agricultural problems were rather ignored in both countries. When the influence of international organisations and foreign-aid missions began to grow in the 1960s, more attention was given to agriculture, but it remained somewhat one-sided. Special attention was given to a few irrigation projects in Ethiopia and to the rubber farmers surrounding the immense Firestone plantations in Liberia; but the mass of farmers were little affected by government policy.[33]

This was perhaps no bad thing before the 1950s when the farming population was fulfilling its primary function of feeding itself and the rest of the population with reasonable efficiency. Population densities were low. For instance, in 1960 the estimated density of population in Liberia was 12 persons per km^2 compared with 34 in neighbouring Sierra Leone, 28 in Ghana and 38 in Nigeria. By contrast Ethiopia, at an estimated 17 persons per km^2 was more densely populated than Kenya (12) and Tanganyika (10) but less so than Uganda (27).[34] Even so, pressure on the food supply was not a serious problem. However, during the 1950s the situation began to change, as the cities, and the non-agricultural sectors of the economy grew, so that more food was needed. Both countries found that they had to spend increasing proportions of their export earnings on imported food. In Ethiopia, which lacked the export resources which Liberia enjoyed from rubber and iron ore, food shortages emerged with increasing seriousness, culminating in famines in 1973 (especially in Wollo province). This, incidentally was the fundamental cause behind the overthrow of Emperor Haile Selassie in 1974.[35]

Agricultural experts in both countries found, however, that proposals to introduce reforms aimed at increasing food production in the traditional sector were difficult to implement. In principle. governments and ruling groups wished to see food production increased – but in practice they were often hesitant to allow some necessary changes (especially regarding land tenure, rights to forced labour, and taxation policy) which tended to undermine their own position.

The problems were most serious in Ethiopia, where the need for a change of policy was acute, but where the ruling Amhara nobles and chiefs were embedded in a semi-feudal system hallowed by centuries of tradition. They were headed by an Emperor who claimed descent from King Solomon and the Queen of Sheba and who enjoyed almost absolute power, at least in theory. In practice he was hemmed in by the ancient traditions and customs of the Empire, enshrined and guarded by the Ethiopian Christian church. This church had been established as early as the fourth century AD and had come to enjoy an immense patrimony in land and titles as well as traditional prestige as the faith of the only ancient African kingdom to have survived the European 'scramble' for Africa.[36]

Ethiopia's unique geography as a mountain plateau state has resulted in an agricultural system very different from that obtaining in most African countries. Despite the considerable size of the country, much of the land is of little use for farming being either tropical lowland desert (as in much of the east and north) or steep-sided, or heavily-wooded mountain terrain. Moreover the mountainous area is dissected into numerous flat plateaux, known as *Ambas*, with almost sheer sides, often descending thousands of metres into valley gorges below. On these plateaux, with their pleasant temperate climate, the ancient Ethiopians were able to defend themselves against all adversaries, whether European, Arab or African. But this situation meant that good land was in short supply and that it was relatively easy for powerful military leaders, commanding cavalry, to obtain control and ownership over it. The peasant cultivators could not move away, deeper into the bush, as they could so easily elsewhere in Africa. At an early date a semi-feudal system of land tenure became established. In theory the Emperor owned all the land, but he could (and did) grant it out to favourites and powerful local chiefs in exchange for their support: and in course of time, many of these local rulers (known as *rases*) intermarried into the extended royal family.

The result was that the typical Ethiopian farmer became a tenant of a very small farm held under onerous conditions of share-cropping, without security of tenure and often having to perform labour services on his landlord's farm and having to pay tithes and land-taxes as well. In his study of the system Gilkes shows that 90 per cent of the farmers hold fewer than 5 hectares each and 66 per cent fewer than 0·5 hectare. In addition these holdings were usually fragmented into three or four pieces.[37]

There was no legal limit to the landlord's share of the crop. By custom it was not supposed to be more than 50 per cent, but cases of

75 per cent or more were known. When it is realised that the farmers had to pay taxes as well (supposed to have been paid by the landlord, but usually passed on to the tenant) and tithes, it is not surprising that farmers could not do much more than subsist on their holdings. If most farmers had been freeholders the situation would have been less serious, but Gilkes believes that the great majority of farmers were tenants, despite some official figures which purport to deny this. According to these official figures, of the 1960s, which relate to all provinces except Eritrea and Bale (which were in revolt), only 42 per cent of rural households were tenants, while 46 per cent were owners, and the remaining 12 per cent were landless. However, Gilkes points out that there are many inconsistencies in the figures, and that tenants on Church lands (and some other categories) had been omitted. He believes that the true proportion of tenants was between 65 and 80 per cent.[38]

The Emperor himself realised that the tenancy system was a major blockage to improvement and that tenants were hardly likely to adopt new methods when their landlords could evict them at will without compensation, or appropriate from half to three-quarters of any increase. He stated his position unequivocally in 1961.

The fundamental obstacle to the full realisation of the full measure of Ethiopia's agricultural potential has been, simply stated, lack of security in the land. The fruits of the farmer's labour must be enjoyed by him whose toil has produced the crop. The essence of land reform is, that while fully respecting the principle of private ownership, that landless people must have the opportunity to possess their own land, that the position of tenant farmers must be improved, and that the system of taxation applying to the land holdings must be the same for all. It is our aim that every Ethiopian should own his own land, in implementation of this principle.[39]

A Ministry of Land Reform and Administration was established, and eventually, in 1968, it introduced a bill into the Chamber of Deputies to abolish the worst abuses, such as eviction at will, excessive shares of the crop passing to landlords, and undue landlord control over the conditions of tenancies. Since the Chamber consisted largely of landlords, it is hardly surprising that there was strong opposition, and the evidence suggests that the government was relieved to see the measure fail. The price, however, had to be paid during the revolution of 1974 and it is not surprising that the new reform government was soon complaining that peasants were ignoring the rights of landowners and were refusing to pay rents.

There were also many other factors which operated against an effective government policy for agriculture. The long neglect of education meant that not only were nearly all farmers illiterate but there was an acute shortage of research scientists, extension workers and agricultural economists. When it is realised that even cabinet ministers were not allowed to take decisions without consulting the Emperor until 1966, it is hardly surprising that ministerial initiatives were nonexistent – and until quite recently there were no trained personnel to carry out any policies which might have existed.

In these circumstances agricultural policy was largely concerned with a few special schemes in selected areas. Some of the landlords were able to increase production on their farms by means of mechanisation, but this was usually accompanied by the eviction of tenants, who had great difficulty in finding new land or jobs outside agriculture. Mechanisation was thus of limited value.

The government sought to help the smaller farmers in 1971 with schemes known as the Minimum Package Programmes, run in conjunction with Swedish and Danish foreign-aid missions. These aimed to help farmers with 20 hectares or less by providing credit for seeds, fertilisers and implements. But the repayment conditions were stringent and tenants found it difficult to qualify; worse, landlords often succeeded in appropriating the credits and leaving their luckless tenants with the obligation to repay loans they had never been able to utilise. Since the courts were controlled by the landlords the tenants could seldom obtain redress.

Another scheme in which the Swedish aid mission (SIDA) co-operated with the government was the Chilalo Agricultural Development Unit (CADU) but this produced such unsatisfactory results for the tenants that the Swedes threatened to withdraw unless changes in the tenancy arrangements were made. The scheme led to large increases in grain and milk production, and was a considerable success technically, but it also led to much eviction as mechanisation spread. The Swedes felt that too few benefits were going to the farmers.[41]

Surprisingly, despite great geographical, historical, and social contrasts, Liberian agricultural policy shows some interesting similarities with Ethiopian. Although the Americo-Liberians, the descendants of the returned slaves of the nineteenth century, did not form a semi-feudal group in the same sense as the Amharan aristocracy of Ethiopia, their control over the Liberian state gave them some of the same advantages until their overthrow in 1980. It gave them effective control over the land. Using analogies drawn from the American west they claimed that all unused land was in the 'public domain' – i.e. belonged to the Liberian State which they controlled. As traditional cultivation systems in Liberia depend upon long-fallow rotations (mainly of upland rice and cassava), there is very little *permanently* occupied land; so that the government could usually arrange to sell or lease land anywhere in the country. Although local farmers were not supposed to be disturbed, their interests were not always safeguarded. This control over the land was rendered easier by the strangely 'colonialist' type of local government in Liberia, whereby chiefs were responsible to government-appointed District Officers.[42]

The parallel with Ethiopia can also be extended to labour policy, for one of the aims of the government was to procure labour to work on the rubber plantations. In their study of the Liberian economy in 1969, Robson and Lury state.

Recruitment for both government and private employers was carried on legally by requisitions on tribal chiefs, resulting in a considerable amount of involuntary employment. In 1960, some 20 000 unskilled workers (almost a quarter of the wage-earning force) were so recruited, largely for rubber plantations and local government service in the interior.[43]

The irony of this situation was that despite governmental neglect of agriculture, traditional rice production paid the Liberian farmer more than he could earn on the foreign rubber estates, on whom the Liberian government relied for their revenue. The policy of granting concessions to foreign companies enabled the government to increase its revenue dramatically for a minimum effort, but if offered little scope for the Liberian people as a whole to raise their standard of living. Robson and Lury worked out the relevant calculations for the early 1960s as follows. They reckoned that a farmer typically had a wife and three children with whom he cultivated about 1·2 hectares a year (0·8 hectare in upland rice and 0·4 hectare in other crops). In fact, the cultivation period lasted for only about three months during which about 500 kg of clean rice (after deduction for seed) could be sold. The price was $6.50 per 45 kg, yielding a total of $71.50. If the farmer then worked for the remaining 250 days as a rubber tapper at the prevailing wage of $0.45 a day he could earn another $112.50 – giving him a total cash income of $184.00. This ignores the value of his food crops grown in addition to the rice. By contrast if he had worked for 350 days as a rubber tapper he would have earned only $157.50.[44] Thus, if the government had had a policy for improving food production it would have made work on the rubber plantations an even more unattractive proposition economically. Yet it was on its immense leases to the Firestone rubber company that the government had hinged its whole development policy. Any alternative occupation which restricted the labour for these plantations (or obliged them to pay higher wages) threatened to reduce the government's revenue from the foreign concessionaires. Since most of this revenue was spent in the Monrovia area, where the Americo-Liberians mainly live, it is hardly surprising that they showed little enthusiasm for proposals to make farming in the provinces more profitable.

Yet, with exports of rubber and iron ore booming during the 1960s, and the number of people involved in export production also increasing rapidly, the demand for rice and other foods naturally rose. However, efforts to persuade the farmers to increase production were largely unsuccessful for the reasons already mentioned. As a result food had to be imported, costing $5.5 million in 1963.

Despite the rapid rise in government revenue from $4 million in 1950 to $50 million in 1967, the proportion spent on agricultural research and advice was minimal. In 1960 it was two per cent of expenditure. USAID stepped into the breach and tried to provide an extension service to farmers, but abandoned its efforts in 1962 after discouraging results. The extension worker tried to persuade farmers to grow rice in swamps, as is done in neighbouring Sierra Leone, where much higher yields can be obtained than on the uplands. However, they found that in the existing uncertain conditions of land tenure farmers were not prepared to make the fairly considerable investments of labour time necessary in building banks, and water channels, etc.

There was no guarantee that land made more valuable by such efforts would not be appropriated by highly-placed Liberians or rented to foreign concessionaires.

In addition to forced labour, Liberian farmers were subject to hut taxes and 'extra-legal tribute payments of rice, money and labour services to a variety of government employees'. Even more discouraging it was found that when efforts were made to improve the very inadequate transportation system by the construction of new roads into the interior, the farmers' reaction was to move away from the road in order to avoid new tribute demands.[45]

Again the comparison with Ethiopia is instructive. There was the same emphasis on 'institutional' blockages to progress, arising not from backward social customs amongst the farming population, but imposed by a ruling elite group in its own interests. Since the mass of the farming population had no influence on the Liberian government, there was very little they could do to alter government policy. It can be no accident, however, that questions of rice supply triggered the coup of April 1980, in which the regime was overthrown.

In the long run, of course, it is in the interests of all concerned for Liberia to diversify its economy, and to become less dependent on foreign concessions. Government policies directed towards improvement in domestic food production would save foreign exchange and enlarge the domestic market for manufacturers, although development along these lines could only be really effective within the context of a West African common market. This question of regional economic co-operation within Africa is another vital policy area, whose importance is highlighted by past failures, especially during the colonial period. Despite increased governmental commitment in principle, there is evidence, not only of lack of progress, but of actual regression. For instance in 1978 the UN Food and Agricultural Organisation warned that the share of intra-African trade in total food imports had fallen, from 18 per cent in 1962–4, to only 12 per cent in 1972–4 – representing a major challenge to programmes of economic integration and co-operation. Specifically they blamed the maintenance of tariff barriers.[46]

Conclusions

It has not been possible to survey all the stages in the development of agricultural policy in Africa, because of the widely divergent conditions obtaining, and because of the length of the time-span involved. It has only been possible to indicate some of the more important trends, and to emphasise certain major achievements and problems. It now remains to try to draw the strands together and to consider some of the lessons which may be drawn from past experience.

Inevitably opinions will differ as to the relative importance and significance of such lessons. The conclusions reached here are not presented dogmatically, but are put forward in the hope that they may stimulate discussion and creative thought about future policy.

First, it seems clear that much of the ineffectiveness of past policies sprang from lack of clarity and decisiveness. There is a need for governments to work out a clear, effective, and above all voluntary policy, which farmers can understand and freely support. Rene Dumont's strictures on the counter-productiveness of force put this point well.

Second, there is a need to break down the 'Balkanisation' of policy resulting from the colonial situation.[47] Regional co-operation can save money and duplication of effort and needs to be encouraged.

Third, governments need to give far more financial support to the machinery for carrying out their agricultural policies. The low prestige and shoe-string budgets of Agricultural Departments have been a serious hindrance in the past, and will be so in the future unless governments are prepared to grant a larger share of national resources for agricultural purposes. This problem of the lack of money lies at the root of some of the major difficulties which policy-makers encountered in the past. For instance, the lack of basic statistical information about fundamental facts of the rural economy made sensible policies almost impossible. It is essential to know the size and ownership of farms, what is being produced, how and where it is marketed, the size of the labour supply and other critical pieces of information. Such surveys have now been successfully carried out in some African countries.[48]

Fundamental research into crops, livestock, diseases, soils, manures and other related aspects is also crucial for policy-making. Here much good work was done, and the co-ordinated regional research stations, such as those for cocoa, rice and oilseeds, in Anglophone West Africa were examples of successful policy decisions. Similar research stations need to be set up, on a full regional basis, in all parts of Africa.

Extension services were also too small, and were insufficiently integrated with research stations (especially in East Africa), so that the advice being given to farmers had not always been fully justified by experiment in local conditions. Recent studies have unearthed a new danger, which is that the work being undertaken in research stations tends to be biased towards the richer farmers (probably unconsciously) and the advice then given tends towards the creation of greater inequality in the rural areas. This conflicts with the policies of most African governments, and needs to be countered by field studies which assess the social and economic effects of research programmes. There is also evidence that the wealthier farmers can benefit unduly when land consolidation schemes are being carried out to reduce fragmentation of farm units, as in eastern Nigeria.[49]

An aspect of past policy, which was generally beneficial, was the swing away from excessive reliance on exports to a greater emphasis on food production, which began as early as the 1930s. However, although this change in *policy* was fairly general, it was not always fully implemented, and there is still room for more progress in this direction. Admittedly this is easier said than done, and a study in 1975 by Polly Hill, of a food-producing village in southern Ghana, suggests that the dynamics of food production are highly complex. She found that because much of the work was done by women the men became dissatisfied and migrated, causing a further drop in production. A local source of income was needed for the men *in addition to* food-crop production. She suggested a cash crop (such as cocoa) or rural industries (such as weaving) to keep the men in the rural areas.[50] This interesting example also shows the need for agricultural policy to be integrated with other aspects of development planning.

The neglect of agricultural economics also has been widespread, so that both research workers and extension workers were not always fully aware of the *economic* effects of their proposals, and sometimes failed to understand why suggestions which were sound technically were rejected by farmers, (because their economic results were sometimes harmful).

Agricultural education was also rather neglected in the past and the ill effects of this on the supply of trained personnel familiar with the modern scientific aspects of farming, is still serious. In addition there was a tendency to make agricultural education in its higher branches too divorced from actual farming. Office-bound, armchair agricultural experts are of limited value.

Finally, there is still a need to guard against the seductive temptations of the large-scale, capital intensive agricultural project. The apparent success of the Gezira scheme in the Sudan, which was producing cotton worth around £3 millions from some 80 000 hectares of irrigated land as early as 1929, encouraged the belief that agricultural problems could be easily solved by 'crash programmes' involving heavy investments in irrigation and mechanisation.[51] This led to a rash of over-ambitious and badly planned schemes, such as the irrigated cotton and rice scheme in Mali (known as the *Office du Niger*) and the notorious mechanised groundnut scheme in Tanganyika. This latter scheme was supposed to lead to groundnut production on 1·4 million hectares between 1947 and 1951, for an investment of £24 million. It was planned to show a profit of £10 million a year. Instead it had to be wound up in 1950, when only 50 000 hectares had been cleared and more than £24 million had been lost.[52]

The experience at Gezira shows that large-scale schemes can be successful, but also indicates that the preparation and planning need to be carefully worked out before heavy investments are made. A critical factor was the active support and enthusiasm of the Sudanese farmers themselves, and the fact that the problems of land-ownership and tenure were fairly and sensibly solved before the scheme began. Even so, the conditions for irrigation were specially favourable at Gezira, and it is noteworthy that its successor in Mali was a dismal failure.[53] However, despite its early success the scheme at Gezira still has some shortcomings which are discussed in the next chapter.

References

1 For a general survey of agricultural conditions and policies see Walter Fitzgerald, *Africa, a Social, Economic and Political Geography of its major Regions*, 2nd ed., 1936. For an outline survey of conditions in the 1960s see Colin Legum (ed.), *Africa Handbook*, 2nd ed., London, 1969.
2 C.C. Wrigley in *History of East Africa*, Vol. II, Vincent Harlow,

E.M. Chilver and Alison Smith, (eds), pp. 245–251. Restrictions on African-grown coffee were first lifted in 1937, but only in a limited area.

3 *Oxford Regional Economic Atlas, Africa*, Clarendon Press, Oxford, 1965 p. 8.

4 *ibid.*, p. 13. See also Lionel Cliffe, 'Labour migration and peasant differentiation: Zambian experiences', in *Journal of Peasant Studies*, **5**, April, 1978, pp. 326–46, and Mac Dixon-Fyle, 'Agricultural improvement and political protest on the Tonga plateau, Northern Rhodesia', in *Journal of African History*, **18**, 1977, pp. 579–96.

5 The best survey of British colonial agricultural policies may be found in G.B. Masefield, *A History of the Colonial Agricultural Service*, Oxford, 1972.

6 *ibid.*, pp. 3 and 63.

7 C. Fyfe, *A Short History of Sierra Leone*, London, 1962.

8 In Sierra Leone the imposition of a house tax caused a revolt in 1898; Fyfe, *op.cit.*, pp. 141–8.

9 *The Gold Coast Handbook*, Accra, 1923, p. 96, and Samir Amin, (ed.) *Modern Migrations in Western Africa*, Oxford, 1974, p. 95.

10 A.G. Hopkins, *An Economic History of West Africa*, London, 1973, especially pp. 231–6.

11 Masefield, *op. cit.*, pp. 19–24.

12 See *East Africa Royal Commission 1953–1955 Report*, London Cmd. 9475, 1955, especially pp. 279–379 on proposed changes in agrarian organisation. See also Martin R. Doorubos, 'Land tenure and political conflict in Ankok, Uganda', *Journal of Development Studies*, **12**, 1975, pp. 54–74; Lionel Cliffe, 'Rural class formation in East Africa', *Journal of Peasant Studies*, **4**, Jan. 1977, pp. 195–224; and Philip Raikes, 'Rural differentiation and class formation in Tanzania', *Journal of Peasant Studies*, **5**, April 1978, pp. 285–325.

13 Masefield, *op.cit.*, pp. 63–104.

14 *ibid.*, p. 151.

15 Michael Crowder, *West Africa under Colonial Rule*, London, 1968, p. 314.

16 John C. de Wilde *et al.*, *Experiences with Agricultural Development in Tropical Africa*, Vol. I, *The Synthesis*, 1967, pp. 93–4.

17 Masefield, *op.cit.* p. 38.

18 *ibid.*, pp. 1–52.

19 *ibid.*, pp. 38–45.

20 *ibid.*, pp. 124–7.

21 Crowder, *op.cit.*, p. 317.

22 *ibid.*, pp. 499–502; René Dumont, *False Start in Africa*, Paris, 1962, Eng. trans. 1966, pp. 126–7.

23 See Robert Harms, 'The end of red rubber: a reassessment', *Journal of African History*, XVI, 1975, pp. 73–88.

24 Fitzgerald, *op.cit.*, pp. 300–2.

25 *ibid.*, pp. 309–11.

26 Crowder, *op.cit.*, pp. 499–502.

27 Dumont, *False Start in Africa*, Sphere Books and Andre Deutsch, 1966, p. 70.

28 Crowder, *op.cit.*, p. 316. See also Jean Suret-Canale, *French Colonialism in Tropical Africa*, Longman, 1975.
29 See de Wilde, *et al.*, *op.cit.*, pp. 245–300.
30 For Portuguese-speaking Africa, see Douglas Wheeler and René Pelissier, *Angola*, 1970; Gerald Bender, *Angola Under the Portuguese: The Myth and the Reality*, Heinemann, London, 1978; M.D.D. Newitt, *Portuguese Settlement in the Zambesi*, Longman, London 1973 and 'Land and labour in early twentieth-century Mozambique', *Iberian Studies*, Vol. I, 1962, pp. 45–52; and W. Fitzgerald, *op.cit.*
31 Legum, *op.cit.*, p. 434.
32 For details see Basil Davidson, 'African peasants and revolution', *Journal of Peasant Studies*, I, 1973–4, pp. 269–90; John S. Saul, *The State and Revolution in Eastern Africa* Heinemann, London, 1979, which has chapters on agricultural policy in Angola and Mozambique; and Robin Palmer and Neil Parsons, eds, *The Roots of Rural Poverty in Southern Africa*, Heinemann, London, 1977.
33 See for instance, Patrick Gilkes, *The Dying Lion, Feudalism and Modernisation in Ethiopia*, 1975, pp. 124–7; P. Robson and D.A. Lury, eds, *The Economies of Africa*, 1969, pp. 287–315, (Liberia).
34 *Oxford Regional Economic Atlas*, pp. 8–9.
35 Gilkes, *op.cit.*, pp. xi-xix.
36 A.H.M. Jones and Elizabeth Monroe, *A History of Ethiopia*, Oxford, 1965, based on original 1935 edition.
37 Gilkes, *op.cit.*, p. 121.
38 *ibid.*, pp. 115–16.
39 Cited, *ibid.*, p. 70.
40 Yet radical supporters of the revolution were pessimistic about the chances of any real benefits accruing to the poorer peasants, fearing that a Bonapartist elite would enjoy the fruits of office, Marxist phraseology notwithstanding. See Addis Hiwet, *Ethiopia: From Autocracy to Revolution* (Occasional Publication, No. 1 of *Review of African Political Economy*, London, 1975).
41 Gilkes, *op. cit.*, pp. 122–36. See also M. Stähl, *Ethiopia: Political Contradictions in Agricultural Development*, Political Science Association, Uppsala, Sweden, 1974; and J. Cohen, 'Rural change in Ethiopia: the Chilalo Agricultural Development Unit', *Economic Development and Cultural Change*, **22**, 1974, pp. 580–614.
42 Robson and Lury, *op.cit.*, pp. 287–315. See also R. Clower, G. Dalton, M. Harwitz, and A.A. Walters, *Growth without Development: an Economic Survey of Liberia*, Evanston, Illinois, 1966.
43 Robson and Lury, *op.cit.*, p. 301.
44 *ibid.*, pp. 304–6.
45 *ibid.*, pp. 287–315.
46 FAO, *The State of Food and Agriculture*, 1978, p. 2–17.
47 See Samir Amin, *Neo-Colonialism in West Africa*, Penguin, Harmondsworth, 1973, for a discussion of the difficulties of embarking on new policies.
48 See J. Levi, with M.A. Havinden, G. Karr and O. Johnson, *The Development of African Agriculture: Economic Action and Reac-*

tion in Sierra Leone, Oxford, 1976, for a discussion of farming surveys in Sierra Leone.

49 A.R.C. Low, 'Small farm improvement strategies – the implications of a computer simulation study of indigenous farming in south-east Ghana', *Journal of Development Studies* **12**, 1975–6, pp. 334–50; Theo C. Mbagwu, 'Land concentration around a few individuals in Igbo land of Eastern Nigeria: its processes, scope and future', *Africa*, **48**, 1978, pp. 101–15.

50 Polly Hill, 'Food farming and migration from Fante villages', *Africa*, **48**, 1978, pp. 220–30.

51 A. Gaitskell, *Gezira, a Story of Development in the Sudan*, Faber and Faber, London, 1959, especially pp. 126–36.

52 See A.T.P. Seabrook, 'The groundnut scheme in retrospect', *Tanganyika Notes and Records*, Vol. 47, 1957, pp. 87–91, for a short account of this fiasco. He notes the lack of detailed studies on the scheme subsequently.

53 de Wilde, *et al.*, *op.cit.*, passim.

9 Development: ends and means

The course of development thought and practice since World War II

Most of the theory and practice regarding economic development in the 20 years or so from 1945 laid particular emphasis on the promotion of industrial production, in emulation of the major industrial powers. Development was essentially conceived of as a movement towards the economic conditions found in the 'developed' countries, it being felt that their greater wealth was founded on their productive technology, and especially their industrial technology.

In the south Asian countries, particularly India, bold attempts were made in the fifties to establish heavy industry and the production of capital goods. In most of the Third World, however, the strategy of industrialising was based on the substitution of domestically-produced, for imported, manufactured goods.

To some extent, these early approaches were influenced by the view that in the rural areas there was a great deal of under-employed labour, especially in the more densely populated countries, and that the stimulation of industry would raise income levels partly by absorbing that labour and by doing it at low real cost in terms of foregone agricultural production. It was generally accepted that Africa was more labour-scarce than other regions, but this did not inhibit the notion that industry was the key to economic development.

W.A. Lewis, in his famous articles on development with 'unlimited supplies of labour'[1] had considerable influence on attitudes during the fifties and early sixties, and his advisory work on Ghana (the Gold Coast)[2] probably reinforced these attitudes in the African context. The latter showed how import statistics could be used to assess both the likely markets for the domestic production of manufactured goods and the technical feasibility of home supply. In any event, most African countries embarked on import-substituting manufacture in the late fifties and early sixties, especially after formal independence from the colonial powers was achieved.

Linked with this focus on industrial development was a concentration on the growth rate of (real) national income per head. There was a belief – at least implicit – that a high rate of economic growth would be beneficial for the whole population because, even if it were geographically and socially limited, it would naturally tend to spread throughout the economy, or 'trickle down'.

Very little attention was paid to agriculture during this era, its role in development being seen as essentially passive: as providing labour for the industrial sector, food for the industrial labour force, markets for manufactured products, foreign exchange earnings with which capital goods might be bought and finally, tax revenue for the support of the non-agricultural sector and government.

By the late sixties views had begun to change and by the early seventies a very marked general change of opinion regarding development was apparent.

This change of opinion arose because of a number of factors, but these can be considered perhaps as symptoms of two fundamental phenomena: first, the failure of the agricultural sector to respond to the non-agricultural stimulus in the way that had been foreseen, and second, the failure of the hitherto prevailing economic strategies to bring about *widespread* development. The symptoms were rising food prices and food imports, migration to the towns, with growing urban unemployment and slums, and increasing dependence on food-aid. The results were firstly, a realisation that the development of agriculture had to be treated as a matter of urgency and secondly, the acknowledgement that much greater attention should be paid to the distribution of incomes and of income-earning assets, a view partly embodied in the campaign for more 'employment'.

Income distribution

Early disquiet about emphasis on plain economic growth without much regard for the way in which that growth might be distributed, can be found expressed in the well-known book on the Liberian economy, with its poignant title: *Growth Without Development*,[3] referred to in Chapter 7. As the authors put it:

> The title of our book, *Growth without Development*, is intended to emphasise a central feature of the Liberian economy, namely, that enormous growth in primary commodities produced by foreign concessions for export has been unaccompanied either by structural changes to induce complementary growth or by institutional changes to diffuse gains in real income among all sectors of the population. (p. iv)

But, more recently, criticism of the use of economic growth as an indicator of the growth rate of a nation's welfare has been even more damning, particularly in the book: *Redistribution With Growth*.[4] The simple algebra spelled out therein shows clearly that the growth rate of national income gives the highest weight to the growth rate of incomes among those who already have the highest income levels; the reverse of what might be considered a more desirable indicator, that would give greater weight to improvement in the poorest classes. Suppose that the households of a particular country are ranked in order of income, and then divided into fifths – from the 20 per cent of the population who are poorest up to the richest 20 per cent. Let Y_1 denote the total income of the poorest 20 per cent, Y_2 the income of the second lowest, and so on up to Y_5. Let Y denote national income and $\triangle Y$,

$\triangle Y_1$, etc., denote income changes per year. Then the national growth rate is

$$\frac{\triangle Y}{Y} = \frac{\triangle Y_1 + \triangle Y_2 + \triangle Y_3 + \triangle Y_4 + \triangle Y_5}{Y}$$

$$= \frac{\triangle Y_1}{Y} + \frac{\triangle Y_2}{Y} + \ldots$$

$$= \frac{\triangle Y_1 . Y_1}{Y_1 \quad Y} + \frac{\triangle Y_2 . Y_2}{Y_2 \quad Y} + \ldots$$

This is the weighted sum of the growth rate in each 20 per cent division, where the weights are equal to the proportion of total national income earned by each division. In a typical Third World country, the richest 20 per cent of the population receives about 50 per cent of the national income, whereas the poorest 20 per cent receives about 5 per cent. In other words, if the richest 20 per cent experiences an income growth of 1 per cent per year, this is given about ten times the weight of the same growth rate experienced by the poorest class, when measuring the national growth rate.

Another aspect of the debate centring on the distribution of income was concerned with unemployment or under-employment of labour. This became prominent in the discussion slightly earlier than did income distribution, but it has been argued, particularly by Weeks,[5] that there is little point in taking 'the employment problem' as a topic separate from problems of income distribution. Perhaps the main reason why it came so much to the forefront was the increasingly obvious fact that the early development strategies outlined above were not absorbing labour to any great extent, if at all. This was true in particular of the cities, where the supply of labour, especially through migration, was increasing very rapidly, while the demand was increasing only slowly or even declining, despite any growth in the manufacturing sector.[6] But there was also some concern about rising unemployment in rural areas as a result of the adoption by land-owners and by government-aided projects of modern labour-saving technology.[7] This has been a less important question for Africa, because of the relative abundance of land and relative lack of inequality in rights, and secure rights, to work the land. However, rural 'employment generation' was given prominence precisely because of the apparent infeasibility of the urban-manufacturing sector absorbing labour to any significant extent – at least with imported technology.

In the Third World the rate of growth of employment in the non-farm sector has typically been only about half the rate of growth of non-agricultural output, and in Africa far less than that. Population growth rates have been about 2–3 per cent per year, and the proportion of the African labour force employed in agriculture has been roughly 75 per cent and often more. If we suppose a hypothetical country has a labour force of one million, 750 000 are employed in agriculture. Supposing this labour force is growing at about 2 per cent per year, i.e. about 15 000, the rate of growth of employment in the non-agricultural sector required just to absorb this rural *increase* must be

$$15\ 000 \div 250\ 000 \times 100 = 6\%$$

So the rate of growth of output in the non-agricultural sector must be at least twice that on the basis of past performance, and this merely to keep the labour force in agriculture constant.

All of the above considerations, then, have brought about a general change of opinion about agriculture: that its development should receive priority and should be thought of as a prerequisite for further development, rather than as having a largely passive or secondary role. So the agricultural sector is tending to receive far more attention than in the past from those concerned with economic development, both in national governments and in international or foreign national agencies. 'Attention', however, quite apart from the possibility of it being mere lip-service, is not sufficient to achieve rural development; and we now go on to assess some of the major rural development strategies carried out in recent years. As we shall see, rural development is not a prize that is easily won.

General strategies of rural development

To some extent, strategies of rural development have tended to mirror overall development strategies. They have tended to be oriented towards injecting external resources and new technology, and concentrating them on a small proportion of the rural population. The basis for such an approach is essentially the set of beliefs, first, that rural development can be generated significantly only if new resources are brought in to the rural sector, i.e. that little, if any, development can be expected from existing rural resources; second, that no other, more satisfactory, way of achieving rural development has yet been found; and, third, that, given the limited availability of these external resources, they must of necessity be concentrated to be efficacious. One cannot deny the internal logic of these views, and it is therefore unreasonable to be overly critical of rural development strategies that have followed this line. Nonetheless it is worth at least questioning the wisdom of the assumptions, and, indeed, of the conclusions. Such an approach in fact has been questioned increasingly in recent years, though more so with regard to other parts of the Third World than sub-Saharan Africa. Johnston and others have employed the simple and useful distinction between 'bimodal' and 'unimodal' strategies of rural development.[8] Unimodal strategies involve farm-level investments that are finely divisible, or neutral to scale, and can be adopted easily by small farmers. The cases of agricultural development in Taiwan and Japan are held up as the major historical examples of unimodal strategy, whose main supposed advantage is that widespread increases in rural incomes provide a large market for new, simple, labour-intensive commodities and so open the gateway for the long-term structural changes that must accompany long-lived and equitable economic development. Bimodal strategy, on the other hand, refers to the intensive injection of new technology, described above, and which in practice has been so common in African countries. This may have a bigger impact in the short run, and on the fraction of the people it impinges on, but from the point of view of long-term general development, it is arguably more or less sterile. Griffin uses a similar typology of approaches to rural development, but includes political ideology as well as economic aspects.[9] At one end of his typological spectrum are 'technocratic' approaches (broadly equivalent to bimodal strategies); at the other end are 'radical' strategies, whose main feature seems to be socialism, rather than any particular type of technology. Griffin's classification is perhaps less useful than Johnston's, however, because it is quite possible, and even common, for professedly socialist governments to embark on bimodal strategies: the State Farms of Ghana and Guinea are perhaps the most famous examples.

Although the green revolution has in practice been of less interest to Africa than to other parts of the Third World, its potential contribution obviously might be considerable, especially if the general technical approach were more adapted to African conditions (and indeed efforts are being made in just that direction). The essentials of the green revolution were the development of new varieties, especially of rice and wheat seeds, which were capable of responding much better to artificial fertiliser than were traditional varieties. Conceivably similar developments might well arise from research on staple foods that are more common to Africa than rice and wheat. But how much would this be likely to contribute to rural development; and how far has the green revolution been truly 'revolutionary'? This is where the two schools of thought, represented by Johnston on the one hand and Griffin on the other, part company. The 'Johnston school' argues that the technology of the green revolution is finely divisible and does not entail any significant economies of scale, nor does it require any marked change in productive techniques, but merely the application of fertiliser, a change of seeds and perhaps extra weeding owing to the effects of the fertiliser on weed growth. It is supposed, therefore, to be essentially a unimodal technology. True it has been adopted mainly by the larger-scale farms; but this, it is argued, is not unexpected, for agricultural innovations are always adopted gradually, the majority copying, and gaining confidence and knowledge from the early adopters.

Griffin's analysis reaches an opposite conclusion, arguing that the new technology has been, in practice, capital intensive, especially in the more important case of rice. Capital is required, he says, mainly in the form of irrigation facilities, but also as pesticides, herbicides and associated equipment; without these the new rice varieties cannot achieve their potential. So the whole technology, in Griffin's view and in the view of many others, is biased against the use of labour and thus against the small farmer and landless worker, and in favour of the larger farmer, for whom the prices of capital and land tend to be relatively low. It is thus essentially bimodal (although Griffin does not use that term).

Whichever side one takes in this argument, the statistical evidence is such as to provide no support for the view that the majority of the people in the countries that have encouraged the use of green-revolution technology have gained any improvement in their levels of food consumption or general standards of living. So, at least, governments cannot complacently suppose that the problems of rural development are solved as seemed to be the view in some quarters in the early days of adoption of the new seeds. On the other hand, the research that is going on into new seed varieties and other technical aspects of agriculture, of course, should not be dismissed out of hand. Indeed, there have been apparent successes; for example, a new variety of maize developed in Kenya was adopted quite rapidly in the late sixties, by large and small scale farmers alike.

Rural-development schemes in Africa that could be described as successful unambiguously are remarkably difficult to find. On the whole, outcomes range from the resounding failure, such as the groundnut scheme in Tanzania, or the Niger Project in Nigeria, from which there were virtually no returns despite large expenditures, to the 'expensive success' which looks impressive and may have given great benefit to those fortunate people affected by it, but at a high cost.

It is, however, easy to criticise but less easy to suggest better alternatives. Let us adopt, therefore, a more constructive attitude and try to analyse development schemes in the hope of extracting useful lessons.

Classification of rural development programmes is probably not a particularly useful exercise because the differences appear to be largely differences of degree rather than kind. There are, however, notable exceptions which deserve separate examination, such as Tanzania's *ujamaa* village campaign and those settlement schemes that entail revolutionary changes in the entire way of life of the peoples concerned. On the other hand, these approaches do contain common elements, both with one another and with other more 'normal' schemes. Surprisingly enough the huge Gezira irrigation scheme in the Sudan and *ujamaa* are arguably similar in many respects, though on different scales. The common elements, though, are only those connected with the *means* of development, which normally involve the injection of resources from outside the rural economy, the introduction of new technologies or new products or both, and possibly the reallocation of land by moving people geographically or by some other means. The ends of different development schemes are likely to be quite different. These will include, for example, the encouragement of cash crops in order to raise finance for other sectors such as government (as with the original Gezira Scheme); the achievement of a 'socialist' society (which may itself mean different things to different governments), as in Tanzania; the raising of food production to facilitate industrial expansion; a vague desire to 'modernise' agriculture; and the raising of output per man-hour of labour throughout the agricultural sector. There may be more than one aim, aims may be unclear, they may change, and they may conflict with one another (for example, the goal of greater agricultural export earnings may conflict with that of higher food production and consumption).

So when making a judgement about the success or otherwise of a development programme, one must relate that judgement to particular goals. Thus, for example, the Gezira Scheme may have been a success in terms of its promotion of cash production, but a failure in terms of, say, equity. Again, many of the schemes in French-speaking Africa have been directed towards the advancement of a particular commodity – usually a cash crop; and these may well largely have succeeded in achieving their limited targets.

Some examples of rural development policy

Gezira, Sudan

The Gezira scheme is interesting for a number of reasons. Firstly it is perhaps the earliest rural development project; the idea was born and some of the foundation work done before World War I, although the beginning of the scheme proper was not until 1926; it is also still the largest scheme of its kind in Africa. Secondly, the technical or engineering, side seems basically quite simple and yet ingenious in that the area affected by the scheme is very large. The idea was to supply irrigation to the Gezira plain, which lies immediately to the south of Khartoum between the White and Blue Niles. This was done by constructing a dam on the Blue Nile upstream from the plain, with a canal leading from the dam lake across the plain so that water could be taken from it to irrigate a huge area by gravitation. Another important feature on the physical side was the fact that the soils were particularly suitable, being fertile and not liable to much seepage, so that canals did not need expensive lining and were relatively easy to drain.

Also of interest is the rather unusual system of administering and financing the scheme. A tripartite agreement was set up between the people who owned the land, the government and a commercial company which was established specifically to help run the project and profit thereby.[10] Ownership remained in the hands of the people, but the government hired the land, initially for a period of 40 years, and paid rent, although the areas required for canals, buildings, etc., were bought outright. The whole system of land use was then totally transformed by the company and government so as to make what was considered a single, efficient, irrigation system, divided into regular, rectangular 'tenancies' of about 12 hectares each. The owners of the land were then allowed to take up these tenancies, to an extent that fell within their managerial capacity, and as far as possible near to their own land. There were in addition certain controls imposed over subletting, mortgaging, etc., to prevent excessive indebtedness and inequality, and also over cultivation practice, so as to ensure the efficiency of the scheme as a whole.

The tenants, in addition to producing their own food, were to grow cotton, which was intended to generate the cash profits to be shared between the three parties to the agreement.

> The Land Ordinance which embodied these proposals ... provided an ingenious way of establishing control over land without outraging the traditional right of proprietorship while preventing the landowner from using that right to extract anything from his future tenant.[11]

Despite its boldness, its auspicious beginnings, its apparent economic and social soundness and its longevity, Gezira has not been without its critics. A recent study by Barnett,[12] for example, looks at the working of the scheme from the point of view of the villagers, an aspect which is neglected in Gaitskell's book. According to Barnett, what happens in practice is rather different from the theory. Thus there is extensive hiring of labour by tenants, heavy and continuing indebtedness, unapproved irrigation methods and unequal access to water. The incomes of tenants are apparently no higher than incomes outside the scheme, too. The problems seem to be mainly associated with the built-in rigidity and inertia of the organisation, although there have been attempts to diversify production. Thus although the inhabitants of the Gezira plain are probably better off than they would be without the scheme, that is a rather static virtue. Moreover, this is a criticism that could perhaps be levelled at many development projects: they provide the conditions necessary for a once-for-all improvement in standards of living, but not for a continuing improvement.

Ujamaa, Tanzania

The practice of rural-development policy in Tanzania has changed quite considerably since the early sixties, although the underlying philosophy and goals have remained much the same. The ultimate aim has been to fashion a rural society and economy based on villages, which would engage in communal production with the common ownership of resources, particularly land. The procedure by which this state was to be achieved has never been fully revolutionary, although there has been a varying degree of compulsion with varying degrees of haste, both greater in the mid-seventies.

The concept underlying the ideology of Tanzanian development goes by the Swahili name, *ujamaa*, which literally means 'familyhood'. *Ujamaa* is a particular type of socialism that attempts to harness the tendencies towards communal living already existing in African rural society, especially in the extended family. These tendencies include common ownership of land, obligations to help those in need, communal labour and an egalitarian attitude towards the rights of the individual. Conversely, the Tanzanian strategy seeks to inhibit or reverse the momentum of growing economic and social inequality which, as we have seen in Chapter 5, is likely to arise, especially where land is relatively scarce.

Initially, in the early sixties, development took the form of the creation of about 1 000 settlements, often by the politically motivated TANU Youth League. Many of these did not succeed and were abandoned because of adverse physical environments.

A classic bimodal strategy was then adopted and in turn rejected because of its inefficient use of new inputs and because it encouraged the growth of inequality.

Then the Arusha Declaration of 1967 put the formation of villages firmly back in the centre of the stage, although the process was still intended to be voluntary. The second five-year plan in 1969 reinforced the position of village formation and established the Regional Development Fund as a source of stimulus for village projects. Also other forms of government aid were directed in favour of those who formed *ujamaa* groups and carried on some communal production. (During this last era, it was envisaged that there could be two steps towards *ujamaa*, the preliminary one being the formation of a plain village, not necessarily with any communal production.)

In 1973 it was resolved by government that living in villages would no longer be voluntary and moreover that the whole of the rural population should be in villages by 1977.

Regardless of the merits or demerits of the *ujamaa* strategy, such a rapid transition in a society as poor as much of rural Tanzania, was bound to meet with difficulties. People are not irrational, after all, and there must usually have been good reasons why some peasants chose not to live in villages in the past; and even if those reasons were no longer valid, the very act of making the change would be costly, especially when the change takes place over such a short period of time. For example, new houses have to be built, new supplies of water found, perennial crops neglected or even abandoned, and so on.

One might, then, wonder what the supposed advantages of *ujamaa* villages are, that they should warrant such draconian measures.

The major social advantage, that of communal production and equality, is obvious, although it is cold comfort to know that one is just as poor as everyone else in the community, if one was materially better off before being moved into the village. The main material advantage lies in the possibility of reducing the costs of providing services such as water supply, credit, medicine, education, extension and transport.

The true *ujamaa* village is distinguished from an ordinary village by having some communal production. Whether larger scale, fully communal, production has definite material advantages over small-scale individual production – with perhaps some communal tasks – is debatable. We have seen in Chapter 5 that labour input and output per hectare tend to be greater on smaller farms, and, perhaps not surprisingly, communal fields do not appear to have been very productive. To some extent, this is the result of a mistaken view of the nature of 'labour', which as we have seen in Chapter 4 is more complex than one might suppose. In particular, the application of labour to agriculture requires judgement, managerial ability, technical knowledge and skill, and not simply a brute, mechanical use of muscle power. But if an individual is obliged to work on communal land so that the fruits of his toil accrue to everyone, he has little incentive to use his own skill and judgement to obtain a higher output per hour of work. Moreover, this is self-reinforcing, for he will see that others behave in the same way; human nature being what it is, work on communal land will tend towards a token level, especially if individually managed plots exist, as well as communal ones. This adverse effect of communal work may be offset to some extent insofar as there is imposed a fairly uniform rate of work when a particular task is carried out by everyone at the same time. The major example of such a task – at least as regards current, non-investment labour – is hoeing or planting, or both if they are done together; and we have seen that co-operation occurs in that type of activity even in rural societies that are not especially 'socialist'. Work done in unison avoids the problem of the individual having to decide how much effort to apply; the system decides for him, and indeed the comradeship, rhythm, etc., may make work sufficiently less onerous as to induce greater effort than would be the case with individual work.

The record of what happened to the *ujamaa* programme during the mid-seventies is, unfortunately, rather confused, not least because in that period agriculture was subject to adverse weather conditions and thus to a drop in production especially of maize, the staple food. Added to that it is reported that coercion of peasants to move to villages was widespread. But by 1975 formal attempts to bring about collective production had apparently ceased, while participation in communal farming was in any case low, even though two or three million people were in villages by then.

To date, the consensus of opinion seems to be that there is most marked resistance to being moved to villages in those regions where commercial crops are important and which are relatively well off. It is welcomed most where people can see clear material advantages, especially in the form of publicly supplied services; but one wonders whether there are enough resources to make these significant on a nationwide scale. Also, despite the fact that the majority of rural people seem to be now living in villages and are apparently reasonably convinced of the advantages, the disadvantages of communal fields in particular are widely complained of.

Development projects in Ethiopia, early seventies[14]

Recent Ethiopian experience in rural development is worth looking at partly because the ends and means, and the changes in those ends and means, have been very clearly stated and assessed. Also, the approach contains the salient elements common to most rural-development programmes throughout Africa, so that the lessons to be derived from it are widely applicable.

The essentials have been a dependence on technical innovations based especially on fertilisers, new seed varieties and other chemical inputs, plus a dependence on spreading these innovations to the farming community by means of what might concisely be termed an imposed bureaucracy.[15]

As we saw in Chapter 8, Ethiopia, along with many other Third World countries, in the late sixties, took the line of 'developing' selected rural areas in an intensive manner, using modern technology along with the requisite trained personnel, and using economic aid supplied mainly by Sweden and the World Bank. This approach represented not so much a bimodal philosophy, but rather an attempt to experiment in an effort to find modes of development that could be applied more widely. Three such intensive schemes were begun in 1967, 1970 and 1972, respectively: the Chilalo Agricultural Development Unit (CADU), the Wolamo Agricultural Development Unit (WADU),[16] and the Ada District Development Project (ADDP).

The main components of the CADU project were:

1 Research to improve crop varieties, livestock and tools.
2 Extension, to the rural community, of new techniques.
3 Credit and marketing.
4 Public works such as roads and water supply, and promotion of soil conservation, small industries, etc.

The implements developed under the research programme were not very successful, mainly because they were inappropriate to farming conditions in the area; for example, the new plough was too heavy for oxen to pull or for transporting. Experiments with fertiliser and new crop varieties were more encouraging, however, and it was on these inputs that the extension efforts were largely concentrated.

The extension method employed was based on the demonstration plot on a selected farmer's land, on which the effects of the new inputs were shown, and which surrounding farmers were encouraged to come and observe.

Most of the farmers, however, even if they were convinced of the effectiveness of the new inputs, were too poor to be able to purchase them in significant amounts, so that a cheap credit scheme became an additional necessary element.

The project did unquestionably have a positive impact on a fair number of farmers, in that between 10 000 and 20 000 farmers were using the new inputs, and over 25 000 in 1974 after the poor harvests and high wheat prices of the previous year. But there were grounds for pessimism about the whole approach as a means for general development.

Firstly, ownership of land was rather unequal, with widespread sharecropping and other tenancy arrangements. This meant that the main beneficiaries were the relatively well-off farmers, who could more easily afford to purchase inputs and were less averse to taking any risks involved. Sharecroppers would have received only a share of the extra production, which is both a reason why they would be less willing to adopt the new inputs and a reason why their landlords would be inclined to evict them, so as to reap all of the benefits.

Larger farmers are also more creditworthy and tend to have better access to the administration. Credit will also tend to be biased towards them because it is far cheaper to distribute to a few rich farmers than to many poor ones.

This, seemingly built-in, bias of rural-development projects in favour of those who are already relatively well-off seems to be a universal problem. The poor cannot afford to pay much for new technology, even when it is demonstrably effective; and an attempt to overcome the bias by means of cheap credit seems doomed to failure, too, for the reasons just given.[17]

More generally, this entire method of development was found to be either incapable of achieving the goal of improvements for a majority of farmers, or, to put it another way, the cost of even approaching that goal was prohibitive. This was found to be the case with the other two schemes, WADU and ADDP as well, and, indeed, with many other such schemes throughout the Third World.

A further attempt was made in Ethiopia, to solve the problems raised by the early development programme. This attempt was known as the Minimum Package Project, its aim being to reduce the cost of spreading new technology, per farmer reached, and thus to spread it more widely and in a more equitable fashion. The 'package' consisted mainly of fertiliser and improved seeds, although there continued to be other minor elements, such as drainage and soil-conservation works.

The organisation of extension was streamlined by allocating each extension agent to an area of 10 to 15 kilometres along a tarred road and 5 to 10 kilometres on either side of the road. Furthermore the provision of credit was deliberately oriented towards smaller farmers (cultivating less than 20 hectares) and was made specific simply by supplying the new inputs on credit; but still, some security was required in the form of downpayments and personal guarantors.

Despite these efforts to make the programme more egalitarian, however, it has not been notably successful, because the fundamental forces at work making for inequality were still present. Moreover, even though extension was more widespread in its impact, there were still not the human and economic resources available to replicate the programme on a national scale.

Animation rurale, Ivory Coast

The approach known as *animation rurale*, embarked on in the early sixties, presents an interesting comparison with CADU. This is because its aims – the spread of new methods to farmers – were superficially the same, but its mode of operating was quite different and indeed probably more successful than CADU and the other Ethiopian projects. The Ivory Coast programme is also of importance because the region exemplifies the typically African conditions of relative land abundance, and farming systems based on shifting cultivation. Linked with this is the lack of any great degree of inequality of wealth – at least within villages and regions if not between regions – in contrast with Ethiopia. That too is perhaps more representative of rural Africa.

The most outstanding feature of *animation rurale* was its attempt to induce farmers, in effect, to develop themselves. Certainly the organisation of the programme, initially in the central Department of the country, with about a quarter of the total population, was concerted by government and its agents, and was based on research into better farming methods, but the idea of imposing 'advanced' techniques from above on 'backward' farmers was ruled out from the beginning. The strategy was one that began by studying rural conditions as they already were, trying to discover what improvements might be feasible under those conditions and testing them under those conditions. Strictly, the term *animation rurale* only applied to the technique of making the rural community receptive to change by instructing, and generally arousing the interest of, particular farmers – *animateurs* – selected by the villagers themselves; the actual communication of new techniques to the villages was considered as something separate, i.e. extension proper. But in practice the distinction was blurred, for the obvious reason that farmers would not have been 'animated' by new techniques unless those techniques were seen to be clearly advantageous. No amount of ingenuity employed in organising the communication of ideas to rural areas will be effective unless the ideas themselves are worthwhile.

Thus the foundation of the programme was laid in the research done, and in the sound attitude to research, before *animation rurale* proper was begun. And the first stage of that research was a socio-economic survey carried out in a pilot area. Following that, pilot development programmes were begun with villagers' consent, consisting of such ingredients as the introduction of short-duration Allen cotton, the regrouping of fields into blocks and the integration of animal husbandry with cultivation.

The programme was not without its problems, despite generally encouraging results. One difficulty was that of finding an appropriate place to test new methods. Technically the best place was on actual farms, but the benefits accruing to those farms chosen aroused jealousy. More neutral territory, such as the experimental station, was also more artificial because, for example, of the high proportion of hired labour employed.

Some fundamentals of agricultural development

These few examples of attempts to develop African rural areas illustrate the essential elements that have been present in most, if not all, cases; so we need now to try and see if any useful lessons can be learned by abstracting and generalising.

We can perhaps single out three major broad features of rural development programmes, that are combined in varying degrees. Other features could well be examined, but lack of space and the need for simplicity dictates their omission.

One of the three elements considered here is institutional change of some sort. It may be completely dominant, as in Tanzania's *ujamaa* policy, or strongly linked to, or determined by, a new technology, or settlement scheme as in Gezira, or of minimal significance, as in CADU and Ivory Coast's *animation rurale*. It is difficult to reach definite general conclusions about institutional change, partly at least because assessment depends on particular values. The changes wrought by *ujamaa* were of the very essence of economic and social policy in Tanzania: they were as much an end as a means to an end. Another major type of institutional change that can be placed under the heading of land reform has already been discussed in Chapter 5. In general, what one can perhaps conclude is that extreme care and popular assent are necessary if imposed institutional changes are not to be damaging economically. Very radical measures in a poor environment can only too easily upset delicate economic and ecological balances, tipping the poor over the brink into destitution. On the other hand, as was emphasised in Chapter 5, the 'natural' evolutionary forces at work that cause institutional change can result in growing inequality unless there is some kind of intervention from an outside authority.

A second major element in agricultural development practice has been the communication of technical knowledge. We avoid the use of the common term, 'extension', because it does not seem general enough, in that it implies the communication of knowledge in one direction only, viz, to the farmers from the developers. Some programmes, such as *animation rurale*, have involved a good deal of two-way communication and appear to have been all the more successful for it, while others, like CADU, were essentially one-way and have tended to yield disappointing results. Communication of knowledge, however, is intimately bound up with our third major element.

This third element is of over-riding importance; and we focus most attention on it. It is the attempted introduction of an agricultural technology different from that already in use. It is necessary to weigh very carefully the terms used at this point. By 'technology' we mean simply 'way of doing things' or 'method of production', where 'production' can be taken to include things like processing and transporting. Note that we have avoided using the terms 'new' or 'improved', in favour of 'different', technology. This is because, firstly, the technology being introduced to farmers by way of 'development' may well not be new to them, but may simply not have been in use for various reasons. For example, intensive methods of cultivation may be known to, but eschewed by, farmers because they involve too much work, or too much work at a particular time, or because the farmers cannot afford to pay for the necessary inputs. Secondly, of course, the 'different' technology that the 'developers' try to spread may well not be an actual improvement on that already in use. Here again, though – and the point has already been emphasised earlier in this chapter – 'improvement' can mean different things depending on ones's values.

It is probably helpful, too, in the context of discussing technology and changes in technology, to distinguish between 'indigenous' or 'traditional' technology and 'modern', 'non-traditional' or 'alien': let us stick to 'traditional' versus 'alien' for convenience. The distinction *is* only for convenience and does become blurred in many cases. Higher-yielding varieties of traditional crops, developed on research stations, represent a good example. Despite this qualification, however, it should normally be possible to judge broadly the degree of 'alienness' (or conversely, of 'traditionality') embodied in the 'different' technologies being encouraged. Mechanical cultivation using tractors, for example, is obviously about as 'alien' a technology as possible, as also is the use of artificial fertilisers, although other components of the technology that employs them may be more traditional. Simple furrow irrigation may be considered traditional, but it may also be part of a large irrigation system dependent on an 'alien' dam.

The point of the distinction is that in practice it would appear that the extent to which the technology being introduced is alien, markedly affects the nature of the outcome of a development programme.

Differing degrees of faith have been placed in our three major elements by developers, as we have seen, but probably most faith has been put in 'alien' technologies. It is obvious why this should be so. Those responsible for trying to develop agriculture have been reared on a diet of Western (or, more accurately, northern) technology, and have justifiably found its results impressive. There is no question that research on new seed varieties, chemicals such as artificial fertilisers and pesticides, powered implements, and so on, can have, and have had, very remarkable positive economic effects in many instances, and especially in the richer countries. The strength of faith is not at all surprising. But there is also little doubt that the faith has weakened in recent years: the majority of rural Africans remain very poor. There has been much less faith in institutional change, except in some circumstances and indeed the results have not been encouraging in general. (Of course, linked with the lack of success in the introduction of the more alien technologies and institutions has been the failure of extension.) The comprehensive study of African agricultural development by de Wilde and others reaches the conclusion:

> By and large it has been the individual farmers working within a gradually changing traditional environment who have accounted for most of whatever progress has been achieved.[18]

Herein lies food for thought and perhaps the basis of tentative conclusions regarding rural development strategies and projects.

The outstanding question that needs answering is this: Why is it that alien technologies, despite their apparent promise, have had such a remarkably small impact on African agriculture in general? Part of the answer – possibly the most important part – lies in their very alienness. By definition, the fact that they are alien means that they cannot be supplied from within the rural economy. This implies that unless they are donated *gratis*, and even if they are subsidised, the rural economy must be able to generate an extra cash 'export' to pay for them, or else must be prepared to forego some of the meagre output it already produces in order to provide the wherewithal for the new technology. Although outside aid has made alien technologies available to some fortunate people, it has never been anywhere near large enough to make them available generally, nor is it likely to be. That being so, there remain the resources of the people themselves, who are mostly very poor. Because of their poverty, any amount of their production foregone, even in exchange for productive inputs, represents a considerable sacrifice: the subjective cost is high. This high cost has to be weighed against the expected returns. Note the term 'expected', which reflects the fact that the supposed returns from the new technology are not certain. Let us leave this problem aside for the moment, so as to simplify the argument, and suppose that there is no uncertainty about the returns from the technology being purchased. Even if this were so, because the subjective cost to a poor family of foregoing a given amount of production is high, the returns required to make the technology worthwhile will be higher than those required by a richer family.

Suppose we have two farmers with total incomes (including the market valuations of output that is unsold) of $200 and $400 per year (and that their families are identical in terms of ages and sexes). Suppose also that $1's worth of a particular artificial fertiliser will increase production by an amount worth $1·50, and that such a result is absolutely certain. It looks as though the fertiliser is clearly worth buying for both farmers. But because the return is not immediate, this is not so. Obviously, a family close to starvation will not exchange or sell food for fertiliser even if the return is certain and attractive – because the *subjective* cost is too high. And this is true to a lesser extent of families that are not so desperate, but still poor. Simply because of the *delay* in the returns, the poorer the family the less fertiliser will it be willing to buy (and in the extreme, the starving family will buy none).[19] Borrowing may be possible, but non-institutional rates of interest tend to be very high, averaging around 50 per cent per annum and often 100 per cent or more on short-term credit. Also, if everyone is trying to borrow cash to buy fertiliser or whatever, interest rates will tend to rise. Institutional credit at relatively low rates of interest has been seen as a possible solution, but inevitably it has to be rationed and in practice has to be channelled towards the better-off if a high level of default in repayment is to be avoided.

So far we have implicitly assumed that there are constant returns to fertiliser. Let us now be more realistic and suppose there are diminishing returns, while continuing with the assumption that the returns are known with complete certainty. The poorer farmer will have a higher subjective cost of buying fertiliser at all levels, and a higher subjective marginal cost than the richer farmer. He will therefore cease buying fertiliser at a lower level than the richer farmer. In general, *ceteris paribus*, the poorer the farmer the less fertiliser he will buy, not only because of his higher rate of time preference, but also because he has higher subjective costs. (See Fig. 9.1.)

All these differences between 'rich' and poor in their economic behaviour will be far greater when we are comparing farmers in the richer countries of the world with those of Africa. So it should not be too surprising that poor African farmers do not respond very enthusiastically to supposedly 'advanced' rich-country, alien, technology.

Next, let us bring in uncertainty. The returns to any input or bundle of inputs will always be uncertain to a greater or lesser degree. But the less the knowledge about their returns, the greater the uncertainty. Such knowledge will tend to be minimal on the part of the farmers themselves (since the technologies are indeed 'alien'), and any risks in production by poor farmers are avoided, because starvation may be the only reward. Even on the part of those who try to induce the farmers to adopt alien technologies knowledge is slight, for the technologies have not been tried and tested to any great extent in Africa – yet another reason, why they have not been very successful. Or they have been tried and found to give nothing like the productivity

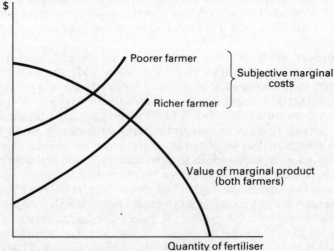

Fig. 9.1 Purchase of fertiliser by 'rich' and 'poor' farmers

they do in their 'natural' environments. Perhaps the best example of this is mechanical cultivation using equipment designed for large-scale, rich-country, farming. Troubles have arisen because, for example, African soils may sometimes actually deteriorate if they are too deeply ploughed, or, more often, because spare parts and the skills required to maintain equipment have not been readily available. Even fertilisers have produced, in general, surprisingly moderate results in Africa, contrary to what many people believe.[20]

Another reason why alien technologies have not succeeded is because they have not been appropriate for the relative factor scarcities found in Africa. Too often, well-meaning developers have tried to introduce new methods that would raise output per hectare, when what was wanted by farmers was something that would raise output per hour of work. The two results are not necessarily compatible, especially where there is plenty of land and yields are not very important. Another, related, mistake has been a failure to recognise the different valuations rural people put on their labour at different times in the farming season. For example, labour required for the new techniques at a particular time might not be forthcoming because it is also a crucial period in essential food production; and food comes first when you are poor. This has been a very common occurrence.

Development from within?

The general conclusion here, then, is that it is not enough to rely on alien technologies and, indeed, that they are of their very nature unlikely to be successful in a rural economy characterised by extensive poverty. The higher and more certain is the rate of return, the more widely they will be adopted. But even if they are widely adopted, they must necessarily tend to reinforce any economic inequalities simply because richer farmers will be able to afford them more easily. (The only type of alien technology it is possible to exempt from this kind of reasoning is that used for public investments of general benefit, such as dams, roads, bridges, etc.) Admittedly, these are negative conclusions; and it is not very helpful, either, solemnly to advise that new technologies need to be devised that are more appropriate to the poor economy and the African environment. That advice is correct, but it is easier given than carried out!

One possible approach could be to give greater consideration to the economics of traditional technologies, to the ways in which they change and to the possibilities of basing agricultural development on them, by, for example, encouraging their more rapid adoption, or devoting research to developing them or to developing new methods depending mainly on resources and materials readily available within rural areas. This approach seems to follow logically from the conclusion reached by the de Wilde study quoted earlier, and from the last few paragraphs. We cannot, obviously, devote any further space to this approach herein, or to the problems likely to be met in administering it, but Chapter 6 at least gives some idea of the economics of existing, traditional, technological change, a part of economics that has been much neglected.

References

1 W.A. Lewis, 'Economic development with unlimited supplies of labour', *Manchester School*, May 1954.

2 W.A. Lewis, *Industrialisation and the Gold Coast*, Government Printer, Accra, 1953.

3 R.W. Clower, G. Dalton, M. Harwitz and A.A. Walters, *Growth Without Development. An Economic Survey of Liberia*, Evanston, Illinois, North Western University Press, 1966.

4 H.B. Chenery, *et al.*, *Redistribution with Growth*, Oxford University Press, 1974.

5 J. Weeks, 'Does employment matter?', *Manpower and Unemployment Research in Africa*, Centre for Developing Area Studies, Montreal, Vol. 4, No. 1, 1971. Also in R. Jolly, *et al.*, (eds), *Third World Employment*, Penguin, 1973.

6 See for example, C.R. Frank, Jr, 'Urban unemployment and economic growth in Africa', in Jolly, *et al.*, *op. cit.*

7 C. Eicher, *et al.*, 'Employment Generation in African Agriculture', Michigan State University, July 1970.

8 See for example, B.F. Johnston and J. Cownie, 'The seed-fertilizer revolution and labor-force absorption', *American Economic Review*, September 1969 and B.F. Johnston and P. Kilby, *Agriculture and Structural Transformation*, Oxford University Press, 1975, Ch. 4.

9 K.B. Griffin, 'Policy options for rural development', *Oxford Bulletin of Economics and Statistics*, November 1973; K.B. Griffin, *The Political Economy of Agrarian Change*, Macmillan, London, 1974.

10 In the early fifties, the company was displaced by the national Sudan Gezira Board.

11 A. Gaitskell, *Gezira. A Story of Development in the Sudan*, Faber and Faber, London, 1959, pp. 85–6.

12 T. Barnett, *The Gezira Scheme: An Illusion of Development*, Frank Cass, London, 1977.

13 M.F. Lofchie, 'Agrarian crisis and economic liberalisation in Tanzania', *Journal of Modern African Studies*, **16**, 3, 1978, pp. 451–75.

14 This section has relied heavily on Tesfai Tecle, 'The Evolution of Alternative Rural Development Strategies in Ethiopia: Implications for Employment and Income Distribution: *African Rural Employment Paper No.* 12, Michigan State University, 1975.

15 No attempt is made to assess events after the Land Reform Proclamation of 1975, when clearly the entire social, political and economic milieu in Ethiopia changed radically.

16 Chilalo and Wolamo are administrative provinces.

17 See Griffin, *op. cit.*

18 J.C. de Wilde, *et al.*, *Experiences with Agricultural Development in Tropical Africa*, Vol. 1, Johns Hopkins University Press, Baltimore, 1967, p. 221.

19 In technical terms: the poorer the family, the higher its rate of time preference.

20 FAO, '*Shifting Cultivation and Soil Conservation in Africa*', Rome, 1974.

Index